SOME DAY I'LL FIND YOU

H. A. Williams was born in 1919, and educated at Cranleigh School and Trinity College, Cambridge. He trained for the priesthood at Cuddesdon College, Oxford, and was ordained in 1943. He held two curacies in London before becoming Chaplain and Tutor of Westcott House, Cambridge from 1948 to 1951. He was Fellow of Trinity College, Cambridge and Examining Chaplain to the Bishop of London. His main work consisted in the teaching of academic theology in the University of Cambridge. Since 1969 he has been a member of the Community of the Resurrection at Mirfield.

Harry Williams is the author of several books, including *Jesus and the Resurrection*, *God's Wisdom in Christ's Cross*, *The Four Last Things*, *The True Wilderness* and *True Resurrection* (the latter two also available as Fount Paperbacks).

D1500674

Books by H. A. Williams
available as Fount Paperbacks

TRUE WILDERNESS
TRUE RESURRECTION

SOME DAY I'LL FIND YOU

an autobiography
by
H. A. Williams C.R.

Collins
FOUNT PAPERBACKS

First published by
Mitchell Beazley International,
London, 1982
Published by Fount Paperbacks,
London, 1984

Reprinted 1984

Made and printed in Great Britain by
Richard Clay (The Chaucer Press) Ltd,
Bungay, Suffolk

Nothing is apt to mask the face of God so much as religion.

MARTIN BUBER

CONTENTS

PREFACE

THIS BOOK IS A MONGREL because I am one. It is partly a description of people and places I have known. I've been lucky in often finding people amusing. I did as a small child in France, though less perhaps as a boy at home and school and more as a curate in London. But it was Cambridge without doubt that was the richest soil for amusement, since dons, for all their intelligence, can frequently be possessed by folly, some of it positively sublime, some with an edge to it which the uninitiated might mistake for malice; while the *naïveté* of undergraduates can on occasion seem very funny if also very touching. But as well as amusement I have of course had my share of troubles – ordinary ones like the pangs of despised love or being (or at least feeling) the slave of circumstances.

I have, however, also had troubles of a less ordinary kind, and the description of these transposes the book into another key and makes it more like a pilgrim's progress. Hence its mongrel quality. In particular I have had to describe how for years on end I mixed up God and the devil, not knowing which was which. It was a muddle which needed a severe breakdown before it could be slowly sorted out. The sorting out led me to discover that in order to love God I often had to hate religion and I began to catch glimpses of God's glory in places where, on any ecclesiastical estimate, that glory had no right to be.

I have tried to be as honest about myself as I can without, I hope, being intolerably earnest (I believe with G. K. Chesterton that it was by the force of gravity that Satan fell). Some people may choose to describe such attempted honesty as "letting it all hang out". If so, the phrase will be theirs, not mine – I saw it used in a review by a religious and theological pundit, but have forgotten the book he was reviewing.

Most important of all perhaps: I am still in transit. I haven't yet arrived. Hence the title – *Some Day I'll Find You*.

I would like to thank Roger Hearn for the skill and patience with which he has edited the book, and James Mitchell for his encouragement, even though he was apt to get the book's title wrong – an easy enough thing to do with the Noël Coward corpus being so large.

H.A.W.

PART ONE

Child,
Schoolboy,
Student

I

HE WAS GUILTY. There was no doubt about that. He was only eight or nine years old, but guilty he certainly was. He had remained silent, and in consequence the gardener's boy got the blame. That was bad. But that wasn't his crime. His crime was that he had forgotten God, his Creator. He ran to his favourite hidy-hole at the end of the garden. But he heard a voice speaking to him, and it was frightening because nobody was there. It said – "Remember thy Creator." Then again, more loudly – "Remember thy Creator." Then yet again, this time like thunder – "Remember thy Creator." In a panic he rushed from his hidy-hole through the garden, but not into the house. He went into the street and ran as fast as he could to the church nearby, expecting it to be empty. But it wasn't empty. It was packed jam full; not with people, but with angels and archangels, and they all turned their eyes on him and with stern faces solemnly chanted over and over again – "Remember thy Creator."

What happened next to the young culprit I can't remember. It was a tale from a pious storybook my mother used to read to me when I went to bed. I was three or four at the time. And I suppose I remember it because that morning I had stolen an apple from a bowl of fruit in the dining-room; my two sisters, older than I was, had informed against me, and my mother had spanked me saying – "You thief. You thief." Clearly it was only playful. I certainly can't remember the slightest physical pain or discomfort. But in my memory the incident got linked with the story. The story's being read that evening was, I am sure, pure coincidence. It was the next story in the book. But it left its mark.

Indeed it is the earliest memory I have of any idea or

thought of God. Doubtless a child of three to four years old can have all sorts of lively pictures of God. But I can recapture only the one I had on this occasion. God was an oak chest we had in the nursery. But in my imagination from the closed lid of the chest arose from its four corners a superstructure which inclined inwards until there was a space small enough to hold a neck and head. The face of the head was not that of an old man with a grey beard but an ageless face, clean shaven, and above it an abundance of thick brown curly hair. It wasn't an angry or threatening face, but it wasn't a smiling one either. It was slightly sinister because it looked straight in front of it at nothing with enormous concentration. In a way it could have been a pictorial representation of Aristotle's Unmoved Mover, except that the Unmoved Mover didn't frighten little boys to death by telling them to remember their Creator.

But I soon forgot the story. At least I can't recall any more thoughts about God from this period, except for children's services where we were taught to sing – "There's a Friend for little children above the bright blue sky," and "Gentle Jesus meek and mild, Look upon a little child." But what meant most to me at these services was the habit of the clergyman of holding his thumbs and forefingers so that they formed a triangle. He always stood and walked with his hands like that. I thought it the essential part of the proceedings, though I asked no questions.

I have begun with my earliest memories of God since this is to be a religious autobiography. But religion doesn't exist in a vacuum. For a small child it is part of home and family, and (as he gets older) of the society in which he lives. So something must be said about these.

The story I have to tell will often be sombre. My childhood was at times somewhat miserable. But that is far from the full truth. There was plenty of light as well as shade, plenty of fun as well as unhappiness, a great deal of love as well as a lack of it. There is much that I can remember with the greatest pleasure as well as things which pain me. I suppose that is the average human lot.

4

I WAS BORN (it was 1919) in Rochester, since my father was in the Navy and was stationed at Chatham at the time.

He was born in 1870. I find it intriguing to think that a great deal of his naval career was spent before ships had wireless. This brought its advantages. His ship was cruising in the China Sea when Edward VII's coronation was supposed to be taking place, and the ship's company celebrated, it appears, with extreme conviviality. When they arrived back in Hong Kong they got the news of the coronation's postponement and were able to celebrate it again with equal conviviality when it actually took place.

I hope I am not being self-indulgent if I tell two of my father's shipboard stories.

In one of the larger ships in which he served the commander (number two in the ship) was disliked because he was so extremely pompous. He looked a bit like George Robey and therefore it was Robey he was inevitably called. He was one day sitting behind a newspaper in a fairly crowded wardroom when a new servant (obviously put up to it by his mates) went up and stood in front of the newspaper and said – "Mr Robey, the Captain wants to speak to you." No reaction. "Mr Robey, the Captain wants to speak to you." Still no reaction. "Mr Robey, the Captain wants to speak to you." At this point a head appeared from behind the newspaper and said with icy self-control – "Are you speaking to me?" "Yes. Beg pardon Mr Robey, but the Captain wants to speak to you." The commander got up and with a voice by this time slightly quivering said – "My name is Arbuthnot, and when you speak to me you should address me as Sir," and with slow dignified steps went out. The laughter which then broke out was so convulsive that the chaplain, who entered the wardroom only at this point, wondered why everybody was drunk early in the afternoon.

The second story concerns my father sitting to hear complaints. I'm afraid I don't understand the technicalities of the procedure, but a petty officer or somebody of that sort brought a charge of insubordination against one of the ship's boys because the boy had twice to his face called him a bloody fool. With tremendous moral indignation the petty officer said to my father – "How, Sir, would you like to be called a bloody fool, supposing that you weren't one?"

During the First World War my father was in the Grand Fleet on board HMS *Collingwood*, which took part in the battle of Jutland. But Jellicoe, of course, kept the Fleet idle for a long period at Scapa Flow. To while away the time my father filled two enormous scrapbooks for the entertainment of my mother and my two sisters – Joan, born in 1911, and Helen, born in 1914 (I had not yet appeared on the scene). These scrapbooks were, and still are, an enormous source of delight to me. I think they reassure me that I belong to a warm humanity.

It is (or was) almost a routine custom for members of the wardroom to write doggerel – very often messages from one ship to another or from one department of a ship to another, not infrequently couched in very meaty terms. For the purposes of his scrapbooks my father's doggerel kept strictly within the limits of what is now called family entertainment. His method was to cut out figures from coloured magazines (many of them, he said, came from *La Vie Parisienne*), paste them in the book in some sort of scheme, and then write a story about them in verse. There were, for instance, stories about three girls, always dressed in the height of Parisian fashion, called Susie Sweetheart, Dolly Daydreams and Katie Kissme. I suspect that what they were made to get up to for us was not necessarily what they were getting up to in the original text. On one page, for example, Katie Kissme (dressed as usual with tremendous elegance in the latest style) was shown speaking on the telephone to her boyfriend, a wounded (but not too badly wounded) soldier in a military hospital:

"Hallo, Hallo, is that you Jack?
I'm awfully glad that you've come back.

6

What's that you say? Shot through the arm?
Well, then there's *no* cause for alarm.
I'm pleased to hear it's nothing worse.
What's that? You've got a pretty nurse?
I always meant to see you soon
But now I'll come this afternoon."

My favourite page must have been cut out from an English magazine, as it showed an extremely angry clergyman holding a golf club, and in another corner of the page a caddie trying unsuccessfully to control his laughter hiding his face with his hands, and in a third corner a quite idiotic policeman looking as if he had just stepped out of *The Pirates of Penzance*. Round these three figures a story was written about the clergyman's progress on the golf course:

"The Reverend Geoffrey Bertram Day,
LLD, BD, MA,
Felt some exercise he needed
So one morning he proceeded
To the Hayling Island Links
Taking with him food and drinks.
Very keen on golf was he
But I think you will agree

"With a niblick or a cleek
That his game was rather weak;
With a putter or a brassy
It was certainly more classy.
And I'll bet an even fiver
With a mashie or a driver
That the Reverend old fogey
Would have beaten Colonel Bogey.

"He took twelve for the first green
Holing out at seventeen.
And on finishing hole two
Found his score was forty-two.

'Not bad, not bad at all,' said he
As pleased he stood by the third tee,
'But my score must not grow bigger;
I must exercise more vigour.'

"So he drove hard, but alas
Missed the ball and hit the grass.
His favourite club completely smashed
He scowled and shouted 'Well I'm dashed!'
A scene which made his youthful caddie
– an intelligent young laddie –
Turn aside a little while
To conceal a furtive smile.
And a policeman passing by
Thought he'd better wink his eye,
And pretend he had not heard
That extremely naughty word."

3

MY FATHER'S FATHER was also in the Navy. He joined it in
1852, retired from it in 1889, then became a magistrate in
Devonport and lived for ever, that is until he was ninety-
eight.

We stayed with my grandparents when I was about
six, and I remember my grandfather as one of the most
delightfully benign old men I have ever met. He gave me
a musical box, which enchanted me for years. I have just
looked up his obituary in *The Times* for 13 October, 1930.
He was an engineer who saw active service in HMS *Vulcan*
during the Crimean War and "was present at the taking of
Sebastopol, for which he received the Crimean and Turkish
medals and the Sebastopol clasp". *The Times'* obituary
sounds like a BBC television send-up of the British Empire:
"He served in China in the gun vessels *Clown* and *Algerine*,
and on this station saw more fighting during the second
China war. He was present at the capture of Canton and the
Taku forts and also at the destruction of pirate strongholds

8

and armed stockades." And so it goes on until he retires as an Engineer Rear-Admiral.

More interesting to me was some information given me by his eldest daughter, my Aunt Nellie, that my grandfather strongly disapproved of the Athanasian Creed, and that when it was recited in church he used to slam his large prayer book shut with the biggest bang he could manage and stand silent, looking furious. I thought of him when I successfully argued for the discontinuance of the recital of the Athanasian Creed here at Mirfield, though I kept completely silent about him as I didn't think his layman's attempt to bully the clergy would help my cause.

My grandfather wrote a book called *The Steam Navy of England*, "dedicated by permission to Admiral His Royal Highness the Duke of Edinburgh" (the Affie of Queen Victoria's letters). The *Morning Post* obituary says that the book "attracted considerable attention at the time". Its main interest for me is that my grandfather's name, like mine and my father's, was Harry, so that in the British Library his book appears in the catalogue near to my own books.

I went to stay with my grandmother and her youngest daughter, my unmarried Aunt Ethel, after my grandfather had died. My grandmother told me a charming story about herself. As a young bride in the 1860s my grandfather asked her to go to an auction and bid for a table, as he would be too busy to go himself. He said, "Don't give more than twenty pounds for it." My grandmother didn't properly understand the procedure at auctions and in any case was almost too nervous to speak. The bidding started at five pounds and gradually went up to eight. "Any offers above eight pounds?" asked the auctioneer. "Any offers above eight pounds?" There was silence, and my grandmother, summoning all the courage she could muster, shouted in a supreme act of bravery – "Twenty pounds." Everybody was dumbfounded. They gasped and gulped. Even the auctioneer hadn't the courage to ask whether there were any offers above twenty pounds. After a stupefied silence, he brought down the hammer and said, "The table is yours, madam." My grandmother went away very pleased and proud of herself.

MY FATHER RETIRED from the Navy in 1924 with the rank of Captain. The prospect of further promotion had been narrowed down to two candidates, of whom my father was one, and the other man got it. My maternal grandmother attributed the success of my father's rival to the fact that his wife at a New Year's party four months previously had opened her front door, seen a strange black cat on the doorstep, and had immediately picked it up and carried it into the house, thus bringing luck to herself and hers. This was a view which my mother severely condemned on religious grounds. She said she was much comforted the Sunday after the disappointment by the psalms at Matins, including the verse: "For promotion cometh neither from the east, nor from the west, nor yet from the south. And why? God is the Judge; He putteth down one and setteth up another." Years later my Aunt Nellie (who was visiting us at Rochester at the time) told me that my mother expatiated on her spiritual consolation subsequently at lunch, her tactlessness rubbing salt into my father's wound. He answered, "So promotion cometh neither from the east, nor from the west, nor yet from the south? But, my darling Nan, have you never heard of the clergyman seeking preferment who preached on that text before Lord North when he was Prime Minister?" My mother, it appears, was not amused.

My father never appeared to feel at a loose end after retiring from the Navy. He read widely, enjoyed playing the piano and bridge and tennis and gardened a lot when he was too old for tennis. By religion he was what used to be called ordinary C. of E., and a very good religion it was too: Matins on three Sundays out of four, while at Christmas, Easter and Whitsun he would stay on for the

Second Service and receive Communion. In Rochester he was Vicar's Warden at St Margaret's, where I was christened. The vicar, Canon Wheatley, must have stayed at the church a prodigious time. He was still vicar over twenty years later, when my father wrote for the baptismal certificate I needed to get ordained. In replying to my father Canon Wheatley expressed the hope on my behalf that "his being at Cuddesdon has not unduly exalted his churchmanship". He needn't have worried.

❧§ 5 §❧

BUT MY MOTHER has been left reading me a bedtime story or sitting a little deflated at the Sunday lunch table. It is time she had her turn.

There is no doubt that she was immensely attractive and that the attraction lay in her vivacity. She was no still-life study. Photographs, whether studio portraits or snapshots, libelled her disgracefully. People buzzed round her, and what made her popular was not only her vivacity but also a large streak of *naïveté*, which disarmed women and made men feel they belonged to the strong, protective sex. The *naïveté* was quite genuine and unselfconscious. It sprang, I think, from the fact that she was academically a dunce, but in a most engaging way.

She had learnt German at school (an extra, as my maternal grandmother complained) for over four years and ended up knowing no word of the language except "Guten Tag", let alone being able to put a German sentence together. But she could tell amusing stories about Fräulein and what the girls did to her.

I discovered at home a heavily bowdlerized (my mother was born in 1887) school copy of *Macbeth* with my mother's name in it, Annie Abbott. The mistress in charge had evidently thought the edition over-bowdlerized, for, at the appropriate place in the text, there was an insertion in a schoolgirl hand of the two words – "Dammed [*sic*] fact."

But my mother did win one prize. I have it with me

now. It is a copy of Stainer's *Dictionary of Musical Terms*, beautifully bound in dark blue calf with anchors, ropes in loose reef-knots, and signallers' flags stamped in gold leaf. There is an imposing label inside which says: "Royal School for Naval and Marine Officers' Daughters", and the label is signed by the *Lady Principal* Jemima Leys, and then by the *President* (in very careful copybook handwriting) George (then Duke of York, later King George V). The volume looks so handsome that I thought when I first saw it, and in view of its title, that my mother had in her schooldays played the piano more accurately than she did after undertaking the care of a family. But the merit for which the prize was given is described with an almost beautiful precision. It was for "Diligence in Music" – not proficiency but diligence. I still find that both amusing and touching.

In her later life I remember in particular two captivating examples of my mother's *naïveté*. They both occurred when we were abroad *en famille*.

In Venice we were walking for the first time from St Mark's Square to the Piazzetta and my father said, "That's the Doge's Palace over there." My mother stopped, looked at it for a moment, and then said quite seriously: "Good Heavens. I wonder how many bedrooms."

The other occasion was in Rome. We were drinking some mid-morning coffee in one of those narrow streets which lead out of the Piazza di Spagna, when my mother, looking up and down the street and surveying the buildings on each side, suddenly said, "I say, this place is quite continental, isn't it?"

Such remarks never irritated people. They liked my mother for them. They gave out a sort of freshness which at its weakest was pleasing and at its strongest enchanting. They had no competitive element in them and people laughed for pleasure or joy.

One of the results of her *naïveté* was that her imagination was quickly stirred so that her feelings overflowed.

Once she was staying with her in-laws and my grandfather gave her *The Mill on the Floss* to read. A few evenings later he asked her at dinner how she had liked it. Her answer was to burst into floods of tears, so that my grandfather insisted that from then on, when staying with them, she should be given only amusing books.

Years later, during the Second World War, my parents (they were by then getting on in years) stayed for some time in a village in Cheshire. The inhabitants were most welcoming and hospitable. For my mother the hospitality included an invitation to join a ladies' prayer group. They met in a drawing-room, knelt with heads in armchairs and bottoms up, and in this posture gave the Deity His instructions as any individual might feel led. All the ladies were surprised, and many of them seriously startled, to hear my mother earnestly praying to God that He would guide and strengthen Scarlett O'Hara to make the right decision. At the time she was reading *Gone with the Wind* and in the elevated atmosphere of the prayer meeting had momentarily confused fiction with fact. What greater compliment could be paid to a novelist than to have a reader who was led to pray for one of her characters?

Of course it was not for nothing that my mother was emotionally excitable. (Here I should explain in passing that we used to call our maternal grandmother Nana because she had taken my sisters to *Peter Pan* one Christmas and they had fallen in love with the dog called that in the play and had transferred the name to her.)

It was obvious to me that Nana had taken it out of my mother. She continued to all her life. My grandfather had died when my mother was a girl of twelve, and there was a younger brother – my Uncle George – who had to be put through Osborne and Dartmouth. Nana lived for her son and, I'm pretty sure, made her daughter feel a bit of an encumbrance. I suspect that it was intimated to her when she was nineteen or twenty that it was her duty to get married and so to cease being any longer financially dependent on her mother. That would leave more money to pay for George's education, my mother's own, German and all, being considered an investment which had now matured.

My father certainly adored her. He first met her at a reception when he had a shore appointment at Portsmouth, and subsequently wrote to invite her and Nana to tea. When they arrived at his lodgings (Nana told me) they found he had bought biscuits with letters of the alphabet on them and had arranged them to form the word ANNIE.

I doubt whether my mother was much, if at all, in love with him, but he was an eligible match. Nana was always very critical of him and once said to me: "Your mother would never have married your father if your grandfather had lived."

My maternal grandfather was also in the Navy (there was a tremendous amount of intermarriage among naval families in those days). His early career had been promising. He had been in HMS *Challenger* when it sailed on its famous scientific expedition in the 1870s. Later (by this time he was a commander) he had an accident on board and was killed. What precisely the accident was I could never elicit either from Nana or from my mother. I suspect that he had one evening dined too well in the wardroom and had fallen down a shaft or something of that sort, receiving injuries which in the end were fatal. It would account for my mother's fanatical teetotalism (Lady Astor couldn't have beaten her), which certainly couldn't have been due to my father, who drank only very moderately and many days not at all.

We saw Nana fairly often. She came to stay with us and we children used to stay with her. She always used the telephone as if she were sending a telegram. The telephone would ring and Nana's voice would say: "Arriving at 2.48 tomorrow. Nana," and then the telephone would go dead.

As children generally are, we were very curious about her own childhood, but we could get very little out of her. I once asked her what her Christian names were and, looking embarrassed, she said: "Emmie Murray." Later I learnt she was called Emily Maria. I didn't realize it at the time, but it is clear to me now that she was ashamed of her background and that was why she was so reticent about it and tended to play the great lady. (Among dozens of tourists she so imposed upon and impressed the attendants on board Nelson's HMS *Victory* at Portsmouth, when as a child she took me there, that we were given a special guide – a fact which gave her tremendous pleasure.)

All this had for over forty years completely passed from my memory, when, about two or three years ago, I was staying with my eldest sister in Farnham, and she said: "I've discovered about Nana." It took me quite a long time to twig what she was talking about. "What do you mean?" I answered. "Well," said my sister, "you remember how Nana would never tell us anything about her childhood or family? By chance I discovered that somebody I met the other day was her great-niece. They run a garage near here. Nana's parents owned a stables and used to hire out horses and carriages. When Nana married she cut herself off entirely from her family and refused to recognize them because they were in trade. Wasn't it disgusting of her? No wonder she used to give herself such airs."

This squalid piece of the worst kind of snobbery says a great deal about the atmosphere in which my mother grew up. It left her, I think, feeling she didn't know who or what she was, except that she was very much a second-class citizen compared with her brother – though he was always extremely kind to her, and to all of us.

It will be seen – and this in many ways has been the purpose of what I have so far said about my mother – how prime a target she was for any religious bird of prey. The bird turned out to be a retired colonel and his wife who were neighbours of ours in Rochester. They were extreme Evangelicals, or, as they would have put it, keen Christians out and out for Jesus.

Lying about in the attic at home I found when I was twelve or thirteen two books which indicated that my mother had for a time been an Anglo-Catholic. She had written her name in both of them. One was an obviously used copy of Father Stanton's famous *Catholic Prayers for Church of England People*. The other was a book for children with brightly coloured illustrations of priests in chasubles and dalmatics, of High Mass going on amid clouds of incense, of young men being ordained deacons and priests by a bishop wearing an enormous mitre, of infants being baptized, boys and girls being confirmed (the bishop again wearing his enormous mitre), people receiving Communion, making their confessions, kneeling before a statue of the Madonna, gazing in rapture at the reserved sacrament, being anointed with oil on their sick-bed – in fact the complete Anglo-Catholic *table d'hôte*. I haven't the slightest idea who brought this Anglo-Catholic influence to bear on my mother. It was over before I was born and never recurred. It was a passing phase, and I have no means of knowing how short or long it was.

Lasting victory belonged to the colonel and his lady who got their religious claws firmly into my mother's flesh. But the results were not to show for a year or two. It needed a personal crisis before their victim was fully conditioned.

❧❦6❧❦

I LIVED IN ROCHESTER until I was four and have never been back there since. I remember only isolated scenes and incidents.

I loved the gramophone – a thing you wound up and with an enormous red horn. I was especially fond of the record of a sentimental song called "Blue eyes, True Eyes" because, after having sung the song, the singer then whistled the tune, and my father told me that it was to that whistle that the dog was listening in the picture on the His Master's Voice label. Another favourite was a song beginning "Sally, do you remember the time when you lived down in our alley?" The record was smashed and my father said: "Sally has fallen down stairs and broken her leg," which I took with immense seriousness.

Then I remember a needlewoman who used to come in once a week and always brought me a carnation because I liked the smell.

We kept chickens at the end of the garden with whom I became great friends. I was unlucky enough to go into the kitchen after one had been killed and before it had been plucked. My reaction can be imagined.

My mother sensibly thought it a terrible mistake of nurses to threaten children, as they often used to, with policemen unless the children did what they were told. Her idea was that if a child were lost, stolen or strayed, it should go to a policeman, if it saw one, as to a friend. I remember being told how kind and nice and wonderful policemen were. I don't remember the result, but Nana did. She said that when out with her I insisted upon shaking hands with every policeman in sight, and kicked up the most appalling rumpus of yelling and screaming unless I was allowed to. The result was that Nana used to keep a sharp lookout for any policeman and, if she saw one, would quickly turn down a side street or go into a shop as if she were a criminal on the run.

I remember seeing a procession of sandwich men carrying placards advertising something. I asked my mother what they were. I suppose that in fact they were wretched men out of work in the aftermath of the First World War. But my mother told me that that was how people ended up if they were lazy and never did any work. I looked with dismal curiosity at these specimens of retribution, wondering if I would work hard enough not to end up like them.

Woolworth's store puzzled me a great deal. There was one at Rochester (or Chatham) and an identical one at Southsea, where Nana lived. I got it into my head that you walked into one end of the store at Rochester and out of the other end at Southsea, and I couldn't understand why, this being so, we bothered to take the train. I could never get an answer to my puzzle as the grown-ups never understood it and my sisters were contemptuous.

My nursemaid, Alice, was a brute. She used to take me out in the push-chair every afternoon, but as soon as we were out of sight of the house she would make me get out and walk until I was absolutely dropping. I naturally didn't understand that she wanted to tire me out before we reached the Castle Gardens so that I would sit quietly in my push-chair while she carried on with sailors. One blissful day she disappeared for good. I never asked where she was as I thought the question might lead to her return. In fact she had been found in the embrace of my father's marine servant, who came up to the house to do odd jobs, and, since the marine was married, it was thought better that Alice should go.

My last memory of Rochester is of a sunny day in the garden with my two sisters, all of us having bare arms with a dab of brown on the left one. The brown dab was iodine. We had all been inoculated against typhoid, since we were going to France. (The inoculation was totally unnecessary.)

It was 1924. My father, having failed to get his promotion, had retired from the Navy. The French franc was much in our favour. My mother was far from well and had been ordered a complete change by the doctors.

After my two sisters my mother had given birth to a stillborn child, a boy with black hair like her own. (This stillborn boy has never been for me an emotional problem, but it has certainly been an intellectual one. How far can I be said to possess the identity which would have been his? Should I have existed at all if he had been born alive? If we are only intelligent animals, then, of course, there is no problem. But if we have immortal souls, did he have one or was it sacrificed that I might have it instead? In my experience, parsons are not trained to answer that sort of question or, more accurately, they are not trained to think that they have the answer.)

The strain of the last few years for my mother must have been very considerable, especially coming after four years of war with worry about my father and her brother George, now a sub-lieutenant in HMS *Queen Elizabeth*, not to mention the terrible general distress, the disorganization of everything, and the malnutrition.

After I was born she had a severe nervous breakdown. What she needed was psychotherapy, but it wasn't available in those days or even thought of. You were either sane or mad. My father took her to a Harley Street neurologist. I doubt whether he was much help. My mother gradually recovered, but it was thought that a complete change of scene would complete the cure. So to France we went. Perhaps my father wanted to get her away from the religious vultures out and out for Jesus. My eldest sister, Joan, was left behind at boarding school and would join us in the summer holidays. I just remember the cabin on board the Southern Railway ship *Princess Ena*, which took us overnight to St Malo.

ᘛ7ᘚ

WE MEANT TO STAY for two or three months and stayed four years. My parents used to visit England every now and then, and my two sisters (the younger of them, Helen, was soon old enough to join Joan at boarding school) used to divide their time between Middlesex in term and Brittany in the holidays.

On one side of St Malo lies the estuary of the River Rance. It takes five to six minutes to cross the estuary to Dinard in motor launches called *vedettes*.

On the other side of St Malo there lies the end (or beginning) of a beach which stretches just over four miles to Rotheneuf. The beach is of firm golden sand – the sea covers it completely every high tide – with rocks dotted about here and there, rather like Cornwall.

Half-way along the coast between St Malo and Rotheneuf is a town called Paramé. It was here that we rented a furnished house about three minutes' walk from the sea.

I could see the sea from my bedroom window. A child between the ages of four and eight is extremely impressionable, and that particular seascape has become part of me, as I realize every time I go back there. The sea is broken by rocky islands which jut up in this and the other place. On one of them there is a lighthouse which flashes green and red. I knew it intimately as a personal friend. I loved it when the evenings drew in again, and it became dark early so that I could once more see my friend speaking to me. The largest island was called Cézembre, and as our house was called the Villa Cézembre, it caused confusion in the shops when we asked for goods to be delivered. They would say that they would have to wait for the *vedette* to go out, and we would triumphantly answer that there was no need as the address we meant was the Villa Cézembre, Rue des Fleurs, Paramé.

In the summer the beach was perfect for building sandcastles, climbing over rocks, examining rock pools, collecting various types of shell and seaweed. The bathing was good too: no undercurrents, the sea increasing in depth slowly and gradually, and easy for the feet. When it was rough the grown-ups used to lie on surfboards and allow themselves to be carried by an incoming wave – though this had the occupational hazard of being given a severe blow in the stomach when the sea played tricks with the surfboard.

The beach is connected for me with a small mongrel dog which turned up in our garden and to which Joan and Helen gave a meal so that he stayed around. Eventually our parents allowed us to keep him and we called him Sammy.

Sammy, my sisters said, was a darling little pet, the sweetest, most loving little thing, obviously full of friendliness and gratitude to his protectors, as indeed events that followed showed. He was also the most intelligent dog alive, as he found somewhere the crumpled and soiled remains of a cap I had lost in the wind a long time before and brought it into the house. But after he had been with us three or four weeks, all of us together saw him walking up from the beach proudly carrying a brassière in his mouth, obviously stolen from a pile of clothes while a woman was bathing. My mother wanted my father to parade round the beach waving the brassière so that its owner could recognize it and claim it and my father explain to her what had happened, my mother not trusting her own French to cope with the emergency. But this my father absolutely refused to do. Instead he went inside and searched a seldom frequented corner of the house. And there he found a pile of stolen clothes: men's trousers, women's underwear, children's jerseys, a panama hat – you name it and it was there. Sammy was a trained thief.

My father went at once to the police station and explained the situation, but the police were merely amused. They didn't even suggest that we got rid of Sammy. So the earnest and tearful pleading of us three children won the day, and Sammy was reprieved, only we should have to keep a sharp lookout on his activities.

Three or four days later my sisters were out with my father and I was at home alone with my mother. At about twelve noon an infuriated man came round to our house. He had discovered from neighbours that Sammy was ours and Sammy had run into their house and eaten the lunch prepared for the man, his wife and four children – arrived from Paris for a holiday only the day before. "My family are starving," he said, "starving, starving, and all because of your dog." My mother gave him the most abject apologies and said that most unfortunately she was not in a position to offer them all lunch at our house, but the least she could do was to go herself to a good hotel nearby, arrange for the family to have lunch, and foot the bill. But the man didn't want that. He wasn't short of money. It was a matter of honour – "*l'honneur, l'honneur, l'honneur,*" he kept repeating. My mother must have looked at her most pleading feminine, for the man gradually ceased to be angry, began looking tenderly at my mother, and finally walked up to her and kissed her twice. Then muttering "*Mille pardons, madame, mille pardons*", he walked slowly away. What he told his wife we never discovered.

It was clear that Sammy had to be put down at once. When my father and sisters returned a council of war was held, and it was decided that the quickest way of doing it was to take him to the local chemist, who was known to be expert in over-anaesthetizing unwanted animals humanely – "It will only be sending him into a lovely sleep. You know how nice that is" – but the owner had to dispose of the corpse.

My father dug a large hole in the garden and Sammy was taken to the chemist, whom we supplied with a wicker basket with a lid you could shut down in which to place Sammy's mortal remains. My father called for the corpse at about six, and Joan, Helen and myself, together with a boy of my own age with whom I had been playing, called Valentine, and my mother, all went reverently into the garden to see the body buried. We mawkishly picked up the basket and were horrified by its stillness and weight. The stark reality of death had fallen heavily upon us. We tried to suppress our tears. Then there was a bit of delay as somebody called and my father had to deal with him. But at last the lid of the basket was opened so that its contents could be decently buried. At that point Sammy barked and jumped out of the basket wagging his tail. He hadn't been anaesthetized enough and had now come to. Valentine in a tone of religious awe whispered to me – "*C'est comme Jésus. C'est comme le Pâques.*"

The next morning my father took Sammy to a vet in St Malo and had him properly disposed of.

8

THERE WAS A CONSIDERABLE ENGLISH COLONY around St Malo, attracted no doubt by the favourable rate of exchange. The rich lived in Dinard, where a Mrs Hughes-Hallett used to entertain her guests on gold plate, and a Mrs Johnson, an American widow of immense fortune, married a Turkish prince, who, to her intense annoyance, renounced his title almost as soon as the marriage register was safely signed.

Those of more modest income, like ourselves, lived in and around Paramé, where there were enough English people to have built an Anglican Church (known to the locals as *le temple*) and to maintain a full-time Anglican chaplain. The church, I regret to say, has now been bought by the Jehovah's Witnesses, who have a smartly painted board outside not only announcing that all are welcome but guaranteeing that no collection will be taken.

In the winter there was a great deal of entertaining, as servants, food and drink were all cheap for English people. For me this meant children's parties, which I loathed, except when (as in two houses) a cinema formed part of the entertainment and I had my first experience of Charlie Chaplin, Harold Lloyd and Felix the cat. My sisters asked my mother whether they need take me to parties. They said I embarrassed them by eating so much.

Their return from school was always a moment of intense excitement for me. The ship from Southampton arrived at St Malo at 7 a.m., which meant an early start from our house. We used in summer to arrive at the port in time to see the ship coming across the horizon. My pleasurable agitation was almost unbearable as the ship grew larger and larger until it was large enough for us to see my sisters waving on deck. My mother by arrangement always wore a red hat for the occasion so that my sisters could spot her as we stood on the mole. In those days St Malo was only a high-tide port, so if it was low tide the passengers had to land in *vedettes* and my sisters were invariably in the last one.

Except for one instance we never had any trouble with the customs, as my father at the end of the First World War had been made a Chevalier of the Legion of Honour and it was the practice then to signify the fact by wearing a ribbon in your button hole. This meant that we went through the customs without let or hindrance. The exception was the occasion when my sisters (conforming to a temporary fad of English doctors) brought with them three enormous jars of a nauseous substance called cod-liver oil and malt. The customs officials looked at the jars suspiciously and held them up to the light. There was much discussion and the senior official was called. He must have been a sensible man, for he stopped the delay by politely asking my father whether he would object if the jars were sent to our house in a day or two's time. My father said he would be honoured and enchanted, and they delivered the awful stuff three days later. I regret to say that none of it was the worse for wear.

The day my sisters returned to school was as black a day for me as for them. In fact they told me later that I always began the crying in which they soon joined.

On one occasion there was a reprieve which lasted a week. About ten days before the end of a holiday Helen had developed a slight rash. We were lucky enough to have the services of a clever Parisian doctor, who ran a sanatorium about a mile from our house (it is still going strong). He visited it from Paris about twice a week and had a few local patients, including ourselves. He had diagnosed Helen's condition as no more than a heat-rash which could be disregarded and would disappear soon of its own accord. My mother thought she had better write to the headmistress and explain this. The day my sisters were due to leave the headmistress replied by cable: "School doctor says it is German measles. Please delay return." The Parisian Dr Page was understandably white with fury at the arrogance and insolence of an English provincial G.P. diagnosing a condition without having seen the patient, when he himself had seen her and knew perfectly well what the trouble was. He wrote a letter to the school doctor, enclosing a translation into English done with real pleasure by my father. Of course Dr Page's opinion was correct. But the incident gave me my sisters' company for seven more days.

I was not allowed to see them off at the port. I was too upsetting a factor, and in any case the ship left at 9 p.m.,

24

which seemed to me the ultimate in lateness. I was left, boo-hooing, with Léonne, my nursemaid.

Léonne was completely different from Alice. She was kind and gentle and considerate and I grew to love her. She was also very devout and spoke to me of figures hitherto unknown to me such as *la Vierge* and *le Pape*. Around this time my mother asked me who always loved me and looked after me from above. I said it was la Vierge. "Who?" she asked. "La Vierge Marie," I said. Oh dear, it wasn't the right answer at all. I think my mother wanted to sack Léonne, but my father pointed out that she got on so well with me that it would be stupid not to keep her. All that needed to be done was to ask her in a friendly way not to speak to me about religion. That was done. Léonne promised and kept her promise.

I recall something which happened when I was out with Léonne which I look back to with interest, as it shows how different is the reaction of a child to things from an adult's. She was taking me for a walk one day when we came across a man standing with his back to a wall and completely exposing his private parts. I had often seen my father naked and the sight of this man aroused in me no reaction at all. He seemed to belong to the ordinary course of events. I couldn't understand why Léonne grabbed me, reversed our direction, and went up to two women who were following us about fifty yards behind. There was a frenzied discussion. All three grown-ups said they were horrified for *le petit*, that it was unbelievably disgraceful that *le petit* should be forced to see such things. In fact *le petit* was the only person in the group totally unconcerned though somewhat puzzled by all the fuss – but then the behaviour of grown-ups was often unaccountable. I don't know what happened in the end as Léonne took me home by another road and the two women rushed off to find a policeman.

These were good times for me because it was not only Léonne who liked me but also our ferocious old cook, Marie Louise, who adored small boys and hated girls. This meant that I was allowed into the kitchen and given all sorts of tit-bits while my sisters were chased out with considerable asperity. I had a small child's (English) edition of *Don Quixote*, which had a picture at the end of Don Quixote being thrown from his horse by the lance of a superior, impeccable knight. I showed it to Marie Louise, who said: "*Ah, Vive la France!*" "*Et l'Angleterre?*" I asked. "*l'Angleterre, non.*" It was too emphatic an answer for me to ask the usual "*Pourquoi?*"

One of the excitements of life was the arrival about twice a year of the circus – there were two of them on the road. I used to go with my father. My mother didn't like circuses much.

I remember the whole set-up rather than the individual performances: the huge tent, the brass band, the combined smells of sawdust, disinfectant and animal excreta. It was a new alternative world, glamorous and arousing. It had about it a wild, loud, gypsy atmosphere quite lacking in Bertram Mills' circus at Olympia, which smelt of Sloane Street and Kensington. At the Cirque Perrier or Pindère even the women who showed you to your seat looked like the sort of person who kidnapped children in storybooks. I was glad my father was with me.

One individual performance I do recall. It was a conjurer who guaranteed to produce in an empty glass under a handkerchief any drink the audience might ask for. He proved his capacity for magic by giving the drink to the person who asked for it to taste himself. People asked for red wine, white wine, cider, pernod, cognac, limonade, crème de menthe, St Raphael, and so on, always getting the drink they asked for. But there was one man in the audience with an extremely loud voice who kept on shouting for Viandox (the French Bovril), and the conjurer had to pretend not to hear him as he obviously hadn't any. "Viandox, Viandox, Viandox," this horrible man kept on shouting. I hated him. For all I know he may have been a paid advertiser of the product, but what he symbolized for me at the time (though I couldn't then have put it articulately) was an aggressive one-upmanship. His shouting summed up all those people who are unable to accept your limitations in decent compassionate silence, but who like to point them out in order to show the world how much cleverer than you they are.

Talking of aggression, one example of it absolutely terrified me because it was so sudden and unexpected. A short walk from our house was a corner shop, a café which also sold groceries and stamps. When I was about eight my mother sent me there to buy some stamps. I was glad to go as I knew the ladies who ran the place, a daughter of around seventeen, her mother and grandmother. When I arrived they were all in the café, no doubt saving fuel as it was winter, and the café was nice and warm with a brightly burning stove. They took no notice of me when I arrived as they were discussing what should happen next to a piece of embroidery the daughter had half finished. What colours should be used in what places in the remainder of the piece? The mother and grandmother disagreed on this, and the daughter doing the work was uncertain whose advice to take. Fingers were pointed at various places and rival colours suggested. After a bit the daughter began to veer to her grandmother's views. The mother then suddenly picked up the embroidery, opened the lid of the stove, and threw the embroidery into it, saying savagely: "*Mettez tout dans le feu*." I dashed out of the shop and ran home as quickly as I could. Nothing would drag me into the shop again. "*Mettez tout dans le feu*" became a proverbial saying shared between my mother and me.

I was taught to read in English and French at the same time, which, I suppose, ought to have been confusing but wasn't at all, except that I can't spell in either language. My father taught me to read in English and later gave me lessons in elementary arithmetic, geography and history. He also taught me to write in ordinary connected handwriting. My sisters came home from school full of the current educational fashion for what was called script writing and bringing a book to teach it. This did muddle me, and my handwriting has suffered ever since – though this is a disadvantage to my correspondents rather than to myself.

In the afternoon a Mlle de Sacconey came to teach me to read in French. She became a close friend of the family and used to come and stay with us when we had returned to England.

Her initial approach as a stranger of foreign speech to a small boy of four was superbly tactful. At my first lesson she read me in English the history of Squirrel Nutkin (my first experience of Beatrix Potter), with us both sitting together at the table so that I could see the pictures. I loved it so much that my Aunt Ethel sent me *Peter Rabbit* and *The Tailor of Gloucester* next Christmas.

Mlle de Sacconey started me on a book called *Je Commence à Lire*. She invented a small boy of my own age whom, she said, she was also teaching and who always seemed to be half a lesson in front of myself. She revealed that she had bought a prize for whichever of us reached the end of the book first and that she did so hope I would win it as she liked me better than the other boy, but she would have to be fair. Naturally I won (just!) and she gave me a toy railway engine. I used to go down on all fours and drag it round the room on its journey to Paris, making it stop at the proper places (learnt from Valentine): Rennes, Laval, Le Mans, Chartres, Versailles, Paris.

It was Mlle de Sacconey who introduced me to Bécassine, a children's nurse, whose adventures in writing and coloured strip cartoons are in France a children's classic. There were a number of volumes – *Bécassine aux Bains de Mer, Bécassine au Pays Basque, L'Enfance de Bécassine*, and so on. A few years ago a friend brought me from France five of the series, a reprint of 1964, showing that they were still being read forty years after I first met them.

Quite a number of our friends from England used to come to Paramé for a holiday, either staying with us or at some hotel or other nearby. Nana was the first to come. She was horrified on her arrival at the house when I and

Helen (aged nine) rushed out to meet her in sabots. Wearing wooden clogs was really to go too native. What on earth would happen to our social prestige? Sometimes my sisters brought schoolfriends to stay.

A more sinister visitor was the colonel's lady from Rochester, who stayed with us for a month. She almost drowned one day bathing before breakfast at high tide. But she survived to tell me of a small girl who was so fond of Jesus and understood so deeply how fond Jesus was of her that she told her mother that Jesus was not merely in her room but actually with her in bed. Wasn't that wonderful?

❧§9§❧

I HAVE KEPT TO THE LAST a description of the English church because it is connected in my mind with the beginning of the personal crisis which bore down upon my mother and gradually began to change the atmosphere of our home, not always but often.

To begin with and for some time all was well in a cosy and reliable world where the English church as a matter of course had its place in our lives.

The chaplain, Julian Turpin, was a man of great charm and vitality. In 1927 he all but won the local tennis tournament, but was forced to leave before the final match since it was Sunday and he had to take Evensong. He preached a stirring sermon, we were told, on the importance of duty. He was married with six children – three boys and three girls. Of the two elder boys one, I believe, was at Sandhurst and the other at Oxford. His eldest child, Phyllis, was a brilliant linguist and had some of the eccentricities and vagueness occasionally found in people of more than average intelligence. She was a delightful companion even if her clothes were liable to cause surprise. Although it was a furnished house we were renting, we had new covers made for the drawing-room chairs out of chintzy material rather loudly patterned. Phyllis, by chance, had seen the material in the upholsterer's window and, having taken a fancy to it, bought a length and had it made up into a dress. She came to tea with us wearing the dress and found herself sitting on a sofa covered with material precisely identical with the material in which she herself was covered. I was spellbound. It seemed to me perfect, exactly the way in which people should relate to furniture, and I couldn't understand why the grown-ups all laughed so much, including Phyllis, who had a great sense of humour. One Sunday she had a quick bathe before morning service and turned up in church in a coat and skirt but still wearing her bathing cap. She eventually became a Roman Catholic and married a German count. To her younger sister, Mary, Joan and I have good reason to be grateful. She married an Englishman. I will call him Gerald Branson. He worked in St Malo and was one of the figures on the periphery of my mother's crisis. After we had returned to England, Mary and Gerald kindly invited Joan and me to stay with them in Paramé, which we did most summers until the outbreak of the Second World War.

It was in the church where Mr Turpin ministered that I attended my first service of Holy Communion. It was, I think, latish on a Sunday morning and my parents took Helen and me presumably because there was nobody that day in the house to look after us. I remember that when my parents went up to receive the sacrament I asked Helen what they were eating and that she answered: "Bread soaked in water." Helen herself claims not to remember the incident, but then, what self-respecting vicar's wife could be expected to?

The service we normally attended on Sunday was Matins. My mother soon sang in the choir. Since she had had singing lessons and been taught how to produce her voice, her contralto practically was the choir.

As in most churches the seats in the nave faced east while the choir seats faced inwards. My mother and one or two other women sat on the south side while the north side was occupied entirely by four men of the same family –

three brothers, of whom Gerald Branson was one, and a cousin of theirs called Eddie.

The harmonium was on the south side of the choir and was pointed out as special as it had a sliding keyboard which apparently enabled you to transpose without tears. It was played by a redoubtable lady called Mrs Sankey, who always wore hats largely consisting of enormous feathers and who, with her husband, a retired coal merchant, was a pillar of the church. Mr Sankey's brother later became Lord Chancellor, first in the Labour then in the National Government, to the undisguisable envy and irritation of the local English community.

On the south side there was between the nave and the choir a wooden partition about four feet high on which brass railings were fixed, and curtains used to hang to about seven feet from the ground. There was a continuous controversy about whether the curtains should be open or closed. Mrs Sankey had them open, and it was complained that she and my mother looked as if they were a picture in a frame. When my father understudied for Mrs Sankey at the harmonium he closed the curtains, and it was complained that the music was muffled.

The singing could not only be muffled but virtually stopped if my mother happened on religious grounds to disapprove of a verse in a hymn, since then she would refuse to sing it. I remember that happening with Faber's hymn, "Jesu, gentlest Saviour, Thou art in us now". The last verse runs:

> Ah, when wilt thou always
> Make our hearts thy home?
> We must wait for heaven;
> And the day will come.

My mother took the view that for keen Christians, like the colonel's lady and herself, Jesus was always within them here on earth. So she was silent.

One Sunday there was an interruption of a more

startling kind. Somebody threw a brick through one of the windows. It didn't injure anybody, but it stopped the service for some twenty minutes. The man who hurled the brick was not a religious fanatic but a patriotic Frenchman. Rather stupidly we were singing one of the hymns which go to the tune of "*Deutschland, Deutschland über Alles*", and the 1914 war was still fresh in many people's minds and feelings.

I remember on another occasion everybody suppressing giggles at a memorial service for one of the English residents called Colonel Paine. He had been in the Indian Army and was almost a caricature of his profession. You were particularly unlucky if you met him in mid-morning carrying home the milk, because it was a chore which made him extremely bad-tempered. Most people sent their servants to get the milk, but Mrs Paine always used to send the poor old colonel, and you could see him fuming as he literally carried the can. He could be angry on other occasions too – for instance, after a controversy at a party with one of Mr Turpin's sons the colonel shouted out: "That fella's a bounder. I'd like to whip the young puppy." Perhaps it was this remark which unconsciously led Mr Turpin to open Colonel Paine's memorial service with the hymn beginning:

> On the Resurrection morning
> Soul and body meet again;
> No more sorrow, no more weeping,
> No more pain!

Even as a child of eight I remember the superhuman efforts of the congregation to look serious.

After we had been in Paramé a little time a new ecclesiastical figure appeared on the scene, a Mr Tambling, who held what was for me the intriguing and hitherto unknown office of lay-reader. I remember playing one whole afternoon at being a lay-reader. Mr Tambling, like Lewis Carroll, was fond of small girls – a schoolfriend my sisters brought to stay with us nicknamed him Slobbery-bom – and used to call at our house every day after lunch (it was summer holidays time) take my sisters (and for decency's sake the unfortunate man had also to take me – I saw to that) to a nearby sweetshop and buy us *suzettes* (large sweets on a stick). We always chose the same flavours: I chose *framboise*, Joan *anis*, and Helen *caramel au lait*, though that was fifty centimes extra. But Mr Tambling asked us each time what we would like. One day the three of us decided to change our choices, discussing it at some length before lunch. But on that very day, for the first time, Mr Tambling ordered the *suzettes* without asking us what we wanted. And we were too shy or polite to tell him of the change of choice we had planned. It was my first robust experience of bad luck.

Mr Tambling left the Paramé scene as abruptly as he had entered it. I thought that that was the practice of lay-readers.

Looking back now, what perhaps strikes me most about the English church in Paramé is the knowledge of the essential genius of the *Ecclesia Anglicana* possessed by our landlady, Mme à Laurent, a hard-headed French Roman Catholic *bourgeoise* living in St Malo, though admittedly always said to be in Paris when we wanted any repairs done. Hanging on one of the walls of our house was what we took to be a china decoration of pious design with a small bowl attached to it. One day it was broken. Mme à Laurent naturally said it was extremely valuable. My mother asked her why, if this were the case, she had left it in the house. Mme à Laurent answered: "Well, you see, if you let a furnished house to a Catholic family they expect it to have a holy water stoup. I ought to have remembered that you are (I can hear her say the words now) *Catholique Protestant*." Who on earth, I wonder, informed her (a previous tenant?) of the delicate poise, the historical compromise, the looking-both-ways of the Church of England? Perhaps it was just her business instinct.

MY MEMORIES of this period are many and vivid, not only, I think, because I was at an impressionable age but also because it was the last time that there was a consistently happy atmosphere in our family and my parents genuinely enjoyed each other's company.

After our arrival at Paramé my mother recovered her health by leaps and bounds. She was happy. She and my father found congenial friends among the English community and in some of our French neighbours such as Mlle de Sacconey. Friends from England (as I have said) came over and stayed for holidays. My parents joined the local tennis club and a small English badminton get-together. They went dancing in the evening at the Paramé casino (a pleasant building now pulled down and replaced by a hideous block of flats). The casino at St Malo was bigger and included a theatre where an opera company from Paris performed for a season each summer. I was, of course, much too young to go. But the repertoire one year must have included Massenet's *Hérodiade*, as I remember talk of John the Baptist's head being brought on to the stage, and my father bought a record of John the Baptist singing an aria in prison. I remember from it the words: "*Salut! Salut! premier rayon de l'immortalité.*"

That was for me the beginning of a fondness for French operatic religiosity which I still find both attractive and amusing. I think it externalizes for me the deep ambivalence of my feelings about religion. Gounod's *Faust* is a prime example of what I have in mind, to which I must add his St Cecilia Mass. But Massenet is the master because it seems to me that he only played at writing opera (however skilful and charming his playing was) and this increases the allure of his religious scenes. I have never had the opportunity of seeing *Hérodiade*. But there is always young Des Grieux at St Sulpice trying by prayer to overcome his obsession with Manon: "*J'ai voulu mettre Dieu même entre le monde et moi.... Ah, fuyez douce image loin de moi, loin de moi*"; and Manon's arriving at the seminary to entice her lover from his priestly vocation, but first, very properly, praying three times: "*Pardonnez moi, mon Dieu.*" But best of all is the long scene in which the now converted and saintly Thaïs dies and describes her entry into life eternal: "*Le ciel s'ouvre; voici les anges et les prophètes et les saints qui viennent avec un sourire, les mains tout pleins de fleurs. Deux seraphins aux blanches sailes ...*" and so it goes on until the final curtain comes down with Thaïs singing slowly four words, the last being on a high note: "*Ah ... je ... vois ... Dieu.*" It is all very moving, and complete tripe.

I I

AMONG THOSE who attended the English church were Mr and Mrs Branson, whom I mentioned earlier. It was their three sons who sang on the north side of the choir. Mr Branson had a brother, Uncle Eddie, whose own son, also called Eddie, was the choir's fourth man.

From before the First World War the Bransons had built up a very prosperous business exporting agricultural produce – chiefly potatoes – from St Malo to England. They owned an attractive château about three miles outside Paramé called Le (yes, *Le*, it was a masculine peculiar) Grand Rivière with lovely gardens, stables and a fairly extensive home farm. Uncle Eddie and his wife lived in Paramé itself; it was from their garden wall that I was allowed to see a pageant organized by the local municipality in which Léonne, to my intense excitement, sat astride an old hack and, although looking extremely nervous, was in my eyes the full and perfect embodiment of Jeanne d'Arc.

The three sons of the senior Grand Rivière Bransons were Clifford and George, who were twins of twenty-five (Clifford being the elder twin), and Gerald, who was twenty. We soon got to know them all extremely well. We seemed to be constantly up at Le Grand Rivière. It was there that I had my first experience of Hornby trains, which one of the sons unpacked from a cupboard for me, and my first – and almost last – experience of riding, on a dappled grey pony called Charley. I didn't, of course, go to Gerald's twenty-first birthday party, but I remember him coming to our house the following day with a bottle as big as himself which had obviously played some part in the celebrations of the previous evening.

The three sons were constantly with us. It was from them that I learnt the jargon of the twenties: of things going west, or being priceless or wonky or a scream. There were games on the beach, motor drives to Mont St Michel, picnics in the country, plans for dancing in the evening. And my mother, although she was then thirty-eight, was always at the centre of it. One evening, at the Paramé casino, she stole the opera hats and white silk scarves of the three brothers and brought them home as trophies. She was in fact far too popular for her not to arouse jealousy, not my father's but Mrs Branson's.

I was with my mother after church one Sunday when Mrs Branson stayed behind in order to give her a talking to. Even at my early age I soon recognized that Mrs Branson was talking to her very much, as they say, for her good. But the only words I remember Mrs Branson saying were a statement of indubitable fact: "My three boys are boys." After this harangue we went home somewhat gloomily. And much of the fun stopped. The boys came far less often to our house and we went far less often to Le Grand Rivière.

But the eldest of the sons, Clifford – he ran the home farm and was quieter than his brothers – began coming to our house more often. It wasn't long before in some sort of way he and my mother fell in love. I say "in some sort of way" because of the difference between Clifford's age, twenty-seven, and my mother's, forty.

I went once to the seldom frequented corner of the house (where the mongrel, Sammy, had stored his stolen goods) and found Clifford and my mother in a close embrace. She was looking rapturously up into his face and

36

saying "Sonny," and he was looking rapturously down into hers and saying "Mummy." For reasons which will become clear soon, their physical intimacy certainly did not extend beyond that limit. In some ways it might well have been better if it had.

After a time the Bransons – chiefly Mrs Branson, her sister-in-law, Uncle Eddie's wife, and her cousin, a Miss Spurrier who lived in Jersey and stayed regularly at Le Grand Rivière – came to the (for them) perhaps not altogether unreasonable conclusion that my mother was an adventuress bent on luring Clifford to some sort of doom. The last straw was a recently acquired and promising horse called Whiskers, who became ill. Clifford harnessed him to a trap and drove him to our house. Whiskers, on arrival, was covered with a white foamy sweat. After an hour Clifford drove him back home again. But Whiskers died that night. Clifford said he thought that exercise would do the horse good, but the Bransons thought that Clifford was so infatuated with my mother that it had made him inexcusably careless about the horse's welfare.

The Bransons thus cut off all relations with us. Le Grand Rivière became forbidden territory. George and Gerald were seen no more. I was walking one morning with my mother near our house and we passed Uncle Eddie and his wife. My mother bowed. Uncle Eddie took off his hat and smiled, but his wife cut us dead with her head in the air. My mother wept bitterly when we got back home and recounted the incident to my father. In the circumstances she thought it best to resign from the church choir.

I can vividly remember our first Sunday in the nave. Clifford had absented himself from the church, but George, Gerald and cousin Eddie were in the choir, having obviously rehearsed with particular care. They sang more loudly than usual, their voices vibrating round the building: "O come, let us sing unto the Lord; let us heartily rejoice in the strength of our salvation. Let us come before his presence with thanksgiving: and shew ourselves glad in him with psalms."

Mrs Sankey tried to bring about a reconciliation, writing to my mother that there would be a choir practice as usual the following Friday at six, and was she by any chance free to come to tea first? But it was no good. By that time my mother was too obsessed by Clifford to make wise decisions.

One of the minor inconveniences of the situation was that we no longer went to the beach. Every day except Sunday all the summer – even when my sisters were home on holiday – my mother and we three children would tramp the long distance to Clifford's farm, taking a picnic lunch and staying there until the evening.

The farm was interesting to a point. There was only one motor tractor, so there were horses we came to know. The farm labourers were friendly. Threshing was fun. The threshing machine was driven by a steam tractor. The bunch of flowers traditionally put through the machine after the last of the harvest had been threshed was given instead to my mother. Clifford (by this time to us children he was Uncle Clifford) laughed at my mother's fear of cows. If we were too late he would drive us home in his trap.

This mutual infatuation had, however, a far deeper, more lasting, and more destructive consequence for us all than anything which had so far appeared.

12

OBVIOUSLY MY MOTHER felt deeply guilty about falling in love. Objectively she had very little to be guilty about, except perhaps a certain lack of discretion, a certain absence of wisdom where it might have been useful. But who can help falling in love? And when in love it is easy enough, God knows, to throw wisdom and discretion overboard. But the guilt still lay oppressively heavy and threatening upon my mother's feelings. She coped with it – and this is central to the story – by turning to the religion of the colonel's lady and becoming now herself a keen Christian out and out for Jesus.

The results for my own life I was to learn only gradually on our return to England. That wasn't in fact far away, since by now I was eight years old and needed to go to school. Meanwhile my mother concentrated on Clifford to make him, like herself, out and out for Jesus. He was an apt pupil. Not only did he become a keen Christian, but, before many months had passed, said he wanted to be a clergyman. His parents were horrified. What would this adventuress and enchantress do to him next? They told him that as the eldest son he was to inherit all they had. It was no use. He was determined. Seeing they could not deflect him from the path he had decided on, they were able to persuade him at least to become a clergyman properly and go to Oxford.

In all these circumstances my mother inevitably somewhat confused being a keen Christian with being absorbed by Clifford, or rather she translated her absorption by Clifford into what was supposed to be expected from keen Christians.

We had, for instance, quite a number of dance gramophone records which she used to like. Now she no longer did. She said she hated some records of Offenbach's *La Périchôle* that my father had recently bought. I heard her telling a friend how the dance and opera tunes had faded for her. "Oh, I know," answered the friend, "records soon get into a wretched state here. I think the sea air must be bad for them." My mother had to expound to her the way of God more perfectly.

Things, of course, never go smoothly when one is deeply in love, especially if one is in an ambiguous position. My mother's suffering was sometimes obvious, though I was unaware then of its cause. I found her once in the drawing-room weeping her eyes out. I asked her what the matter was and she answered, rocking to and fro: "I want to go home. I want to go home." I deliberately misunderstood her in order to reassure myself. "We can always go back to England when we want to, can't we?" I said. She answered: "I don't mean that. I mean I want to die. I want to die and be with Jesus." She thus activated in me a misery equal to her own, I thought my heart would burst with grief.

She continued, unwillingly and listlessly, to accompany my father on public occasions. She went with him, for instance, to the opera in St Malo. Next morning at breakfast she said how thrilled she had been by a severe thunderstorm which had broken out as they were driving home. "It says in the Bible," she continued, "that Jesus will come again during a thunderstorm and I thought it might be last night."

I mustn't give the impression that she was always as distressed as that. She was often cheerful and in spirits. But when she was in the depths, it used to stab me like a knife. The worst thing was that I knew I could do nothing, nothing at all, to comfort her.

But all in all she hadn't done too badly for herself. She had converted the man she adored to her own fanatical brand of religion, and he was going to England (for Oxford) just at the time when she was going back there too. She might well have meditated thankfully but blindly on Romans 8:28 that all things work together for good to those who love God.

In retrospect there was at this initial period a lighter and more amusing side to her decision to be out and out for Jesus.

When we first arrived in Paramé our Protestant susceptibilities were somewhat shocked at Christmas by the confectioners selling the Holy Family in chocolate. Brittany was at that time the most devoutly Catholic of all places in the world, and nothing could have been done of which the church authorities disapproved. But they were Roman Catholics and couldn't be expected to know better. However, our prejudices were quickly overcome, even at our first Christmas, and we were each given a delicious Holy Family to eat. A psychoanalyst could no doubt have discovered a great deal about us from the bits of chocolate we ate first: St Joseph's legs, Mary's head, or the manger itself with the Christ child in it. At my mother's coming out (why should the phrase be reserved exclusively for gays?) the prohibition of the chocolate Holy Family became absolute. I was very disappointed. No chocolate tasted as good.

An addition, too, was made to our Christmas tree: a Nativity in carved and painted wood now hung at its centre. That in itself was appropriate enough. But it wasn't considered enough, not by any manner of means.

At our Christmas children's party the Christmas tree was in the dining-room, which was separated from the drawing-room by folding doors. The doors were shut while the Christmas tree was being lit up and then, when it was ready, the lights in the drawing-room were switched off and the folding doors opened. It was an exciting moment. But this year the Nativity on the tree was used by my mother for an embarrassing discourse about giving your heart to Jesus. I thought it would never end. The other children were restless, some crying, some giggling. It was awful.

A few days later a similar party was held for the children of Clifford's labourers at the farm. Luckily my mother couldn't trust her French to give a religious discourse to them. Instead, when the folding doors opened, she stood silent and still like a *tableau vivant* of Britannia, except that, instead of holding a trident, her arm pointed to, and her hand touched, the crib in the most melodramatic of gestures. It didn't matter. The French children were clearly prepared for anything from people who were bourgeois, English, and Protestant.

Another thing I recall is that from now on we were taught never to put any book on top of the Bible. If that was a piece of sheer ritualism, it was in keeping, for the Bible had come with my mother to rank with Jesus as an object of worship. She now read me bits of it every evening, pronouncing the plagues of Egypt as "plags". And she didn't know what Jesus meant when he said: "For if they do these things in a green tree, what shall be done in the dry?" She said she would have to ask Mr Turpin, though I don't think she ever did. We were warned sternly against jokes about the Bible. (I remember four or five years later the thrill of horror which swept over me when a member of a concert party on the pier at Southsea said: "The wages of gin is breath." I thought it desperately wicked and terrifyingly attractive.)

Medicine was now administered with prayer, even syrup of figs or calomel, though not the Eno's fruit-salt in the morning. When my mother was sleeping, her eyes used to close completely like anybody else's. But when praying her eyelids covered her pupils, but an area of white below remained uncovered. In this posture she would hold half an aspirin in a glass eyebath with a stem and call down upon it the divine blessing. I got the impression – it was the stem, I think – that there was something particularly solemn about aspirin. It was all very far from being unattractive.

❦ 13 ❦

WHAT MY FATHER'S FEELINGS WERE while all this was going on is difficult to tell. He was too sensitive and loyal a person to speak adversely about our mother to us children, and, in any case, he was by nature reticent.

I can remember only two occasions when he might have been directing a shaft against her, but it was done with such lightness of touch and humour that it delighted us children and we were certainly then totally unaware of any *arrières pensées*.

At the time when we were not yet exiled from Le Grand Rivière, my mother was determined to walk there with my sisters in spite of the fact that it was absolutely pouring with rain. I was left behind, and because I felt sore about it my father adapted a nursery rhyme for me:

> Three drowned rats
> See how they run.
> They all run up to the Grand Rivière

To see Clifford and the horses there
Also to see Miss Spurr-iair
Three drowned rats.

He used at times to stand in for the British Vice-
Consul at St Malo, Sir George Curtis, (whom I am happy to
mention, as his son, Geoffrey, was one of the most loved
members of our Community. He died about a year ago.
Community legend has it that Geoffrey as a young man
used to read weighty theological works sitting on the steps
of the Casino at Dinard). One morning my father came
home with two or three bottles of champagne. I think some
old friends of ours from England had turned up in Paramé
and there was to be a celebration. But my father said: "You
know I stood in at the Consulate for Sir George Curtis
when he went to England? Well, I thought that as acting
consul I had the power to marry people, and I did marry an
English couple. When Sir George came back he told me I
hadn't the power and that in consequence the couple
weren't married at all. I wondered how soon they would
hear about it. I was very frightened. I expected the man to
turn up one day at the Consulate and shoot me. Every step
I heard outside the door I thought might be him. Well, this
morning he did turn up. (We were trembling with
pleasurable fright.) He'd learnt he wasn't married. But he
didn't shoot me. Instead he gave me these bottles of
champagne."

Looking back I think that my father understood my
mother's falling in love with Clifford and hoped it would
pass if he didn't make any fuss about it. But he couldn't
begin to understand her taking to religion in such a
fanatical way. Here he was completely out of his depth.
Evidence of his pathetic attempts to understand and meet
her on these religious grounds were scattered about our
house in England: Bibles and Prayer Books, Bunyan's
Pilgrim's Progress and *Holy War*, Jeremy Taylor's *Holy
Living*, William Law's *Serious Call*, all inscribed at different
times "To my darling Nan with much love" or "To my

43

own darling wife, Nan, with much love" (I have one of these prayer books in my stall here at Mirfield). But it was no good. My mother's religion was for Clifford and to protect herself against sin with Clifford. In any case my father could never have become out and out for Jesus. While still in France we had in church one Sunday the hymn:

> I could not do without thee,
> O Saviour of the lost,
> Whose precious Blood redeemed me
> At such tremendous cost.

At lunch my mother said fiercely, almost savagely, to my father: "I meant every word of it." I realized at once that she was passing a vote of no confidence in him.

He used to take for me a children's weekly called *La Semaine de Suzette*. The Christmas number that year had a religious story about a saint, which my father read to me. He obviously liked it as, at the end, he said: "I must read that to Mum. She'll love it." I knew she wouldn't at all. And I was right. To begin with, it wasn't in the Bible.

My father had some French friends called Miriaux, who had a holiday house in Paramé but lived in Paris. He went to stay with them once or twice, or at least that is what I was told – I'd been to tea with them in Paramé. They had three attractive daughters in their twenties. My favourite was Madeleine. She once sat with my father and me on *la digue* (the seafront) and said that if we watched the passers-by closely we should notice that, whether expensively or cheaply dressed, all the dowdy women were English. I agreed, feeling illogically superior.

My father went on a tour of the Loire with the Miriaux. I still have guidebooks and picture postcards of the trip. But to what it all added up I have no notion, except that I have no reason to doubt it was perfectly innocent, though I don't really care one way or the other. After all, as far as my own life is concerned, what passes for virtue has been a far more destructive force than what passes for vice.

When my parents were deciding where it would be best to settle in England, my mother's religiosity did, on one occasion at least, irritate my father. She kept on telling him that if they prayed about it they would be guided where to live. I remember him answering: "Do you mean we shall see Plymouth, Portsmouth or Rochester written up in the sky?"

We went in fact for six months to a flat in London, in Carlisle Place, near Westminster Cathedral. From there my parents house-hunted.

Seven years later, when I was fifteen, I went with Joan to Paramé as the guest of Gerald and Mary (née Turpin) Branson. The old people – Gerald's parents – couldn't have been more friendly and welcoming. They invited us up constantly to Le Grand Rivière. But, as far as I was concerned, the old early days could not be left behind. It so happened that the first Sunday of our stay was the eleventh after Trinity with the Prayer Book collect beginning: "O God, who declarest Thy almighty power chiefly in shewing mercy and pity." Instinctively I applied the words to Mr and Mrs Branson and their kindness to offspring who must themselves be undesirable because their mother was undesirable. Later on during our visit a young naval lieutenant who was chasing after Joan, having discovered where she was holidaying, turned up unexpectedly. I felt it was dreadful and frightfully unfortunate, as Mrs Branson would think like mother, like daughter – a curious feeling to have about an eligible bachelor who was courting your sister in the company of friends.

One of my main quarrels with traditional Christianity of most varieties, not just Anglican Evangelicalism, is that it does not try to exorcize this kind of guilt from people, but plays upon it. It impresses guilt upon people ever more savagely so that it may then graciously offer them the free gift of salvation, if in some Low or High Church way they take the trouble to buy it.

The trick was copied by the advertisers: frightening you with bad breath for which the product advertised is the only reliable cure.

14

I ENJOYED our time in London. My father took me round to see the sights. To many of them I haven't been since – the Tower, the Houses of Parliament, Madame Tussaud's. I preferred Westminster Cathedral to Westminster Abbey because its atmosphere seemed to me warmer and more homely. But the two places I liked most were the London Museum, then still in Lancaster House, and the Tate Gallery. I liked the interior of Lancaster House. I was fascinated by the clocks in the hall which told you what time it was in all parts of the world. And I was thrilled by the working model (if that is the right name) upstairs of the Great Fire. There was also in a dark corner the waxwork of an eighteenth-century sailor with a pigtail, which, coming on it unexpectedly, gave you a delicious fright. In the Tate Gallery I loved the Victorian story pictures: Sickert's husband and wife bored to death with each other and Martineau's "Last Day in the Old Home" (my mother was very keen on this painting and pointed out for my attention how everything was being sold up while the bankrupt householder was drinking). But the picture which impressed me most was called "The Magic Circle". It showed a tall and youngish witch of very forceful personality standing by a boiling cauldron while with a stick she was tracing a circle around it on the ground. Ominous birds, ravens I think, were standing about just outside the circle. It was a pleasantly terrifying scene. The painter, I've recently discovered, was J. W. Waterhouse and it reached the Tate in 1886.

The church we went to, St Andrew's, Ashley Gardens, was bombed in the war and not rebuilt. The vicar called and I think he and his wife came to dinner with us, but I can't remember having any contact with him myself.

46

During this period there was a state visit of some foreign potentate, and men in the street were selling what they advertised by shouting "Programme and Guide". To my own considerable amusement I applied the words to the collect for the fourth Sunday after Trinity – "that thou being our programme and guide, we may so pass through things temporal, that we finally lose not the things eternal".

I was taken once again to children's services (perhaps the vicar suggested they were more suitable than Matins). At one of these we sang the hymn:

> We are but little children weak
> Nor born to any high estate;
> What can we do for Jesus' sake
> Who is so high, and good, and great?

It was a curious choice as the typical inhabitants of the area were Tory MPs with houses in the country. Perhaps they had gone there for Sunday and that was the point, or perhaps they sent the children to church with the servants. I can't remember. What I do remember is the effect the sentiment of the hymn had on the boy in front of me: he gave his younger sister's hair a violent tug so that she screamed horribly. Looking back on the incident it makes me feel that there is much to be said for Feuerbach's notion that man abstracts and alienates from himself all that is best and strongest within him, and, projecting it upon the heavens, calls it God. Many Christians do that with regard to the figure they call the risen and ascended Jesus. Mrs Alexander's hymn is a case in point.

But, on the whole, St Andrew's church was harmless enough. It gave me my first taste of West End religion, which I have continued to like as I like French operatic religiosity.

Uncle Clifford didn't appear at the flat. Presumably he was settling up his affairs in Paramé to be ready for the October term at Oxford.

But keen Christian friends of my mother did

appear. One of them called Margaret (I've forgotten her surname) gave a tract to the lift-boy which he stuck up for a day or two in the lift. It was the size of a lady's visiting card and had on one side a large question-mark in bold red print. At the bottom of the other side in small black print were some texts and explanations about the return to earth of Jesus in glory, while in red capitals at the top was the question: "Will He Come Today?" I couldn't understand why the lift-boy found it so amusing. I asked my mother, who said that worldly people always did laugh at the Word of God. The lift-boy was, I suppose, about eighteen, and I studied him closely to discover what I could about the species labelled worldly.

But the most important thing which now began to fall on me was first the shadow and then the hand of moral and religious blackmail. Both occurred while my sisters were home for the holidays and Nana was staying with us.

Nana and Joan went out for a day's shopping, getting back at about five o'clock for tea. They had lunch out, and, during it, Nana said to Joan that they ought to buy a paper and see what was on, as it would be fun to go to a film. Joan answered, so Nana informed us: "Wouldn't mum disapprove of us going to a film? Wouldn't she be angry?" This was news to me. I hadn't yet heard of the prohibition. Nana pooh-poohed Joan's objection, and to a film they went. "Really," said Nana, "it is too ridiculous to bring children up like that, too wickedly absurd. Why, people will begin imagining that you are lower-middle-class nonconformists, especially with a name like yours." That was the shadow of blackmail.

The hand itself had to do with my mother teaching us that if we were given any money by relatives we were to give one-tenth of it away to foreign missions. Nana said that Uncle George was angry about it and had declared that no money he gave to anybody was to go to missionaries. He had seen them at work abroad. The main function of uncles is to tip their young nephews and Uncle George always gave me a pound when he came to see us. He was coming to see us at the end of the week, and the visit put me in the most terrible position. If he forbade me to give any money to the missionaries I should have to refuse it – a boy of eight standing up against a man who was now a lieutenant-commander. I dreaded his arrival. His whole visit was an agony, because it was on leaving that he always tipped me. The moment came. But, of course, he was far too sane and far too nice to say anything at all. He just pushed the small folded-up note into my hand and said good-bye. It is difficult to describe the extent of my relief. And I was able to give two shillings to the Church of England Zenana Missionary Society.

15

MY PARENTS finally bought a house in Cranleigh on the Surrey–Sussex border. It was still then a village of about two thousand inhabitants. Its attraction was that it had three schools for boys – a pre-preparatory Dame school where I could be broken in as a day boy, and a Preparatory and Senior School where I could go as a boarder.

Two years ago (we had left our house then over two decades before – my mother sold it when my father died) Joan and I motored over from Farnham to see it again. We found that it had been pulled down by a speculative builder, who had built nine identical houses on the site. There was only one tree left from our garden for us to recognize. It was like dying. We felt that something of our identity had been destroyed. It was as if we had expected to meet an old friend and had seen a tombstone instead. We drove quickly to a pub and had a large drink. Yet it was a house in which we had both, in different ways, had a great deal of unhappiness.

When we first arrived my mother enjoyed herself (she had hated London). It looked as if she and my father might get back to their old footing. People, as they used to then, called and left cards, and my parents would return the call; the wife left one card, the husband two smaller ones.

I enjoyed the Dame school. It was owned and run by a Miss Tapp. To assist her she had a staff of four mistresses and a matron. A man came in to take us for soccer and cricket. I particularly liked being a Wolf Cub and adored what the Wolf Cub book described as trekking. I found the work in form fairly easy, though I got rather stuck in arithmetic (all forms of mathematics were always an almost organic weakness with me). I was only once acutely unhappy. The two senior boys in charge allowed us all to go into the school field. Miss Tapp objected to this and reprimanded them. They said I had told them she had given permission. I hadn't. But Miss Tapp said she trusted the two senior boys and knew that they couldn't both be lying, so I must be. The three of them went on at me so much that in the end I confessed to the lie, though I hadn't told it. I was given an order-mark, and when the order-mark book was read out on Saturday morning, Miss Tapp commented on mine and said it was for lying, a particularly nasty offence. We were standing in a line and I hung my head in shame, perfectly innocent though I was. It seems to me now that there must have been something wrong between me and my parents for my not telling them anything about it. Perhaps I thought that, if I did, I should be given too big a dose of Jesus. I don't know. In any case the incident wasn't at all typical. The school was extremely well run and I enjoyed it.

We were lucky in having Heath Robinson as a near neighbour. His youngest son, Tom, was my age and went to my three schools as his three elder brothers had done. Tom and I spent a great deal of time together.

His father's studio was an outhouse in the garden which had an old-fashioned speaking-tube to the house, and Heath often let us play with it. He was a very gentle person, full of humour (that was hardly strange) and marvellous with children. He had drawn the map of an imaginary island for Tom which was called Biglands, and also one or two pictures of its towns and country. Tom used to govern and administer it, and he allowed me to join him in this work of government. We spent hours discussing the affairs of Biglands, agreeing and disagreeing about them. Tom had great spirit. Later on when we were at preparatory school together the master in the changing-room told us not to whistle. So Tom started us singing. The master told us not to sing, so Tom started us humming. As far as I remember he won and the master fled in despair.

The elder brothers used to have tennis parties with my sisters. Quentin was then eighteen and Helen told me of her daydream of marrying him, adding: "Of course I should convert him first so that he was a keen Christian." There was a sort of racialism among those out and out for Jesus. They were supposed only to marry each other so as not to be unequally yoked with an unbeliever.

Heath Robinson's second son, Alan, was converted in another sense. He became a Roman Catholic and then a Benedictine monk at Prinknash, ending up as Dom Basil. Mrs Robinson became a Roman a year or two later.

But before this they had moved from Cranleigh to Highgate, where I went to stay with them in Shepherd's Hill. By chance their house at Cranleigh was bought by a Roman Catholic lady, who turned Heath's studio into a chapel. In those robust old unecumenical days all our friends made jokes about Heath Robinson's studio being very suitable for a Roman Catholic chapel; you wouldn't notice the difference, they said.

What I have called the moral and religious blackmail now began disturbing me quite often. *Hiawatha* was being produced at Miss Tapp's (in those days it used to be done annually at the Albert Hall). I took home a notice saying that there would be a rehearsal the following Sunday at 3 p.m. I gave it to my mother, and having by now learnt her recently acquired strict Sabbatarian principles, I said the only thing I could: "I don't want to go." (In fact I did want to go because I enjoyed the easy rhythm of the poem and thought it very grand.) "Quite right," she said with a kind of thankful satisfaction. So I didn't go.

Even worse: another neighbour of ours was a widow

whose younger son was my age and also went to Miss Tapp's. We used sometimes to play together. I went once to his place for the day and his mother wanted to take us both to the cinema. I had to tell her that I disapproved of the cinema. She didn't try to persuade me, but, by chance, met my father that same afternoon and told him about it. When I got home my father scolded me and told me I mustn't be a little prig. Torn thus between father and mother, I longed eagerly for the day when everybody would have the same views as my mother's. And I looked forward to it by singing the lines of a hymn:

> And the great church victorious
> Shall be a church at rest.

When I went to stay with the Heath Robinsons in Highgate, my mother and Joan came to fetch me at the end of the week. Heath, his eyes twinkling, said of Tom and myself: "Oh, they've been dreadfully wicked, these two young things. I tried my best to stop it, but you know what young people are. They've been to the cinema and to the theatre." It so happened that, soon after, Joan and I were left alone in a room for two minutes. In the excited voice in which, had we been some years older, she might have asked if I had really been to a brothel, she said: "Have you really been to the theatre?" I had to say "Yes". Mrs Robinson had taken Tom and me to Daly's to see *Charley's Aunt*. The film was Harold Lloyd's first talking film, *Welcome Danger*. My mother on this occasion said nothing, realizing, no doubt, that she couldn't get the better of Heath's gentle humour.

During my stay he told me that he had had a curious dream. He dreamt he had woken up and seen ten Harrys in his bedroom. This was a bit uncomfortable, so he had gone down to the dining-room and found ten more Harrys there. He opened the front door, but found a still further ten Harrys on the doorstep. Then all thirty Harrys chased him down the street and made him wake up. His dream made me feel very important.

❧ 16 ❧

OUR GENERAL PRACTITIONER at Cranleigh, Dr Cameron, was a youngish man but in the best tradition of the family doctor. It seems strange now that if, say, you had a slight attack of 'flu, you telephoned the doctor at nine and he was at your house by eleven.

It was the medical fashion then for children to have their tonsils out. Dr Cameron said it would be a good thing if I had mine out before going as a boarder to the preparatory school. I was examined by a consultant surgeon from Guildford, who said that certainly they must come out. There was no difficulty as the village had a cottage hospital (the first, it was claimed, of its kind in this country) which had been extended and included what would now be called a private wing. So I went in for a week. I quite enjoyed it. Visitors could come at any time as I had a room on my own, and my parents and friends called. My mother read me a book of Norse legends called *Heroes of Asgard*. I was so obviously thrilled by them that my mother thought it necessary to point out that the Norse legends were nothing like so interesting or good as the stories in the Bible. I thought otherwise, but kept my views to myself.

I soon recovered from this very minor operation. But after about a week at home, I fell ill. It was thought that I had swallowed some blood. Anyhow I became very seriously ill, my temperature one evening rising to 105.4. Needless to say my mother nursed me with devoted care and Dr Cameron seemed to live at our house. There were then, of course, no antibiotics. I passed the crisis and recovered. When I was convalescing Dr Cameron came to see me one Sunday morning as I was sitting in an armchair in my bedroom. With a broad smile he said to me – obviously for the benefit of my mother – "You see what you've done to me? You've prevented me from going to church because I had to come and see you." Some weeks later his car passed me while I was walking in the road. He stopped about three hundred yards ahead, opened the window, and beckoned me. Naturally I ran to him and he told me some funny story. Later he told my mother that he had done this in order to see me running and so discover how much my strength was restored. He was satisfied. But it was thought best that I should go to the preparatory school, at least to begin with, as a day boy. My father easily arranged this with the headmaster.

The headmaster was an unmarried clergyman called Mr Mertens. I thought him a kind, pleasant man. In the chapel he used to take the service, preach and play the harmonium. It was a sort of one-man band. The chapel was bright with religious pictures. It had a warm atmosphere. Mr Mertens used to take us for divinity and once warned me that I must think carefully before I spoke. He had asked us why Christ had died and I immediately shot up my hand and said: "To save our sins." He told us always to write the word God with three capital letters. He liked beating us with a clothes-brush. A stroke with the clothes-brush on the bare bottom was called a charlie (I don't know why), and punishments were awarded from one to five charlies according to the gravity of the offence. If, for example, a master caught you talking in class, he would say "Williams, you will take one charlie." Mr Mertens reserved for himself the duty of inflicting the punishment. I never minded, as there was not even the slightest hint of guilt about charlies. They might hurt a bit at the time, but they didn't make me unhappy or leave me feeling wicked. They were clean.

Another master, Mr Marcon, married but with no children, had some prestige as a former hockey international. He was fond of small boys and once contrived that two of the most attractive ones should pick him a bouquet of wild flowers which was placed on his desk in class. Unfortunately that morning – it was after break – Mr Mertens came in first to give out a notice. He asked what the bouquet was doing. When told, he was very angry, said he couldn't possibly allow it, and took the flowers away. Hindsight suggests to me that he was a little jealous of Mr Marcon.

54

The nicest of all the masters was Mr Stone, the music master. He was a quiet, gentle person, but with authority enough to keep perfect order. He made me as sensitive to music as a boy of from ten to thirteen can be. He once set a tune-guessing competition for the whole of the upper part of the school and I won it. He gave me in lovely golden covers a book called (it was at the end of the autumn term) *Christmas with Dickens*. I won other official school prizes, but this one I treasured far above the others. I don't know why, but when I think of Mr Stone I still get a lump in my throat. I think it was his extraordinary kindness and sensitivity.

At a school concert one of the boys sang a song about "Bonnie laddie, Highland laddie", correctly pronouncing "Highland" as "Heeland". I was horrified as I thought he said "heathen" and the word kept on being repeated in the jolliest way. My parents were present; what would my mother think?

It would have been far better for me if the original plan of sending me as a boarder had been followed. I was happy at school and needed badly to get away from the increasingly guilt-ridden atmosphere of home, and the turmoil caused by my mother's feelings for Uncle Clifford.

Clifford arrived at Oxford for the Michaelmas term 1928, joining St Catherine's Society (then non-collegiate, my mother always called it non-collegius), and lodging in the Bullingdon Road with a Mr and Mrs Lambourne. Mr Lambourne was kitchen manager at Brasenose. Both he and his wife were very Low Church, active supporters of the Bible Churchman's Missionary Society and worshippers at St Clement's, where Clifford also worshipped. The vicar, Dr Braddle Johnson, had some allure for me as he wore a D.D. hood. Years later Eric Graham told me at Cuddesdon that Dr Braddle Johnson always took the precaution of thanking visiting preachers for their sermon before the service, just to be on the safe side. Mrs Lambourne said you could always have a nice spiritual talk with him.

My mother and I used to go and stay with the

Lambournes, or rather with Clifford. He was reading for Classical Moderations, and used to go through the set texts, with my mother reading the English while he went through the Greek and Latin originals. I was once heard in the house to say "Ye men of Athens," and my mother said how good it was for me educationally to sit in on her sessions with Clifford.

He sometimes rowed us on the river, teasing my mother because she said she couldn't possibly take her knitting with her in the boat as she would be too busy holding on. We went to Keble to see the original of Holman Hunt's "Light of the World". Some old man in the chapel told us a long story about Holman Hunt, the gist of which was that friends had told him he was mad when he began painting the "Light of the World". My mother seized on this with alacrity: "They would say he was mad, of course they would, naturally, if he were painting Jesus."

Clifford also did social work in some Oxford slums and my mother went with him. What, apparently, distressed them was not the conditions in which the people were living, but the fact that they had seen some young boys playing cards – "It was terrible. They couldn't have been more than thirteen or fourteen years old. If only it could have been ludo or snakes and ladders."

But the highlight of all the visits for me (for we paid several between 1928 and 1931) was a University Mission sermon preached one Sunday evening in St Mary's by William Temple, Archbishop of York. St Mary's was packed out and we had to sit in the gallery. I couldn't understand a word Temple said, but the sight of an archbishop in convocation robes uttering a ceaseless stream of words in a rotund style and fruity voice absolutely mesmerized me. From that moment I knew I wanted to be a clergyman. It was nothing to do with piety. It was the glamour.

The next day I preached, using the open window of my bedroom at the back of Bullingdon Road as a pulpit. It ended badly as, after I had gone on for five or six minutes, the infuriated voice of a man in a house nearby shouted out: "For Christ's sake shut up, can't you, you bloody hypocrite?" I have often deeply envied that unknown man his freedom from inhibition, and wished it could be mine. But at that time I was too full of myself becoming a clergyman to think of anything else. My mother inevitably interpreted my being the victim of glamour as a spiritual triumph for herself, thanks, of course, to God and Jesus and all that.

Clifford passed Classical Mods and went on to read for the Honours School of Theology, in which he got a Third – a creditable result for somebody who, as a farmer, had not studied for eleven years after leaving school and had to learn Greek from scratch. From Oxford he went to Lincoln theological college. He stayed with us often at Cranleigh.

We children liked him because he was so obviously a nice person. He was much younger than my father and hence a brisker companion for us. His visits, too, made my mother happy – or did, at the start. Inevitably, however, he became increasingly unable to give her the intensity of response for which she yearned. Her resultant misery led her either to hysterical weeping, or to ever more eager exercises in religiosity.

One Sunday evening when Clifford was staying with us I was upstairs while the others were listening to a broadcast service. I heard my mother rush up to her bedroom and weep violently. I went in to see what the matter was. She said: "It was so lovely and peaceful and calm while the service was on, and I was just beginning to feel at rest when Dad put some coal on the fire, and he made such a noise that it ruined everything." Not understanding the real cause of her distress, I wondered how so small an incident could evoke so severe a reaction.

Meanwhile for us children Sabbath rules were tightened. Only sacred music could be played on the piano or gramophone. Sunday, we were told, was to be spent to the glory of God, the good of others, and our own salvation. On weekdays more and more things became wicked – dancing especially, while the cinema and theatre became even more wicked than before. At the theatre the actors and actresses were supposed every evening after the performance to indulge in sexual orgies at what were described as stage dinners. I can't imagine where my mother picked up this fantasy. But it led to the conclusion that it was endangering the immortal souls of the performers to encourage them by payment to continue in their profession. By the same token, amateur theatricals were all right. It was only the professionals who led lives of vice.

One summer my mother brought together Clifford and the colonel and his lady from Rochester. The latter ran a beach mission at Westgate, renting a school to house the missioners. Clifford went, and my mother took us three children along. There were services on the beach at which we were made to sing:

> "Out and out for Jesus I will always be,
> Not ashamed to own it letting others see,
> Altogether always His and everywhere I go,
> By His grace I'll do it and the world shall know."

Sometimes as an alternative last line the colonel would make us sing: "And the school shall know."

For the purposes of another sacred song we had to sit holding a Bible in our right hand tucked beneath our left arm. In this position we would sing:

> "Draw your swords,
> Use your swords,
> For the battle is the Lord's.
> Trust in His almighty power
> and draw your swords."

At this point we would draw our Bibles from under our arms and hold them up in our right hands, saying: "The sword of the Spirit which is the Word of God."

But my own chief concern at this beach mission (I was now nine to ten years old) was not the religion but the fact that my sisters had arrived at the age to take notice of the undergraduates among the missioners, thought safe by my mother because they were all keen Christians. My sisters naturally wanted to spend as much time as they could with the undergraduates and had no time left for me. This made me feel left out and miserable. One day I was lying on my bed crying when one of the missioners, a mild and friendly old man called Mr Miller, tried to comfort me. His intentions were gentle and benevolent, but they were expressed in the only terms he understood. He asked me why I was crying. Getting no answer, he suggested a reason: "Is it", he said, "because you have conviction of sin?" His remark made little impact on me except as a memory – Mr Miller's lovable face and his grotesque question to a child of my age.

At the end of our visit the colonel gave me a book called *The New Boy*. I put it on my shelves at home but never read it.

An uncompromising biblical fundamentalism was at the heart of the religion preached at the beach mission. It meant that everything in the Bible was considered the authoritative statement of scientific, historical, moral and religious truth. Divergence from this view was by its adherents labelled modernism. Numbers in the Bible, however, could be taken less literally, since the Bible itself said that with the Lord a thousand years is as one day and one day as a thousand years. It was therefore possible, for example, if you wanted to, to reckon that Methuselah, who is said to have lived 969 years, had in fact died the day he was born. This decidedly lax view of numbers in the Bible was severely attacked by some of the more rigorous fundamentalists. But it was held by most of the missioners.

My mother, as an out-and-outer, was of course a biblical fundamentalist. And one of the ways in which she measured Clifford's devotion to herself was the degree to which he strayed or didn't stray from the fundamentalist straight and narrow. This caused no trouble while he was at Oxford. For the lecturers there in theology were considered a bunch of men misguided by their own cleverness into a pit of unbelief. You had to listen to what they said, remember it, and repeat it in the exam. But there was every reason for not believing it. After all, by no stretch of the imagination could they be considered keen Christians.

Soon after our arrival at Cranleigh, the curate, a clever man who had been a barrister until five years previously, organized what he called tutorial classes on the Bible. My mother went to the first one with Clifford. About twenty people assembled, and the curate began by asking whether anybody present did not agree with Bishop Gore's critical approach to the Bible. My mother and Clifford alone put up their hands, glad to bear witness to the truth at the risk of ridicule. "I felt a warm glow coming over me," said my mother afterwards. She thought the warm glow came from her faithfulness to her convictions, but some of it at least must have come from her standing with her adored Clifford against the world.

But when he went to the theological college at Lincoln, things began to change. Here he came to know the lecturers well and could not help seeing that they were devoted Christians and men of prayer in spite of their not being fundamentalists. Hence his views began to change. The first sign of it was during a walk we three children took with my mother and Clifford. We said that there was clear geological and palaeontological evidence for a universal flood in the world. Clifford said there wasn't. We misheard him and thought he was backing up our opinion. He had in honesty to set us right about this. There was no evidence for a universal flood. It was like walking serenely in the middle of a frozen lake and then hearing the first gentle cracking of the ice beneath. Not that I (or my sisters) cared tuppence about the Bible. What I felt cracking was the stability of my mother's feelings. What she called modernism was disloyalty to herself. And Clifford's disloyalty caused her a great deal of distress.

Meanwhile I was driven against my will to the conclusion that I didn't count much with my mother compared with God and Clifford. When my mother was occupied with religious meetings for our friends or with attempts to convert the village children, all other interests had to give way. During this time I once cut myself slightly and found that there was no iodine or its equivalent in the house. My anger gave me the courage to tell my mother that she ought to think more of us and less of missions. She was first angry and then hysterical, and left me feeling miserably guilty. As far as Clifford was concerned, it was on my thirteenth birthday that I was given no option but to accept the truth. A birthday dinner was planned which was to include some special and expensive ice-cream brought from Guildford, eight miles away. Clifford was due to arrive in time for dinner and I was reasonably certain that the dinner was for him, not for me. My certainty became absolute when Clifford failed to turn up (he arrived the next day). My mother couldn't conceal her anger and frustration, and the atmosphere at dinner was colder than the ice-cream.

❧ 17 ❧

DURING THIS PERIOD my father began more and more to accept the fact that his marriage had failed. He put up with Clifford's frequent visits. In the matter of religion he did for some time battle bravely on. One Sunday the first lesson at church was the magnificent Song of Deborah from the Book of Judges, in which Jael is celebrated (like Mary in St Luke) as blessed above women because she lured Sisera, her nation's enemy, into her tent, gave him a lavish meal, then told him to rest in peace because he was perfectly safe, so that, when he was fast asleep, she could drive a tent-peg through his temples. My father, in an obvious attempt to pull my mother's leg, said he thought Jael's conduct was underhand and despicable. My mother hotly defended her and a sharp contention arose. I wonder at how many lunch tables in the British Isles that Sunday there was acrimonious wrangling about the moral status of Jael, the wife of Heber the Kenite.

But my father soon ceased to challenge my mother in this way. He retired into himself and faded into the background. His apparent self-sufficiency was taken for granted. It never occurred to us to wonder what his feelings were or indeed whether he had any; though once, after one of my mother's hysterical outbursts, Helen, in a fit of unusual insight, said: "It isn't very strange, is it, that Dad's not a Christian?" – she meant, of course, a keen Christian. In classical form he became an unspoken joke between my mother and Clifford, though she was always very careful to run the house properly so that his material needs were met. His elder sister, my Aunt Nellie (by now a widow with a son in the Navy), used to come and stay with us and he with her. He had one or two cronies in the village with whom he used sometimes to go out for a day's drive. He belonged to a bridge four which met weekly. He was honorary librarian of a local men's institute. He read a lot and gardened a lot. From what I've learnt later he began to confide in Joan when she was about twenty. But, to all intents and purposes he led his own life, apart from ours.

When Aunt Nellie stayed with us, there would be a quarrel with my mother which invariably ended with my mother shouting in violent hysterics. They absolutely terrified me, and I was always waiting for them to flare up. After one of these outbursts I heard my father say to Aunt Nellie that he would have to get a divorce. But that was only in the heat of the moment. I don't think he had any real intention of doing it. In any case, although my mother was jealous of her, Aunt Nellie was a kind and wise woman who was always a conciliator. I once in her presence broke a glass lampshade and denied the fact to my father when he subsequently came in. Aunt Nellie said nothing. But for several years afterwards, if she thought I was telling too tall a story, her eyes would wander absent-mindedly to the electric light. Finding me once howling in a state, she pretended that I was a drowning man in process of being rescued. It was such an interesting and amusing performance that in about a quarter of an hour she had me laughing.

Nana was less subtle. After all I have so far described had occurred, she asked me on one of her visits to go to her room after lunch. I wondered what she wanted. As was fitting when talking to a grown-up man of twelve or thirteen she came straight to the point. "Your mother," she said, as if announcing something totally new and unthought of, "your mother is in love with Clifford."

❧❧ 18 ❧❧

TO ALL THIS (while I was at prep school age, from ten to twelve years old) I had two reactions, a minor and a major one.

The minor one consisted of becoming very High Church. I wrote several copies of a parish magazine for a church to which I gave the most Anglo-Catholic dedication I was then capable of imagining – St Joseph and All Saints.

I wrote Vicar's Letters urging people to go to sacramental confession, to attend daily Mass, and to follow a practice that the new rector of Cranleigh, Charles Lyttleton, was reported to have used on one occasion, to pray through the Virgin. The recital of Compline was also recommended, but with less zeal.

In those days London shops produced extensive illustrated catalogues. By some chance I got hold of a catalogue from Mowbrays, then a High Church shop near Oxford Circus. I spent hours and hours poring over this delicious catalogue. It had pictures of every kind of Anglo-Catholic contrivance possible: candlesticks and candles of all sizes, censers and incense containers, tabernacles, aumbries, pyxes, bottles with holy corks and holy spoons for holy oil, chalices, patens, crosses, crucifixes, statues of the Virgin, pries-dieux, copes, chasubles, albs, girdles, cottas, birettas, soutanes – the lot. These had for me a compulsive attraction as if they were a kind of ecclesiastical pornography.

All, however, I was able to afford was a wooden altar cross costing five shillings and a crucifix with a metal figure costing seven shillings and sixpence. But Woolworth's at Guildford came to my aid – nothing there cost more than sixpence. For three shillings I was able to buy six candlesticks, for sixpence twelve candles, while at a Roman Catholic shop in the next street I was able to buy some incense for ninepence.

From the linen cupboard at home I was able to take a tablecloth and some face towels. Thus equipped, I was able to set up an altar on the dressing-table in my bedroom; the crucifix I hung on a piece of twine fixed to a nail at the back of the dressing-table so that it was over the altar-frontal, which was a tablecloth. I punched a lot of holes into a tin and fixed wire into it for a handle to serve as a censer. A silver ashtray served as a paten. A silver sugar bowl which was in the shape of a shell supported on a stem of entwined snakes served as a chalice. The bread was ice-cream wafers. The wine a red liquid called Parish's Food, a tonic supposed to give children iron. In a ragbag I found an old nightdress of my mother's to wear, bits of wide ribbon were stoles, and a piece of half-done embroidery about four foot by two I used as a vestment. I was thus fully supplied to celebrate the Holy Communion, or Mass as I preferred to call it. Sometimes I brought in the gramophone to add to the occasion, but this was rather limiting as we only had one record of hymns – "Onward Christian Soldiers" on one side and "From Greenland's Icy Mountains" on the other. Sometimes I conducted an ordination sitting on a commode which was kept in a cupboard upstairs and singing:

> "The earth, O Lord, is one wide field
> Of all thy chosen seed;
> The crop prepared its fruit to yield,
> The labourers few indeed."

I suppose this pantomime must have been performed for about a year, generally on Sunday mornings. Nana once came in unexpectedly and was most dreadfully shocked to find me at it. You could play at being soldiers or sailors, but church was going too far. Joan said she was embarrassed at a tennis party because her host asked her what my hobbies were. "I could hardly say church, could I?" she commented rather crossly.

But the craze soon died a natural death to be replaced by Meccano, fretsaw work, stamp collecting, and the other more usual pursuits of boys my age.

I am glad that I got through my Anglo-Catholic fixations so young. Some people continue hooked on them for life.

My major reaction to the state of affairs was what I believe now to be an unconscious bid for attention and love. It took the form of what I would now call a psychosomatic illness.

For weeks on end my temperature used to go up to anything from 100 to 101 degrees and I had occasional spasms of convulsive twitchings. Our own Dr Cameron could not find the cause and called in other doctors in consultation, including a Dr Abrahams from London. But none of them could make anything of it. I was continually in bed. Clifford wanted me to go to a favourite quack osteopath of his, but my father forbade that. In the end I was taken to the most distinguished paediatrician of the day, Sir Hector Cameron. I suspect that he saw fairly quickly that I was suffering from what would then be called a nervous disorder, as he prescribed daily doses of glucose and glasses of Vichy water.

I can remember one tell-tale event of this time. I had one evening taken my own temperature, which I was strictly forbidden to do. My disobedience produced nervousness which made me clumsy and I broke the thermometer. This terrified me. I knew my mother was in the garden with Clifford, so I put a table outside my bedroom and on it the broken thermometer, a china bowl I had been given recently, and a note asking my mother to accept the bowl (I can't remember the actual words I used) as a peace-offering or act of reparation for the broken thermometer. Unfortunately when my mother came upstairs to my room she was with Clifford, who saw my note and the bowl. I think this wounded my mother's pride. She stormed into my bedroom in a fury and gave me a good dressing-down.

By the time I was thirteen and ready to go to the senior school at Cranleigh I had "outgrown" my illness. But by then it had imposed upon me its own penalty. Once again I was not allowed to escape from the guilt-ridden atmosphere of home, since it was thought that my health was too delicate for me to go to the senior school as a boarder. I thus found myself one of ten day boys in a school of four hundred. It didn't mean at all that at school I was a second-class citizen, but it did mean that at home I continued to be exposed to its explosive and chilly atmosphere – explosive because my mother might at any time break out into one of her hysterical fits, chilly because her relationship with my father was at times below zero.

My mother didn't go to Clifford's ordination as his parents were to be there. But she seemed not to mind, chiefly, I think, because she received from one or two people letters of congratulation on her success. As an old friend of hers – a Roman Catholic – wrote: "Who can deny, dear Nan, that you were the first to point the way?"

Clifford continued off and on to stay with us while he was a curate in England. He then went for a few years to South Africa, where he became engaged. It was felt by my mother as a terrible blow. She coped with it partly by taking it out of my father and partly by increased religious zeal. When the three of us were sitting in a room she would point at my father and say: "How I hate that man." She began having anything up to thirty village children to our house each week to evangelize them and encourage them to work for a mission in India (Mrs Munn, our cook, had the job of putting down a drugget over the drawing-room carpet before she began to cook the dinner). An Indian child was "adopted" and photographs of her sent for the children to look at. My mother went continually visiting poor people. After some misdemeanour on my part she told me bitterly that she doubted if I were converted. She kicked up the most awful rumpus when Joan in London led Helen into the sin of going to the theatre – a dramatized version of *Jane Eyre*. When she was upset I (and Helen if she were home) tried to comfort her with her own brand of piety. We would embrace her and tell her that underneath were the everlasting arms, that as her days were so would her strength be, that she was kept by the power of God, that Jesus loves, He knows, He cares. She used to nod a feeble assent to these propositions, but naturally they didn't do any good.

Clifford's fiancée came to England before he did and was adopted into our family. She was a bridesmaid at Helen's wedding. Then she faded completely from the scene as Clifford broke off the engagement. However, some years later he married somebody else in England. By that time the torturing fires of my mother's passion had begun to die down. She became calmer, less unhappy, and less religious. She even went to the cinema and theatre and played secular music on the piano on Sundays. And a sort of swan song of affection developed between her and my father. The last twelve or fourteen years of his life were happy ones. It was marvellous to see them together. When he died aged eighty-four I was already a Fellow of Trinity. Aunt Nellie (who had witnessed so many quarrels and hysterical scenes) wrote to my mother and said, "You have been such a good wife to Harry and gave him so much happiness." When my mother showed me the letter, I cried. She thought I was crying because of my father's death. But it wasn't that. It was because of Aunt Nellie's generosity. Of such, I thought, are the kingdom of Heaven.

FOR THE PURPOSES of narration I have abstracted what was indeed a central feature of my life, but by no means the whole of it. I must inevitably have given the impression that existence for me was one long tale of misery. But that was far from the full truth. As well as what I've described there was much happiness, laughter and love.

Christmas, for instance, was always a marvellous time at home. My parents were agreed about its religious significance and its consequent call to fun and festivity. It was the one time when religion made us more human instead of less. We had Christmas dinner at lunch time followed by a satisfied somnolent afternoon until (I've forgotten what year it began) King George spoke to us on the wireless. We listened with reverence and always stood up when the band played God Save the King. Then, after tea, we had our presents. They had all to be attached to a long piece of string with a card at the end saying who they were for, because they were all put into a large laundry basket with a counterpane over it. The basket was put on a table, and each of us in turn drew a present which had to be opened, inspected and rhapsodized over before the next person was allowed to pull a string with the appropriate name on it. I remember one Christmas my father advising me not to pull a certain string until the end. The self-control required was enormous. But at last the time came, and it turned out, to my delight, to be a complete recording of *The Mikado* in twelve records by the D'Oyly Carte opera company, including Henry Lytton. Theatre people on the gramophone were all right. Presumably a studio was considered to provide little opportunity for sexual orgies – though I used to wonder (entirely without knowledge) what Henry Lytton's relations were with Bertha Lewis, the D'Oyly Carte contralto.

I said that I now think my high temperature and convulsive twitchings were an unconscious demand for attention. If so, it was a strategy which worked. For not only was I wonderfully nursed by my mother, but also she read to me a great deal. My illness involved missing school quite frequently, and my parents were naturally concerned about its effect upon my education. But in fact I am certain that I learnt infinitely more from what my mother read to me than I ever would have done at school.

She read a great deal of Dickens: *David Copperfield, Nicholas Nickleby, Dombey and Son, Martin Chuzzlewit, Bleak House* and *A Tale of Two Cities*. The characters in these books, especially the minor ones, became people I felt I knew and about whom my mother and I could gossip. What would Aunt Betsey or Traddles have done? How would Mr Mantalini have coped with this or the other situation? What would Miss Tox or Mr Toots have said? My mother applauded the flight from her husband of the second Mrs Dombey, leaving every jewel, every trinket, every present Mr Dombey had given her in a heap on the floor. That, she said, is what she herself would have done, indeed would do (she implied) were she not a keen Christian. When, however, Dickens portrayed moral or religious monsters – Mr Pecksniff, Mrs Jellyby, Mr Chadband – we were able to laugh together at what to me was in some sort a portrayal of my mother's own moral and religious attitudes. I found this laughter very reassuring. The favourite of all was Jerry Cruncher, who used to get extremely angry with his wife because she would pray against the success of his felonious schemes. How, he stormed, can a man hope to bring off a robbery if his wife spends all her time at home praying against him?

We read a little Thackeray: *Vanity Fair* (my mother was furious with Amelia Sedley for not immediately spotting the virtues of Captain Dobbin and marrying him) and *Pendennis*.

This reading out loud started me reading for myself. Between the ages of eleven and seventeen I read most of the works of the nineteenth-century novelists: Jane Austen, Walter Scott, Charles Reade, Anthony Trollope and George Eliot long before Dr Leavis had made her once again intellectually respectable. I was started off on George Eliot by a motive which was less than pure. Aunt Nellie one day told me that my grandmother would not allow her as a girl to read *Adam Bede* because it was considered too improper. When I went to my scholarship interview at Trinity, in an answer to an enquiry, I told Jim Butler and Steven Runciman that I had read all George Eliot's novels. They were both quietly amused and Jim asked me how many of my contemporaries, did I think, had read her. That was still before Dr Leavis had spoken.

Among the books at home I found a volume called *King's Regulations and Admiralty Instructions*. I began reading it and was surprised when my father, finding me at it, said: "Oh I shouldn't read that if I were you." It seemed to me a bit boring but quite harmless. It was in fact much too boring for me to wade through the book. I can only conclude that it contained instructions about punishment for cases of sodomy. But I have since had no access to the volume to check.

At one stage I thought that *Three Men in a Boat* was the funniest book conceivable. I remember reading a bit of it out loud after lunch one day while we were still at table – the scene in which Harris at an evening reception offers to sing a song and muddles up the Judge's song from *Trial by Jury* with the First Lord's song from *Pinafore*. My father shook all over with laughter and my mother was very amused. Fashions in humour are the strangest of all to account for. The book now seems to me feeble in the extreme. But then so do *Pickwick Papers* (I never took to them) and people used to laugh themselves silly over them when they first appeared.

My mother could be fun when she forgot to be religious. She generally did if we went abroad on holiday. One summer we joined forces with Uncle George, who, with his wife and two sons, rented a house at Le Touquet. The holiday was especially memorable because my mother was at her most mellow, partly because she was under the impression that *sirop de cassis* and a certain peppermint cordial were teetotal drinks, although the peppermint cordial had clearly written on the label "*Alcool de Menthe*". She had a large glass of cassis and soda before dinner and a large glass of alcool de menthe and hot water after, and said she knew the holiday was really doing her an enormous amount of good. None of us had the heart (or foolishness) to enlighten her innocence. She was never a prude on lavatory matters; in fact she liked not locking the door so that we would go in and find her sitting there before she had time to say, "Can't come in." Before starting anywhere she would say: "I must just go and have another squeeze." I mention this here because she was as delighted as the rest of us to find in a shop window in Étaples a cruet with two chamber pots for salt and pepper and a lavatory bowl and brush for mustard. We all said it was delightfully French, but nobody had the courage to buy it. A lurking suspicion of French morals, however, remained with her. When not long before the Second World War King George VI and Queen Elizabeth went on a state visit to Paris, and the newspapers published what entertainments had been laid on for them, my mother said gravely: "I hope they keep it decent for them." Her remark conjured up in my mind wildly funny pictures of their Majesties proceeding in state to displays of live pornography.

Nana was much less inhibited. When I was about nine she chatted to me while I was having a bath. During this she pointed at my penis and said: "When that is firm and stiff, it means that you are strong and well. When it is soft and flabby it means that you are weak and ill." I wasn't very certain what she was referring to, except that it was embarrassing, so I didn't ask any questions. About the same time she and I danced together in the drawing-room and, after a short time, I let down my trousers in mock abandon. At that very moment my mother came in and was (not unreasonably) furious. "Oh Annie," said Nana, "we were only having a bit of fun." But fun of that kind – no doubt very wisely – was not tolerated by my mother.

Nana told me once that we could make ourselves roar with laughter simply by pretending to. This we did. And she was quite right. After a minute or two our pretended laughter became real and was so long and loud that my sisters came in to find out what the joke was when there wasn't any.

Nana loved the card game pelmanism. But while you were having your turn and thinking where such or such a card was, she would turn up the corner of a card to see if her memory were correct and it really was the six of diamonds. This fed my inclination to make fun of everything, and I enjoyed it.

In time she sold her house in Southsea and came to live at a private hotel near us. One summer she came up on a Sunday for tea and, meeting a Stop Me and Buy One ice-cream seller on the way, bought some for us – not, I suspect, entirely unmindful that this Sunday trading would tease my mother in her Sabbatarian principles. But my mother on that day was not in a religiously militant mood. We had tea in the garden. The ice-cream was divided and she took her share. But she preserved her religious integrity by surreptitiously, teaspoonful by teaspoonful, feeding it to the cat, who thus became a beneficiary of this violation of the Lord's Day.

In spite of my mother's Sabbatarian principles, Sunday for us children was not at all a dull or boring day.

Morning church was an excitement we looked forward to. It included a great deal calculated to amuse.

In the pew in front of ours sat five sisters, old ladies to us, all of them spinsters and very short. They were the Misses Woodfine, each of them a character. We loved going to their house, for not only did they give us the most delicious tea and organize charades and other enjoyable games, but their house was lit by oil lamps, which we found intriguing. In 1938 my father met one of them in the street and she crossed the road to speak to him. She said she had the most exciting news. They had just had gas-light fitted into their house. Unexpectedly, in the early 1930s, they suddenly produced the most ravishingly beautiful niece of seventeen called Flora. She was the child of a brother who lived in South America. Aunt Nellie's son, my cousin Jack, when he stayed with us, went crazy about her. Once she was at our house and she lured him into the pantry, then quickly left it herself, locking him in and pocketing the key. He was a prisoner there for twenty minutes. When she let him out he was in a dream of bliss. But, bad luck for him, he had almost immediately to return to his ship at Malta and Flora's aunts refused to take her there to join the fishing fleet. I adored her. I had never seen a vision like her, with her dark complexion, glittering eyes and a smile which was a combination of kindness and mockery or amusement. It was marvellous from now on to be able to look at her safely from behind in church.

Then there were two middle-aged women, inseparables, who always came to church in tailor-made coats and skirts, collars and ties, and porkpie hats. Their speciality was a half curtsy which they would make to the altar, at the name of Jesus, when the word "holy" was said or sung, or any mention of the Trinity. At each half curtsy my sisters and I would catch each other's eye and laugh so that my mother would nudge us and shake her head severely.

A retired general read the lessons. This was in itself worth coming to church for, as his false teeth went clickety-click at certain consonants and it was anybody's bet how often those particular consonants would occur in the lessons for that Sunday. We used to count and have arguments about our differing results.

Then there was a retired insurance agent and his wife. He always said "Hallow-ed be thy name". We used to wait for it. It came twice each service.

A nabob who had an enormous family used to come to the church. They were somewhat ostentatious. Charles Lyttelton (I was, said my sister, cracked on him) was then our Rector. He died comparatively young of pernicious anaemia. Years later at Barbon I met his widow once again (she was by then married to Roger Fulford).

She told me that when she and Charles went to dine with the nabob they had fourteen courses, while at Charles's parental home, Lord Cobham's, they never had more than four. Anyhow what used to amuse us children was that the nabob and his large family, on their arrival at church, used each to give to the altar the sort of curt nod which on a bad day you might give to an under-gardener. Actually, as often, many of them were charming, and one of the daughters, Joyce, was an absolute darling and the salt of the earth. She married a clergyman and their son became a pupil of mine at Trinity. Joyce was once at a meeting at the Mothers' Union headquarters in Westminster. She saw a dowdy-looking woman standing alone while coffee was being served and, characteristically, went up to her and asked her whether she knew London well. She later learnt to her embarrassment that the dowdy-looking woman was Amy Wand, the Bishop of London's wife. Amy was herself a dear. She once invited me to stay at Fulham before addressing a meeting for her the following morning. I was very young and didn't know whether I was expected to dinner or not. Instead of telephoning the chaplain to ask, I turned up at Fulham Palace round about ten o'clock. Amy greeted me sternly with the words: "We waited for dinner until half-past eight and had a chicken." The chaplain whispered in my ear: "Don't worry. It's only the Berkshire farmer coming out." In fact both the Bishop and Amy were marvellously kind and warm-hearted. Their own son had been killed mountain climbing, and it made them particularly fond of young men of my age. For a holiday, what they both liked doing more than anything was to go on a coach tour round some part of Britain. They did it regularly every year.

Charles Lyttelton was succeeded by Hugo Johnstone – the man with the golden voice, curate at St Martin-in-the-Fields, who pioneered the daily morning religious service on the wireless at 10.15, and had published a devotional book in connection with it called *New Every Morning*, full of prayers for things like "gallant and high-hearted happiness". He was, I think, reacting against the ecclesiasticism of his father, who had been successively Principal of St Stephen's House and Cuddesdon – both theological colleges in the environs of Oxford.

One Christmas morning a woman who was mad about Hugo Johnstone distributed a notice which she had herself duplicated telling us that when the Rector wished us all a happy Christmas we were to stand up and say: "And the same to you." The unsuspecting Hugo opened the service with his good wishes. There followed the most awkward atmosphere of silence, and one poor woman in the front, who couldn't see that the rest of the congregation had remained seated, stood up and said alone: "And the same to you." It was heady stuff for a Christmas morning.

Hugo Johnstone preached incessantly about love, once, to our delight, announcing his text as "Perfect love casteth out love." He told us of a London taximan to whom, at Christmas time, rude words were shouted from a car decorated with holly. The taximan replied: "You need some holly in your heart." "Rather prickly," whispered Helen to me and we both shook silently. Then Hugo went a bit Oxford Group and preached a sermon on moral rearmament. At least that is what he thought he was saying. What he actually said each time was national rearmament. "Bang, bang, bang, bang, bang," Joan muttered under her breath.

All in all church on Sunday was the best form of family entertainment.

And at home too Sunday was far from irksome. On Saturday evening we had a sort of family prayers (my father didn't come) in which my mother prayed that all preachers the following day might be "emptied, cleansed, purified vessels through which the Holy Spirit can flow". Alas, she seldom considered them such when she heard them. She usually greeted their efforts with a sort of spiritual condescension – not bad for them, the sort of thing in these days found chiefly when Anglo-Catholic clergy-men are talking about their non-Anglo-Catholic colleagues.

The sacred music rule left us *The Messiah*, excerpts from Bach's *Matthew Passion* and Mendelssohn's *Elijah*, not to mention Clara Butt singing Liddle's "Abide with me". It was possible too to cheat. I thought the barcarole from the *Tales of Hoffmann* so lovely that it must be religious; it was rather a pleasant shock when I first saw the opera and discovered it was in fact the music for an orgy in Venice. You could get away, too, with records of Paul Robeson, because one of them was "Steal away to Jesus" and they all sounded much the same from a distance.

After tea we often played sacred games of which our favourite was called Scripture Lotto. Each player was given four cards marked out in squares. Each square contained a word or sentence with a number. These were the answers to questions on small bits of card the size of the old kind of railway ticket on which the appropriate number was also printed. The question on the ticket would be read out. The first to give the right answer (shown by its being the right number) would get the ticket-question to cover the answer-square with. If you gave a wrong answer you forfeited a ticket already won. Hence: Question – "How does Scripture teach us to have good manners?" answer – "Be courteous 43." Question – "What is the shortest verse in the Bible?" answer – "Jesus wept 28." Question – "What four insects are said in the Bible to be very wise?" answer – "Ants, conies, locusts, and spiders 18." It was just as exciting as any other children's game. When the questions and answers in Scripture Lotto became too familiar another game was bought working on identical principles and called Flora and Fauna of Scripture. We never took to this much (it was a bit too erudite), though I do remember one question: "What produce grown in Egypt did the children of Israel think about in the wilderness?" answer – "Cucumbers, melons, leeks, onions, and garlic 83."

There was nothing my mother liked more than sending out Bible notes. At first it was the Scripture Union. She formed her own branch which she modestly called The

Gleanings. Later she switched to the Bible Reading Fellowship. Somehow I made quite clear to her that in no circumstances would I discuss the Scripture Union or any other biblical portion with her, as in fact I never read it, but I had to pretend I did in order to keep the peace.

Once on the first day of a visit by Aunt Nellie I was asked to go to her room and tell her that dinner would be ready in about twenty minutes. I found that she had finished dressing and was sitting in an easy chair hastily studying the Bible Reading Fellowship notes for that month. She was preparing herself for whatever questions or comments about them my mother might direct at her. "Oh dear," she said, "your mother always sends me these Bible notes."

About ninety to a hundred of them were sent out to various places by post each month. I sometimes addressed the envelopes. This I was pleased to do as my mother paid me for the work and it brought with it also another advantage.

From the age of nine, off and on, I had smoked, stealing the cigarettes from my father's box. Later I bought them. They were very cheap in those days. When addressing envelopes for Bible notes I knew I should not be disturbed in the room I was using, for, even though being paid, was I not doing the Lord's work? So I could smoke as much as I liked in peace.

But it ended badly when I was sixteen. In my bedroom my mother discovered a tin with the stubs in it of about four cigarettes. She rushed to her own bedroom, knelt down at her bed, and sobbed loudly and violently as though she had caught me raping a small girl. I think she had a fantasy of me as a lamb without blemish offered to the Lord.

I was careful to hide my smoking until I was eighteen, when I asked for and received my father's permission and disregarded whatever reaction my mother might put up. She accepted it grudgingly with a sort of disapproving acquiescence. Nobody, of course, in those days thought that smoking could damage your health. It was just wicked in itself, like the cinema.

❦❧20❦❧

FOR SEVERAL SUMMERS my mother took us for a fortnight to a kind of house party organized by a military and naval group of Evangelical persuasion.

Although we had misgivings about them, these house parties proved to be very enjoyable. There was always a sprinkling of older people there, but mostly they consisted of young people, girls and boys between, say, sixteen and twenty-five. A school near the sea would be rented and generally it would have ample grounds. So there were opportunities for tennis, bathing, expeditions, picnics and so on. After dinner, groups of us got up revue-type entertainments which were fun both to take part in and to watch. But the best fun, naturally, was each other's company. True, there were large doses of religion inserted into the day's programme, but most of us young people didn't take it at all seriously and were willing to put up with it in order to be there, on the principle of taking the rough with the smooth. Our elders had no notion of what went on after everybody was supposed to have gone to bed. Admittedly, in terms of today's standards, it was only a mild kind of necking. But I found this easy mixing of the sexes and a certain degree of physical familiarity between them extremely reassuring. Preach as much and as loudly as you like, it seemed to say, human beings will still, thank God, be human beings. It was my first vague intimation that God was to be found much more in non-religion than in religion.

Although, like most of the other young people, I was not in the least affected or influenced by the religious routine of the house parties, I shall describe one, as, looking back, it seems to me a curiosity which deserves to be recorded.

It began in the morning at a quarter to eight when

the more elect used to gather for a prayer-meeting. It was a free for all. Sometimes you scored a hit in your prayer. If so, one or more people in the group would breathe deeply and sigh a long A–men (A to rhyme with hay). I once scored three A–mens at one meeting and felt pleased with myself in an amused sort of way. It would be something to laugh over with Constance, to whom that year I was rather close.

At eight o'clock there was Bible study. The Bible meant the Authorized Version. The leader quoted a long dead Dean of Canterbury as saying that the Authorized Version was a most accurate translation in all ways, adding severely: "I tell you this because people prefer the word of man to the Word of God." A subject was then chosen for the two weeks – the devil, for instance, or angels, or sin, or blood – and for the purposes of investigation you divided your notebook into six headings: Who? Where? When? How? Why? What? Then you searched the Scriptures to find individual verses which seemed relevant, totally disregarding their historical context or the type of literature they belonged to, and fitting them into one or other of the six question headings. What? was a very useful receptacle for any verse which obviously didn't answer Who? Where? When? How? or Why?

After the Bible study there were formal prayers which the servants attended. It consisted of the Scripture Union portion for the day and two Prayer Book collects.

At ten o'clock there was what was called Assembly. It consisted of a hymn and an address on the Scripture Union portion. I remember in particular two of these addresses. One was by a major in the Engineers, who had to grapple with one of the more complicated descriptions of sacrificial ritual in Leviticus. It was marvellous what light he elicited for us from God's instructions to the Israelites in the wilderness regarding the fat and the kidneys. Incidentally, since it was axiomatic that new light was to break forth from God's holy Word, it was common after a piece of biblical exposition to say: "I never saw that before." It showed the promise being fulfilled among us. The other address I remember was by a delightful old admiral, flowing with the milk of human kindness, who told us of some woman in Europe (France perhaps) who was accused of a serious crime and was strongly advised by her friends to engage the services of the leading advocate of the day. The woman dithered and delayed applying to him. Finally she did. But the advocate said, "I would gladly madam, have defended you. But it is too late. I can no longer accept your brief because yesterday I consented to be the judge at your trial." This story the admiral applied to Jesus. Better not delay in asking him to be your advocate, since at any moment he might turn into your judge. It was on account of this address that it first began darkly to dawn upon me that people are invariably much better and kinder than the religion they think they profess.

At about six in the afternoon, before we changed for dinner, there was another bit of religion. This varied. It could be testimonies. If so, it generally worked out like this: Betty, we knew, was in love with John. John, we knew, was pious. So Betty would reveal her piety in the hope of impressing him. She took in fact a verse from Ezekiel about God taking from her a heart of stone and giving her a heart of flesh. She was much commended for this by her elders, but it didn't get her the man she wanted. One afternoon an earnest subaltern gave us what he called an object lesson. It consisted of a glass of clear water into which he poured a few drops of iodine so that the water turned brown. This stood for man defiled by sin. He then covered the glass with a silk handkerchief. But the water was still dirty beneath. That was our attempt by good works to be redeemed. He then put some photographic hypo crystals into the glass and the water cleared completely. That was how the blood of Jesus Christ his son cleanseth us from all sin. Geddit?

There was one evening of the house party we always looked forward to, but for reasons other than those envisaged by the organizers. We didn't change for dinner that evening because after it we all assembled in the biggest room in the house with cushions, pillows and mattresses to put on the floor and lie on. The lights were then completely switched off, and some pundit would talk about the Second Coming, proving from Scripture that world events indicated it was about to occur in the immediate future and giving a graphic description of the series of events involved, beginning with the converted being caught up to meet the Lord in the air. I remember once when the lights went up again a young wife saying excitedly: "Perhaps it will be tonight." But we younger people made use of the darkness for a canoodle, inevitably giggling at the ambiguity of the phrase to which the evening had been devoted. It was the triumph of warm humanity over escapist religion, of life over death.

Yet that can't be the last word. It is easy enough to laugh at the kind of thing I've been describing. But it should be remembered that one of the important functions of religion is to give people something to do with their lunacy. And that was something the religion of the house parties did very well.

21

BUT I HAVEN'T YET SPOKEN of the Senior School at Cranleigh. It was a happy place. I used to bicycle there early so as to arrive as the others came out from breakfast, and very often didn't leave until eight or nine in the evening.

I never got to know my housemaster at all well, and he remained a cipher as far as I was concerned. But I was extremely lucky in my headmaster, an unmarried clergyman in his middle thirties called David Loveday, who was admired and adored by successive generations of boys during the twenty-two years of his headmastership. He subsequently became Bishop of Dorchester. I shall call him David, as that is how I came to know him after I had left school.

He had been at Magdalene in the early 1920s while

A. C. Benson was still Master. Benson had had one of his periodic breakdowns and his doctor had advised him to choose a congenial undergraduate, making of him a close friend and constant companion. Benson chose David, and no doubt partly because of it he was nicknamed Joy by his contemporaries.

I think it likely that some of Benson's eccentricity had rubbed off on him. (When he came to visit me as a deacon in Pimlico, the housekeeper, telling me of his arrival, warned me against him, saying "I should be careful. He looks like a tout come for books." I was very surprised to discover who my visitor in fact was.) He was, none the less, an extremely efficient administrator and could be quite terrifying when he chose. His authority in the school was absolute. In that sense nobody could have been a sterner disciplinarian. And, as I appreciated later, he collected round him a group of very able teachers.

But his estimate of things was never conventional. He had his own decided opinions. What he hated above all things was cant. And beneath appearances he was always very kindhearted and human. It was characteristic of him that when a worried housemaster sent him a boy who had been discovered masturbating in an airing cupboard, he asked the boy why he had chosen that particular place. The boy said that it was warm and the day was cold. "I think you ought to be a lawyer," David answered; "you would make a very good defence counsel. Now you can go." While he saw to it that things didn't get out of control, it was clear that sex among boys amused rather than worried him. He was the last person to sow any seeds of destructive guilt.

What was particularly lucky for me was that he had no high opinion of games or sport, at which I was always very bad. He used to go down to the fields to watch matches, partly as a matter of duty and partly because – he didn't conceal it – he was amused by the energetic movement of young limbs and the apoplectic efforts of old housemasters (before he had replaced them) to goad their teams into winning. Under a master called Gower, Cranleigh had built up a reputation for rugger. (I remember in class Gower telling us that boys thought the Rockies were confined to Canada because they were rocky in the head.) David was not impressed by a reputation for rugger. His concern was for a civilized atmosphere in which academic ability and achievement was given its due measure of respect.

In those days in country districts telephone numbers were often only three or two figures. This enabled David to memorize people's telephone numbers by the hymn of that number in the old *Ancient and Modern*. He was particularly pleased that the telephone number of an assistant bishop of Guildford he thought a bounder corresponded with the hymn "Great God, what do I see and hear?"; while a master whose wife had a very loud and ugly voice constantly in use could be telephoned at the hymn "The voice that breathed o'er Eden".

He took a delight in eccentric clergymen: somebody called Raper who was eventually unfrocked for rape; a vicar in the Fens who for a long time presented his housekeeper each year for confirmation. He once accepted an invitation to preach a Harvest Festival sermon in a remote country church in the heart of Suffolk; the vicar said it would be best if he stayed Saturday night at the vicarage. He was unpacking when the vicar knocked at his bedroom door. "I must warn you," he said, "that my wife is a teetotaller, a non-smoker and a vegetarian. However, I have put a bottle of whisky and a tin of corned beef in your wardrobe." During the psalms at the service the following morning the vicar came over to David and asked him if he knew where that bit was in the Bible about seed-time and harvest, as he thought it would make a good first lesson.

Winnington-Ingram, then Bishop of London, was very fond of David and used to come regularly to preach at the school. He liked playing tennis and golf with us (the school has a nine-hole course), and we were told it wouldn't matter if he were allowed to win. I regret to say I remember only one of the sermons I heard from him; it was about a statesman of the time who denied God's existence until the bishop took him out into the garden and showed him the flowers.

David himself was a brilliant preacher. All his sermons were memorable, but the one which made the most impression on me was on a text from the Song of Songs: "Jealousy is as cruel as the grave." Here was no conventional public school religion.

We had a daily compulsory service at a quarter to nine – a psalm, a lesson, prayers and a hymn. Nobody considered it an imposition or a bore. In fact we found it rather fun, especially when we sang psalm 81: "His hands were delivered from making the pots." We had a master called Potts (he was killed in the war) and we all came down on the word with concentrated gusto. I watched a master who used to get justifiably irritated by my mathematical obtuseness singing "Before Thy throne we sinners bend" and wondered what he felt like as he sang.

On Sundays we had a compulsory morning or evening service with sermon. Holy Communion was voluntary at eight. There was a complete disaster on one occasion when an archbishop preached on the theme of fighting the battle of life with borrowed tools. He kept on repeating the phrase until we were all hysterical. We were severely reprimanded the following day by David. He naturally didn't tell us what he told me some years later: that it was all he could do not to laugh himself.

He took a special care of boys who were ordinands. It was because of that, I think, that I came to know him well. He described himself as a pre-Tractarian High Churchman. It was in effect the clerical equivalent of my father's layman's religion: in this case Holy Communion every Sunday and Prayer Book Saint's Day, together with a real and deep, though entirely unostentatious, devotion of which the fruit was a rich and kindly humanity, wholly unconcerned to win any mystical honours in the spiritual life, but laying great emphasis on tolerance and just allowance. One of his most moving sermons as Bishop of Dorchester was on the Christian duty of always allowing and enabling people to have a second chance.

It was he who prepared me for confirmation. His teaching was simple and profound – the very fruit and flower of Anglicanism. On using sacramental confession, for instance, he said that the Anglican rule was that nobody must, many do and some should. When I asked him about fasting communion he said I should fast if I felt drawn that way but that he could not imagine the Almighty with a watch in His hand.

The confirmation itself by the Bishop of Guildford (Dr Macmillan) didn't make much impression on me. He spoke to the parents afterwards and advised them to give their sons a book called *A Religion of your Own*. I can't remember who the author was. What was clear to me on reading it was that its title was a misnomer. It presented you with a prefabricated religion and rule of life which you could make your own only by buying the package deal.

My closest friend at school, whom I loved dearly (our birthdays were on the same day as well as year), was killed as a paratrooper at Arnhem a few months after his marriage. I still have the edition of Boswell he gave me and inscribed. I don't want to say any more about him here. I kept all his long letters in a box at home. My mother, with a woman's flair for clearing things away, put them on a bonfire.

I left Cranleigh in a religiously divided state. To use St Paul's phrase, with my mind I served David Loveday's religion, but with my flesh (i.e. my conditioned and perverted subconscious) I served my mother's religion. I felt the sweet and attractive reasonableness of sober Anglican piety, but somewhere I had a sneaking feeling that only people out and out for Jesus were really Christians. It was a conflict I was to live with for fourteen years until, thank God, it broke me up completely.

Out-and-out religion (whether it be of the Evangelical or Anglo-Catholic variety) tramples upon your humanity with hobnail boots and violates your intrinsic tenderness. Both varieties in their very different ways – so at least it has been in my own experience – are founded upon an Old Testament text which Jesus quoted but which they invert: "I will have sacrifice, and not mercy." As an instinctive protection I developed a kind of religious voyeurism, which has remained with me permanently. However sincerely I am, with one part of my being, joining in a religious service or talking religion with a conventionally pious group, with another part of my being I am a spectator – bored, amused, angry, disgusted or absolutely terrified, as the case may be.

In religious matters the only other person I've seen who actually revealed by his unintended facial expression his involuntary non-participation was a pupil of mine at Cambridge. His father was a bishop who was pious in a rather High Church way and whose spiritual counsel was much sought after by upper-class women. No doubt his son, my pupil, had also had many extra offers of spiritual guidance as he was extraordinarily handsome. When in college chapel lessons were read or sermons preached the boy's face perfectly expressed what I was feeling inside. Perhaps religious voyeurs should get together for sessions of co-counselling. They could then bore each other, which would certainly be most therapeutic.

❧22❧

WHEN I LEFT FOR CAMBRIDGE my mother gave me a picture of Jesus standing in a boat next to a young man with his hand on the tiller. The colonel told me I must join CICCU (the Cambridge Christian Union) and wrote to somebody to see I did.

But I had made up my own mind what I was going to do. Apart from attendance at College chapel on Sundays I had decided not to have anything whatever to do with any religious concern – be it groups of pious people or of ordinands, or societies, or missions, or talks or anything. I wanted to live a life free from the manipulative inhibitions which I had come to associate with keen Christianity.

Before the war Trinity had almost as many undergraduates as now. Nobody from Cranleigh was there. I had a number of school friends dotted about in other colleges, but I knew nobody at my own. In spite of its size, Trinity has always been in my experience a very friendly and homely place, and I soon made a lot of friends. Being a scholar obviously helped: it threw you up against the other scholars of your year and you met their friends. Also you were invited to the Commemoration Feast at the end of the Lent term where you got roaring drunk. And there is nothing like an initial bout of drunkenness for making friends.

I still wanted to be ordained. I didn't know why. The glamorous appeal of William Temple in St Mary's Oxford had long since died away. It seemed to me now rather a down-at-heel and threadbare sort of existence. But I still wanted to go through with it. I was rather nervous of how it would be considered by my non-pious undergraduate contemporaries. Would they laugh at me and think me a fool? I discovered that this was not at all the case. They obviously respected my intention – not me, but the life I had chosen.

With regard to religious observance, what I did, I think, was to put it in a state of hibernation. If I were to be unkind to myself I would say that I went to Sunday chapel to keep up appearances. But that would be less than the full truth. An animal in hibernation needs to breathe, and Sunday chapel was the breathing. David Loveday had written about me to the Dean of Chapel, Dr H. F. Stewart, somebody with masses of white hair and one of the most beautiful faces I have ever seen – as beautiful as that of Hardy, the mathematician, whom I saw only at a distance. Stewart was friendly and hospitable and I enjoyed his sermons. He was an authority on Pascal, and much of his preaching was in French, consisting of quotations from the *Pensées* and the *Lettres à un Provincial*. My moral tutor was

Patrick Duff, later Regius Professor of Civil Law, a devout Christian whose piety consisted chiefly of doing good by stealth. My theological teacher was John Burnaby, later Regius Professor of Divinity. He was a most stimulating teacher and supervisions (tutorials) with him sometimes lasted for two hours instead of one. Immediately after teaching me – if we had exceeded our time – he saw his moral (tutorial) pupils. I used to find them in his waiting room, their eyes full of sympathy and concern for me, as they had heard excited voices in Burnaby's study and imagined I had been accused of some misdemeanour and was hotly defending myself, when in fact all we were discussing was whether some verb in the Epistle to the Galatians was or was not to be taken in the resultative sense.

I found the academic study of theology exciting. It was treated as an intellectual discipline with no connection of any kind with devotional piety.

Altogether I have never been so happy as I was during my undergraduate years at Cambridge. I desperately needed this religion-free interlude where I could experience the delights and rewards of being human in an atmosphere free from guilt and where intellectual integrity was valued instead of dogma and warm companionship instead of zeal. I remember lying in my bath every morning feeling grateful for my happiness but being worried by the speed at which the days were slipping by. Yet my memory of that time is very hazy. No details of it stand out at all sharply. I think that is because I was to return to Trinity in ten years' time and stay there for nineteen, and my detailed memories inevitably belong to that later period.

When the war came I was declared to be medically C3 because of my bad eyesight. I was told I should be called up only for home duties. In the circumstances I availed myself of the permission given to ordinands by the Government to continue their training. I thought it best when going to theological college to get away from the numerous contacts I had in Cambridge. The best alternative seemed Cuddesdon, eight miles from Oxford.

G. M. Trevelyan was installed as Master of Trinity while I was an undergraduate. He took his new duties very seriously and summoned me to the Master's Lodge just before I left. His publisher was Longman, and Longman's warehouse had just been burnt out in the blitz. Trevelyan said to me: "As a clergyman it will be your very responsible duty to be a guardian of British culture and civilization. Your services will be badly needed. With Longman's warehouse gone, for instance, there are no new copies available in this country of Lecky's works." Lecky, best known for his *History of Rationalism*, was the Marghanita Laski and much more of the Victorian age. That in all honesty Trevelyan should think it a main responsibility of a clergyman to propagate Lecky's views gave me a great deal of amusement as I left Trinity. I think I should take the idea much more seriously today.

❧❧ 23 ❧❧

HAVING AT THIS POINT mentioned Trevelyan, it's not possible to pass him by without another word. So great a man not only excuses a digression. He calls out for one.

As an undergraduate I took it as a matter of course when he appeared in the Master's stall in chapel on Sunday evening. His predecessor, J. J. Thomson, always had. But then J.J. was a regular communicant. It didn't dawn on me that Trevelyan was the first Master of Trinity who wasn't in matters of belief a Christian, and that his coming to chapel on Sunday evening was by no means a foregone conclusion.

I later learnt that while several Fellows were wondering what he would do, Trevelyan summoned John Burnaby and Kitson Clark, both of whom he greatly liked and respected, and gave them for some forty-five minutes an account of his religious beliefs from the time when as a small child he was terrified by a Calvinist nurse's threat of a Day of Judgement about to be detonated at any moment, to the agnosticism of his present position, following what in his *Social History* he was later to describe as the typical religion of Englishmen which "eschews dogma and is content to live broadly in the spirit". Without a pause he concluded his narrative with the question: "So where can I buy a surplice?"

It was said that Trevelyan thought that God was a mathematician and disbelieved in Him. Then one Sunday in chapel he heard in a sermon that God was a landscape gardener, and believed. Be that as it may, he was in due course persuaded by John Burnaby to preach. (His sermon, entitled "Religion and Poetry", is published in his *An Autobiography and Other Essays*, Longmans, 1949.) But he still had little use for matter: ecclesiastical. As a member of the Order of Merit he attended the coronation of Queen Elizabeth II. When asked for his comments he said that the ceremony contained "too much Church of England stuff".

It was Trevelyan who signed the letter offering me a Fellowship, but he had retired from being Master the summer before I arrived back. He continued, however, to dine in Hall fairly regularly, and this enabled me to get to know him better than was possible as an undergraduate. It was easy to see that he had a leonine quality of ferocious honesty (quite lacking in the passive figure of the portrait by Nelson) combined with a deep humanity. It was an attractive mixture, and it led me, for my own interest and amusement, to put him through a sort of test.

Trinity's opposite number at Oxford is Christ Church, and the two colleges annually exchange visits. One year our Christ Church guests included Hugh Trevor-Roper (now Lord Dacre). I sat next to him at port on Sunday evening. I wasn't surprised to find him virulently anti-clerical, and was rather pleased when he told me that he thought that "all theology was sophisticated ninnery". It is always amusing when, on meeting people, you find they live up to their reputation. (It was some ten years before Labour politicians began referring to doctrinaire political theory as theology.) But Trevor-Roper had also given me an added bonus. I was fairly certain that his view of theology was shared by Trevelyan, but I was also more than fairly certain that Trevelyan was far too nice a person to say so to a young theologian, even though I wasn't one of his hosts. If I told Trevelyan what Trevor-Roper had said, in what proportions, I wondered, would conviction and courtesy be combined in his reaction? It was certainly worth discovering. I was lucky enough to sit next to him the next time he dined. "On Sunday," I said, "Trevor-Roper told me that he thought that all theology was sophisticated ninnery." Trevelyan took the situation in his stride. He turned to me and said immediately: "How damned rude." It was a delightfully characteristic reply, and I think I remember the entire incident because of it.

When Master he used to invite Fellows to his country place in Northumberland. On one occasion he invited a clutch of scientists (my informant was among them). After dinner the first day they were just about to settle down over their claret and port to a relaxing evening, when from the host's chair Trevelyan looked at them sternly and confronted them with the poser: "What would history have been without Christianity?" They were all struck utterly dumb. But the conversation must have revived somehow, as before the evening was out Trevelyan delivered himself of the obiter dictum: "All novelists since Conrad are cads." It must have been a far cry from those cosy conversations about the General Board in which many dons are apt to find their peace.

Because he hadn't the slightest degree of self-importance, neither did Trevelyan have an idea of the impact he would make on people, especially the young. He used to join Kitson Clark in interviewing the entrance scholarship candidates in history. Kitson told me that he would appear from an inner room, go up to the candidate, briskly shake his hand, and say: "Hallo, I'm Trevelyan," without noticing at all the terror inspired in schoolboys by this sudden epiphany.

Perhaps the lion who cared about people is best represented by what happened at the college council towards the end of his Mastership. The future of a particular Fellow was being discussed, and it looked as if Trevelyan had sunk into a senile doze. Proposals which were less than generous were gradually gaining acceptance round the table. But Trevelyan wasn't asleep. For at this point he suddenly thundered out: "Is this a college or a bloody institution?" The proposals were at once dropped and considerably more generous ones adopted.

If some really deep conviction of his about what was right was challenged by anybody, Trevelyan would often answer: "If that's what you think, you're quite right to say so" – a combination of intensity and tolerance which left you in no doubt about his estimate of your opinion.

On his eightieth birthday we gave him a dinner. His speech afterwards was short, and he made no attempt to disguise why: "I must hurry home now to hear what Bertie Russell has to say about me on the wireless."

When Stanley Baldwin died Trevelyan said of him: "He was an Englishman indeed in whom was much guile." Trevelyan himself was an Englishman indeed in whom (like Nathanael) there was none.

24

AFTER THREE YEARS in Cambridge unobstructed by religion, I realized that I was going to theological college at Cuddesdon in order to brace myself up and take religion seriously.

Cuddesdon was Anglo-Catholic, but in a sober, restrained, Anglican way – no incense, no devotions to the reserved sacrament, no prayers to the Virgin. It was what called itself Prayer Book Catholicism. The name was not altogether appropriate. The Book of Common Prayer was indeed used for the service of Holy Communion, but it was monkeyed about with: what is called the Prayer of Oblation, set appropriately in the Prayer Book after the Communion of the people, was recited before it, immediately after the Prayer of Consecration, thus completely ruining the structure of the service designed by Cranmer.

Those technical details are not very significant, however. The really important thing was not recognized by me until some ten years later. I then came to see that the Catholicism taught during my time at Cuddesdon was fundamentally identical with my mother's extreme Evangelicalism. There was, of course, an apparent contrast which, while I was there, seemed to me basic. But I discovered eventually that the contrast was merely cosmetic. It was the same religion, attired only in a different wig with different makeup and different clothes. What I mean is that it was still the same old apparatus for producing religious results by whipping up guilt feelings and branding people for life with neurotic compulsions, sold as the voice of God. The rules were slightly different, but the game was the same.

For instance, Cuddesdon religion in my time allowed you to employ what was claimed to be a fully critical approach to the Bible. But in practice your researches had to be restrained enough not to contradict any tenet of Catholic orthodoxy. The Bible, and in particular the New Testament, had to be critically examined in such a way that your apparently free and unfettered criticism produced only such material as was calculated to support the structure of Prayer Book Catholicism. Thus what we called true scholarship could not and did not come to conclusions which were too Protestant (justification by faith alone and the inward religion of the heart) or Roman Catholic (the claims made for St Peter) or what was called liberal modernist (Jesus as one of the great Hebrew prophets). It was a sort of sophisticated fundamentalism, much cleverer than anything my poor mother could have thought of, but in essence the same.

There were also a number of taboos and a resort to moral blackmail. The forms these took were different from those at home, but in essence they were identical.

You could go to the theatre and cinema all right and you could drink and smoke in moderation. But taboos about these things were replaced by others, impressed upon us with equal force and equally absurd. The stress, for example, upon the absolute necessity of fasting before communion was fanatical in its intensity. The Principal told us that some people didn't clean their teeth before communion for fear of accidentally swallowing a drop of water. I thought he was going to say that if in these circumstances you did, it didn't matter. But no. He said: "It is quite possible to clean your teeth without swallowing a drop of water."

The chief use of moral blackmail was to bludgeon us into the practice of sacramental confession. In address after address, sermon after sermon, we were told that by not going to confession we were withholding from God the entire consecration of heart and life which He demanded. We were being cowards, who, by means of our cowardice, were impeding the work of God's grace within us. We were resisting the Holy Ghost. In the end the blackmail worked and I gave way. I was broken down as I was at my Dame school when, under pressure, I admitted to telling a lie which in fact I hadn't told. I admitted a need to go to confession when in reality I felt no need. So I made my first confession to the Principal on a Holy Saturday. When he shook hands with me on Easter Day he gave me a beaming smile. I was now one of his spiritual successes. But I had at least courage enough to dampen his exuberance just a little. Cosmo Lang, recently retired from Canterbury, made his confession immediately before me. So I said to the Principal: "I didn't realize that I should be in the company of such distinguished sinners." His radiant smile faded a bit. Did that remark really betoken entire consecration of heart and life?

I am not in the slightest degree against people making their confession if they feel a genuine need to do so. What I am totally against is the artificial stimulation of a bogus need in order that a certain piece of ecclesiastical machinery may be employed and the priest concerned feel useful. The result in my case was entirely destructive. It led me to try and build up an artificial ideal self which excluded over three-quarters of what I was.

It was with my flesh (my conditioned and perverted subconscious) that I served the religion taught me at Cuddesdon. David Loveday noticed something wrong in my letters. He wrote to me: "Don't let the mephitic atmosphere of the seminary clothe you quite."

My induced inhumanity to myself led me to inhumanity to my neighbour, in this case my elder sister, Joan. She had become engaged to a man whose wife had left him eight years previously and from whom he was divorced. He was in the army in the war, but in peacetime he had trained at the Savoy in London and was manager of the Headland Hotel at Newquay. He was a kind, sensitive and altogether delightful person – brave too, as he had gained the M.C. in the First World War when only nineteen. I asked the Principal for his advice on what attitude I should adopt to my sister's proposed marriage. Without making any further enquiries, let alone meeting the parties concerned, he said I should oppose it absolutely. Before I spoke to him I was hoping that humanity would be possible. But he pushed me away completely from humanity right into taboo. His concern was not in the slightest for the tender vulnerable people affected, but only for the rigid abstract principles he mistook for Christian morality. It is hardly necessary to add that my mother's view of the matter was the same as his. I wrote a stern "loving" letter to Joan. It is a wonder she ever forgave me. She was able to, I think, because she remained true to herself and married the man she loved and who loved her, disregarding all our perfervid and condemnatory ad-monitions. She was by then serving in a hospital ship in Indian waters and her fiancé was also by chance sent out to India. So it was in India that they were married. The marriage proved to be a very happy one. It was only later that I myself was to pay the price of disavowing my own humanity which led me to disavow Joan's.

Rigid abstraction was applied by the Principal not

only to morals but also to matters of belief. I suggested to him once that in the prayer in the Book of Common Prayer Communion Service – "Grant that all they that do confess Thy holy name may agree in the truth of the holy Word, and live in unity and godly love" – that the word "truth" should be understood in a deeper, more subtle, and more real sense than that of cut and dried doctrinal definitions. Such an idea was unintelligible to him. Truth meant doctrinal definition or nothing. It is true that at that time the Anglo-Catholic party felt threatened by a proposed scheme for uniting the divided churches of South India. It was thought that the scheme would involve the loss of the apostolic succession understood as a tactile continuity between the first apostles and contemporary bishops by the process of successive hands being laid on successive heads. I was to hear much more of this when I became a curate in London. For Anglo-Catholics of that period the three great fundamentals of Christianity were fasting communion, sacramental confession and apostolic succession. The first I swallowed at Cuddesdon. With the second I was forcibly fed. But the third I never ceased to regard as a piece of superstitious nonsense.

Once again for the purposes of narration I have abstracted certain features (albeit very central) of my experience of Cuddesdon: the small-minded, dehumanizing, guilt-producing instruction and practices sold to us as the Catholic Faith. But, of course, there were many other factors which gave me a great deal of immense value and for which I remained permanently grateful.

To begin with, there was an excellent theological library where I had plenty of time to pursue my particular interests, since, having read theology at Cambridge, I was exempt from most of the papers in the General Ordination Exam.

The country round was then quite unspoilt by commuter houses and was some of the most beautiful in England. Its loveliness was part and parcel of Cuddesdon existence. We used to walk a lot in its lanes and woodlands.

Then there was all the wonderful quiet which positively invited you to think and to pray. This opportunity to combine study and prayer was, I believe, the most valuable thing Cuddesdon gave me (I had to wait twenty-six years to experience it again here at Mirfield).

And then, of course, there were the other students, from many of whom I learnt a great deal as we discussed whatever was on our minds.

But any account of my time at Cuddesdon would be incomplete without the description of a most pleasurable event which occurred when three of us were in a bathroom together getting ready for bed. First of all there were only myself and somebody I shall call Cecil (now an overseas bishop), who imagined himself very much a spiritually superior person and was therefore extremely self-righteous about keeping the rule of silence after Compline. Then the third person, called Jack, came in, a man of irreverent spirit after my own heart. He made signs to indicate that he had a most urgent and important message for Cecil. Cecil, with a solemn face, bent his head to hear. Jack put his mouth close to Cecil's ear and in a loud whisper said one word – "Balls". It was a supreme moment for which the only possible sequel was the recital of the Nunc Dimittis.

PART TWO

London
Curate

I WAS SENT round from Cuddesdon to look at various parishes. What I took chiefly into account was not what sort of church or parish it was but whether I liked the vicar. Eventually I chose St Barnabas, Pimlico, not because I knew anything about its history or traditions but because I felt that its vicar, Hugh Worlledge, was a saint.

My intuition was not wrong. Hugh Worlledge's religion was an affirmation not a denial of his humanity. He cared enormously about people. He would do anything for anybody if he thought it needed to be done. And he saw that what needed to be done could not be achieved only on the private personal level, important though that was. It meant public political action. He found a home for his politically left-wing aspirations in Sir Richard Acland's Commonwealth Party. Acland and he became close friends and Acland preached at St Barnabas.

I admired as well as loved Hugh Worlledge because his left-wing politics were not of the armchair kind characteristic of the Hampstead intellectuals who think it enough simply to preach social justice. He had a considerable amount of capital and gave most of it away to various worthy causes (his brother told me this). He made himself into a comparatively poor man because he didn't see how, without doing this, he could campaign with any sincerity even for the mild kind of socialism Acland proposed. I wasn't myself at all impressed by the wisdom of the Commonwealth Party. It seemed to me more than a little half-baked. But I was immensely impressed by Hugh's dedication to the underprivileged and its very practical manifestations.

He was a tremendous dear as well as being a saint. He filled the clergy-house with a homely atmosphere. His housekeeper, Mrs Riches, was the widow of one of his churchwardens at a previous church at Bury, Manchester. He had promised the dying man to look after his wife and daughter. The daughter, Dot, was now grown up and worked as a secretary, living with her mother in the clergy-house. Mollie Raynes, the sister of Raymond, then Superior of the Mirfield Community, lived in the parish, and often had supper with us. So we were a family. I had thought it was going to be a lonely life. It was exactly the opposite. On his birthday Hugh used to give us all a lavish dinner at Kettner's. He loved fun. I envied him his ability to finish *The Times* crossword before he had finished his breakfast; and I enjoyed reading his short but interesting history of Pimlico.

The Westminster Estate had given us at a pep-percorn rent an attractive house which had survived from the time when Pimlico was a farm. It had been the bailiff's house. It had a garden in front of it, in the middle of which was an early Victorian lamp-post. This didn't indicate that we were an exaggerated example of carriage-lamp people. The lamp-post had never been taken down since it stood on the towpath of the River Bourne, now piped underground to feed the Serpentine in Hyde Park. At the back of the house was the Chelsea Barracks.

We were having tea one day in the garden when a man dashed over our roof, climbed down into the garden, ran through the gate and disappeared. Five minutes later two military policemen followed. The deserter was caught a week later and the vicar and I had the unpleasant duty of identifying him. I saw how strongly Hugh was tempted to say it wasn't the man. But we couldn't because we were reasonably certain it was.

Hugh once arrived back at the house in a police car. He had been bathing in the Serpentine and had left in the pocket of his coat a pipe lighter of a kind where the flint ignited not a wick fed on petrol but some cottony stuff. The cottony stuff was still a little alight and the wind fanned it into flame, so that Hugh returned from his bathe to find his clothes a heap of ashes. Dressed only in bathing trunks he had appealed to the police for help. I told him I would start the most blood-curdling rumours in the parish as one or two people must have seen him get out of the police car naked with two policemen with him. Actually he claimed fire-insurance on the clothes and got it!

I was once riding with Hugh on the top of a bus while he was smoking a pipe. A man sitting behind us tapped his shoulder and said in a condemnatory voice: "Can you imagine Christ smoking a pipe?" Hugh immediately answered: "Well now, can you imagine Christ sitting on the top of an Eleven bus?" The man got off at the next stop.

The area of the parish was roughly a triangle. Its tip was the north end of Chelsea Bridge; the two points of its base were the air terminal in the Buckingham Palace Road and the south end of Lower Sloane Street. Its inhabitants were chiefly people who lived in fairly recently built Westminster City Council flats. Most of these people belonged to the place, having lived in the area all their lives. St Barnabas had a church school (it still has) for children from five to eleven. Most of the inhabitants had been to the church school, even the old ones. This made the parish into a community – almost everybody was an old boy or girl of the school. It was, in fact, one of London's many villages, and very conscious of its identity. There were no smart shops or restaurants at that time in the Pimlico Road, but just a newsagent–tobacconist, a grocer, baker, dairy, laundry, two pubs and, not least important, a pawnbroker.

I was attracted by the native snobbery I found in our London village. Most of the people worked for the Westminster City Council as dustmen, charwomen, road-sweepers, and so on. But if, say, for the baptismal or marriage register, you had to ask one of them what his occupation was, he would invariably answer: "I am on the Council." This showed me that snobbery of some kind is a human rather than a middle-class phenomenon. As I said, I found it attractive. Why shouldn't we all put on our best front?

Two characters in particular deserve mention. One was a retired charwoman called Mrs Harris. She lived in two rooms and was a devoted member of the Conservative Party, telling me proudly that she had been a member of the Primrose League and the Primrose Association, and that the treats and jaunts organized by them had been most enjoyable (so that, I thought, was how they managed Tory democracy). Her old age had unintentionally been made happy by a long past vicar of St Barnabas who had told her that she must never read any of the novels of Marie Corelli as they were extremely wicked. She now felt free from this ban, and been able to buy the set of novels second-hand for next to nothing, and spent her days in what she considered the most delicious moral danger, devouring *Barabbas*, *The Sorrows of Satan*, *The Master Christian* and the rest.

The other person lived just outside the parish in Lower Sloane Street. He was a retired married priest who had been a curate at St Barnabas. His name was Oscar Wilde and he was eighty-nine, exactly the age the one and only Oscar would have been had he lived. He had had rotten eggs thrown at him at the time of the trial by those who confused him with the defendant. By the time I arrived as a deacon he was senile and used to embarrass my inexperience and leave me not knowing what to do. I used to take him Holy Communion. At the short service I would say: "Make your humble confession to Almighty God," and instead of reciting the confession he would say: "You were at Trinity College, Cambridge, weren't you?" It was difficult to know how to proceed.

When the bombing was bad, if the vicar and I were not on ARP or fire duty, we used to sleep in the crypt of the church. Two pews put together and a mattress made a comfortable bunk. And we didn't lack company as Mrs Riches, Dot and Mollie Raynes used to be with us. Mollie was a moral welfare worker south of the river and used to entertain us by telling us the true stories of her wicked girls.

During my time five parishioners were killed in the bombing. I don't want to tell war stories except for one. By then parents had almost entirely recalled their children from evacuation and St Barnabas school was full. One day at lunch-time a flying bomb fell fairly near us. As soon as the explosion was over, I rushed from our Anderson shelter to the school. The windows had all been broken and bits of ceiling had fallen. Some of the children had been cut slightly by flying glass. But in general the children's morale couldn't have been better, and for a very simple reason. The headmaster had been doling out a huge bowl of custard for school lunch, and as a result of the blast he was covered with the custard from head to foot as in the best slapstick film. The children didn't know what to do for laughing. The headmaster and his staff knew how lucky they were to be alive, so everybody was in good spirits.

By the time I arrived at the parish Hugh Worlledge had become disillusioned with the Anglo-Catholicism he had inherited. He was much condemned by other Anglo-Catholic vicars for abolishing the eleven o'clock High Mass at which nobody communicated and which was attended by the rich from various parts of London who liked that sort of thing, and putting in its place a Parish Communion at nine-thirty to which the actual inhabitants of the parish used to come and communicate. This was called selling the pass, though I never understood why. One of the symbolic gestures which has remained in my memory was when the verger put out a lace alb for him to wear. He picked it up and threw it across the vestry floor. His patience with Anglo-Catholic pieties was all but exhausted. He refused to use the English Missal, which was *de rigueur* among Anglo-Cats in those days.

I think I saw the man pretty accurately when I went to the clergy-house on a visit. It was a privilege to be his curate.

2

I WAS ORDAINED DEACON on Trinity Sunday 1943 at St Paul's Cathedral by Geoffrey Fisher, then Bishop of London. While staying at the clergy-house in Pimlico I spent the three days prior to the ordination at Fulham Palace with the other candidates, about twenty in all. We did the same when we were ordained priests.

I didn't share the common view of Geoffrey Fisher as no more than a schoolmaster. I thought him a most impressive person, chiefly because he carried an enormous weight of authority without the slightest hint of self-importance. He was easy to get on with and in his presence you felt you really were with your Father in God. His two charges (before our ordination as deacon and priest) were particularly striking. I shall repeat only one point he made: the vital importance of remembering the distinction drawn by Greek philosophers between *episteemee* (knowledge) and *doxa* (opinion).

Fisher always listened to what you had to say. He might well in consequence tell you that you were a complete fool, but at least he had taken in what you said. He always replied carefully to letters. When he was Archbishop of Canterbury he wrote me an intriguing rebuke to a letter I had written him complaining of what I considered the foolish and prejudiced opposition of a certain bishop to the recommendations of the Wolfenden Report. Fisher ended his reply thus: "In short, even if the Bishop of X is taking himself too seriously, it is a serious thing if you do as well." What answer could be more calculated to turn away wrath?

The first time you wear a dog-collar in public is very embarrassing. You think everybody is looking at you. I hated standing with it on in the Pimlico Road waiting for an Eleven bus to take me to St Paul's. And when it arrived I hoped the people on it wouldn't notice me as, no doubt, they didn't. My parents had come to London for the occasion and were staying in a hotel near Victoria, but went to the cathedral under their own steam. The service was at ten o'clock and lasted two hours. Afterwards I went with my parents to their hotel and immediately lost my temper with a waiter for failing to produce the pot of tea I thought it wise to have before lunch. This, my first act after ordination, made me feel dreadfully guilty. But now I think the fault lay with the stupid people who laid such absurd emphasis on fasting communion. To have gone through what was inevitably a taxing morning without so much as an eggspoonful of water was positively to invite frayed nerves. The arrogant foolishness of that tyrannical demand still makes me angry. It is said that there is no tyranny worse than petty tyranny. There is. It is petty tyranny successfully internalized: in other words, a neurotic compulsion.

From the congregation at St Barnabas I learnt many things. Of them all I think the most profoundly valuable was the fact that I was a greenhorn, a raw hand, a novice. I was stuffed full of ideas learnt at Cambridge and Cuddesdon and felt I had a great deal to teach these dear simple people. With the greatest possible kindness they made me realize that it was I who was the dear simple person. They listened to my sermons and addresses with true Christian indulgence, paragons of patience who knew it would be wrong to discourage a young deacon. By their forbearance, by the very affability of their faces while I spoke, they brought me as painlessly as possible to the recognition that, compared with them, I knew next to nothing about life. I did once overhear a parishioner ask a friend: "Why did Father Williams preach again this Sunday?" The friend laughed and answered by what I recognized as a quotation from the Second Epistle to Timothy: "Endure hardness as a good soldier."

Four times a week I used to go and teach the top form of our church school – boys and girls of ten and eleven. What I found difficult was not so much the size of the class – I suppose it consisted of thirty-five to forty children – but the different levels of intelligence it contained. It was tempting to concentrate on the brighter ones and ignore the rest. But that was to make the period a waste of time for the majority of those present. By a process of trial and error I discovered the obvious: that if you told a story all the children listened and most of them could make something or other of it. When I first started going to the school I used to ask the children questions. I soon stopped it since, whatever the question was, the reaction would be identical. The children would assume that because I was a priest the question would be about religion. And religious questions, they had apparently been conditioned to believe, invariably had the same answer. They would all put up their hands. I would point to one of them; and he or she would invariably answer: "The Body and Blood of Christ." That at least, they thought, was the safest bet, the answer most likely to be right. It was the fruit of good Catholic teaching by a succession of curates full of earnestness and zeal: "How did Jesus tell us to behave towards our enemies?" – "The Body and Blood of Christ." "What do you think that pearl of great price was which a man sold everything to buy?" – "The Body and Blood of Christ." "Why do people say their prayers?" – "The Body and Blood of Christ."

I found it a relief that Hugh Worlledge was in favour of non-denominational Christian teaching in schools. This was a matter of considerable controversy at the time, since Rab Butler was drawing up his Education Act, and High Church clergymen were liable to a fantasy that he was conspiring to undermine the Church of England.

But the controversy about religious education in schools stopped short of hysteria, thanks no doubt to Rab Butler's characteristic tact. The same cannot be said of the controversy about the scheme for reuniting the churches in South India. The Catholic party in the Church of England went berserk about this, suspecting a plot to extinguish them altogether. The fires of fanaticism were kept well stoked by Anglican Religious (monks) from Cowley and Mirfield, some of whom seemed to have little else to do except to rush about London keeping susceptible clergymen at fever point.

It is not my purpose to plot the course of this exercise in bigotry. Hugh Worlledge showed not the slightest sign of excitement about it. I don't think he was at all interested (as a neighbouring curate of keen Catholic views commented with withering scorn: "What can you expect from a man who abolishes the non-communicating High Mass?"). But I was persuaded to go to a meeting in the hall of St Mary Abbot's, Kensington. About a hundred clergymen turned up. Enthusiastic support was given to a proposal that a motion should be drawn up condemning the South India scheme and a vote taken. At this point F. C. Synge (he was then chaplain to Geoffrey Fisher, Bishop of London) got up and said that he was all in favour of a vote being taken, but that it seemed to him that only those who had actually read the proposed scheme were eligible to vote. This was found to disqualify all but nine of the clergymen present, and so no vote was taken.

Why do people imagine that in order to have God you must also have all this kind of nonsense? It is because (as I've already said) religion is to a large extent what people do with their lunacy: their phobias, their will to power, their sexual frustrations.

It has long since ceased to be fashionable to talk with Bonhoeffer of religionless Christianity. But I think I found it at this time in Pimlico among the dustmen, charwomen and road-sweepers who lived in the Westminster City Council flats and never came to church.

One way and another the area had suffered considerably from German bombs. People had been killed and maimed and homes destroyed. Yet when our bombers were heard overhead on their way to Germany, there was no sign of pleasure or satisfaction. "Poor wretches, I'm afraid they're going to get it tonight. Poor souls, I hope it won't be too bad," was the characteristic comment.

If anything is loving your enemies, then that was. And I was forced to ask myself: who was the more

Christian – these people in Pimlico without a sign of hatred for those who had injured them but who were on the contrary full of sympathetic concern, or those Anglo-Catholic pundits too obviously full of hatred for those sponsoring or supporting a plan to reunite separated Christians in South India?

It was a question which chimed in with something else which worried me a great deal at the time. I had no real desire to persuade people to come to church. If I tried to, it was only from a very dry sense of duty. I didn't see how what went on in church could possibly have any meaning for them: what on earth, I thought, would they be able to make of a Sung Mass or of Evensong? I didn't see how they could be other than puzzled and bored. My deepest feelings told me that what I ought to do was to get to know people, to establish with them relations of confidence to whatever degree was possible, and thus perhaps be invited by them to share their joys and sorrows and problems and aspirations. It was in that communion with them, I felt, that God's real presence was to be found, and not in trying to sell God to people as if He were a patent medicine with the church as the chemist's shop where it could be obtained. Yet God as a universal patent medicine had been so drummed into me both from my earliest years at home and during my training at Cuddesdon that I felt horribly guilty by my own lack of desire to make people technically religious and church-going. Wasn't that, after all, what I had been commissioned specifically to do? So I did it. But my fundamental lack of conviction always made it sound artificial in the extreme. Inevitably it was recognized for what it was – a piece of obligatory ritual to which the correct ritual response was known and performed: the people said that they would try to come to church next Sunday. Of course they never did, nor, I think, did they expect you to believe that they would. It was like their saying "Pleased to meet you."

Another facet of what worried me was that I didn't possess that passion for changing people which seems to belong to the heart of every zealous clergyman and is, I believe, called a love of souls. I was distressed to find that I liked people as they were and didn't want them to be different. They seemed to me lovable and, because lovable, amusing. It must be remembered (as I've said) that this part of Pimlico was a village community and that it was during the war. For the war seemed to bring out the best in Londoners and they went about loving their neighbours in the most practical ways. Naturally enough, that was not always the case, but it was typical.

Of the exceptions to the rule I remember one mother of three at whose flat there always seemed to be an abundance of sweets in spite of the strict rationing. I once commented on this and she answered: "Yes, I've a nice lot of sweets, but I had to tell a white lie to get them." "What", I asked, "do you mean by a white lie?" "Oh," she answered, "I had to tell them at the food office that I'd lost my ration books, so they gave me another lot, so now I've got two lots." I said to her as sternly as I could: "Don't you understand that that is a very serious offence indeed for which you could be put in prison?" But as I walked home it was clear to me that my real concern was that the woman shouldn't get into trouble with the authorities, and that her description of a completely black lie as a white one I found very amusing, since she was only doing blatantly what most of us try to do with artifice. It was an exaggeration of self-deception and was funny as a caricature is.

But – the question nagged at me – wasn't I enjoying myself at the expense of her immortal soul? Didn't I believe that God hated her sin and that it was because of it that Christ had suffered and died? What sort of a priest was I to be amused at it?

But there is one thing I did in Pimlico of which I am inordinately proud, not because I did it well, but because (like Dr Johnson's dog walking on two legs) I did it at all. I was the scoutmaster of the church troop.

I have always been unable to tie a single knot, and boys have only to take one look at me to riot at once. I used to dread Fridays, when the scouts met in the church hall. But I got through the meetings somehow; it is extraordinary what you can get away with by bluff. The local scout commissioner (he was called Hitch and the boys inevitably called him Scratch) was extremely helpful. He called often at our meetings, always addressing the boys as "Folk": "Now, Folk, what is the best way of lighting a fire without matches?" "Tell me, Folk, what would you do if you met a mad dog?" His questions had an almost metaphysical quality about them, so divorced were they from everyday life. He once stayed behind to tell me some news he thought would encourage me. I thought it a horror story. It was that in St John's Wood a scoutmaster who was a retired sergeant-major in the Guards had had to disband his troop altogether as he had been unable to keep even a shred of order. The story terrified me. I used to dream that I was myself a retired sergeant-major and wake up in a cold sweat.

Luckily the worst boy, in an excess of energy, accidentally jumped through a plate-glass window into the street. A taxi happened to be passing at the time, so I was able to wrap him in my clergyman's cloak and take him at once to St George's Hospital, where they took over two hours to patch him up. His injuries though messy were only minor. But I'm glad to say they had a permanently sobering effect on the other boys.

What I am most proud of is that one year I took the troop camping for ten days in Berkshire. I was shown in the most marvellous way that, if you do your duty, God looks after you. We were in a field near the village of Inkpen. I called on the vicar, Father Driscoll, who most hospitably invited me to dinner each evening. The food was so outstandingly good that I congratulated him on his cook. "Oh," he said, "I do it myself." He must have noticed that I looked surprised. "You see," he said, "I didn't become a clergyman until I was almost forty and before that I was a chef at Claridge's." I could have kissed him. When I returned to Cambridge I discovered to my great pleasure (it was nothing to do with me) that he had been given a Trinity living. It was encouraging, I thought, that the college livings committee should have so civilized a sense of values.

My final reminiscence of Pimlico shall be of a parade of church scout troops drawn from southwest London (north of the river – we were not without standards) for a service in St Martin in the Fields. I had to march down Whitehall in shorts as scout uniform in those days demanded. I hoped that none of my contemporaries, working in this or the other government department, would see me. The preacher at the service was Father Farrington, at that time vicar of St Gabriel's, Pimlico. His sermon was completely above the heads of the boys, but they behaved well and looked extremely solemn through-out, especially at Father Farrington's opening words: "Hallo, scouts. I'm going to begin by telling you a parable. You know what a parable is? It's a heavenly story with no earthly meaning." I can't remember any more of the sermon.

3

MOLLIE RAYNES'S BROTHER, Raymond (as I've said he was then Superior of the Mirfield Community), told me that if I were offered a job by the vicar of All Saints, Margaret Street (near Oxford Circus), his advice was that I should take the offer very seriously.

I was an ecclesiastical innocent as far as London churches went. All I knew about All Saints was that its music was supposed to be very good. I had never even heard of Dom Bernard Clements or Prebendary Mackay – famous past vicars of the church you were expected to know about as you knew about Lloyd George. The vicar at this time was called Cyril Tomkinson. I decided that if he were to ask me to be his curate my answer would depend on what I made of him, since I knew nothing about the church.

In due time a friend of mine asked me to dinner and said that Cyril Tomkinson would be the other guest. I found a short man in the middle fifties who, when he stood or walked, looked like a small, cheeky bird. He was able to manipulate his eyes like a born comedian so that they gave exaggerated expression to whatever feeling he wished to parody. At dinner he said how very lucky we were to have been at Cambridge rather than Oxford. I asked him why. "Well," he said, "if at Oxford you say something smart, they tell you – 'Clever boy. Do it again.' But at Cambridge if you're smart they look down their noses at you as if you had done something in the worst possible taste. And clever remarks always make a person unpopular. People hold it against you that they didn't think of it first themselves." By this time I was quite fascinated.

After dinner our host deposited Cyril Tomkinson and myself alone in the drawing-room with coffee and brandy. Cyril poured out the coffee and, taking a taste of it, gave a deep sigh of satisfaction. "Thank God," he said, "for good coffee. There's far too much bad coffee about nowadays. People seem to think that God is pleased if they make it weak." He then said that Father Raynes had no doubt told me that he was looking for a curate. Would I be interested in the job? I had indeed become very interested – I had never met a clergyman like Cyril – and I answered "Yes." "I ought, then, to ask you a few questions. Do you mind?" "Of course not," I said. There was a slight pause, and Cyril then asked me: "Are you the sort who falls in love with choirboys?" "No," I said, "I'm afraid I'm not." "Don't apologize," said Cyril, "a clergyman's interests should never be confined to his church. Do you read Henry James?" "No. I haven't read anything of his." "That's a pity. However, it can be arranged." By this time I realized that he was enjoying playing Lady Bracknell and was observing both whether I had identified the rôle and also whether I would be crass enough to say so. I had noticed and I wasn't crass. So he offered me the job. He later told me that clergymen at All Saints, Margaret Street, had to have a certain degree of sophistication. "Holiness is necessary. But it is not enough," he added.

Later that week he showed me round the church. Over the high altar there is an enormous silver hanging pyx given in the early 1920s by the then Duke of Newcastle in memory of former members of the choir who had died in the First World War. At that time the pyx went up and down by electric motor. An enormous key, which looked as if it had strayed from a pantomime, had to be inserted in a lock in the surface of the altar to work the machine, which made a horrible buzzing noise. "My dear," commented Cyril, "in this church the good God lives in a lift."

Cyril was in fact a man of prayer and profound spirituality, but (like David Loveday) what he hated above all things was cant, and he was always pricking the bubble of bogus piety. And this made him make fun of himself as well as of others. After my first sermon at All Saints, which had obviously gone down well, he said to me at once in the vestry – "We shall be scratching each other's eyes out."

As a vicar in Brighton he had shocked the local clergy by saying that the only way to get through Holy Week was on champagne. As I knew, he spent a long time in private each day praying, but in conversation with some nauseatingly over-religious church people I once heard him say – "People speak about prayer. But the only prayer I ever say is to thank God that my father was a stockbroker." He composed two collects. One was in honour of a well-known and spiritually haughty director of souls called John Briscoe: "O God who hast given unto thy servant John Briscoe a proud look and a high stomach, mercifully grant that as we have been chastened by the rod of his correction, so we may be aided by his condescending intercessions." It was a perfect imitation of the English Missal idiom. The second collect was for a fine Ascot. Unfortunately I can remember only the end of it, but that is worth quoting: "... that the rich may glorify Thee by their clothes and think well of Thee in their hearts."

He loved the theatre. Alec Guinness and his wife (then Anglicans) used to come to the church, and also Hugh Sinclair. Cyril quoted with approval what Father Mackay was supposed to have said to couples he was preparing for marriage: "Until after the wedding you mustn't do anything which couldn't be put on to the stage at the Haymarket theatre." But he was inclined to think that Mackay had introduced too many theatrical effects into the church. Once, before a High Mass, as we were putting on our elaborate costumes and the servers and so on (all grown up) were standing round looking frightfully solemn, Cyril said to me: "My dear, I wonder Mackay didn't introduce make-up." You could feel the loutish disapproval this evoked. And once when a committee was discussing how money could be raised for the church, Cyril with a poker face suggested: "Couldn't we hire out opera-glasses at the back of the nave?"

He was not himself above bringing off a *coup de théatre*. VJ Day fell on 15 August – the feast of the Assumption. The church was packed to capacity in honour of the double occasion. Cyril began his sermon in a very slow portentous voice: "Today is ... Napoleon's birthday."

❦❦|4|❦❦

ALL SAINTS led a double life. Most obviously there was what we called the Sunday Theatre – the High Mass at eleven and Solemn Evensong at six. But much more important, in our view, was the continuous work of what would now be described as counselling. There was no parish; or rather, there was a parish the size of a postage stamp which consisted either of Oxford Street stores like Bourne and Hollingsworth or mini-factories where women's clothes were mass-produced (known as the rag trade) and which closed down from five o'clock on Friday evening until ten o'clock Monday morning. Hence the clientèle at All Saints was entirely eclectic.

The music of the Sunday Theatre was superb.

Owing to the generosity of Lord Nuffield the choir school had been kept going somewhere in the country for the entire war, and thanks to the magnificent efforts of Father Roy Foster, the headmaster, the morale of the school never ceased to be of the highest order. After five years, the European war being now over, the boys returned to Margaret Street and sang as if they had never left it, though, of course, no individual boy had ever sung in the church before. The organist and choirmaster was Bill Lloyd Webber (for many years now he has been Professor of Theory and Composition at the Royal College of Music and he is also the author of a good number of instrumental, choral and educational works, not to mention being the father of Andrew of *Superstar* and Julian the cellist; Bill's own father used to sing in the choir at Margaret Street). Under Bill the choir was not only good; it had a touch of exquisite perfection that I have never heard anywhere else, not even at King's, Cambridge. Bill was also an organist of rare distinction. His playing had about it a vitality and colour and crispness which were unequalled.

Each Sunday and Festivals we used to sing masses by Mozart, Schubert, Saint-Saëns and Gounod; it made me sorry that Offenbach had not written a mass. In Advent and Lent the music was even better because it was more austere – unaccompanied Palestrina and Viadana.

Since only the choir could sing the music of the mass, it was our policy to have extremely popular hymns from the old unrevised *Ancient and Modern*. The congregation joined in with gusto, shouting their way through "All people that on earth do dwell", or sobbing it through "Rock of Ages cleft for me", or purring it through "Shall we not love thee, Mother dear?"

The part played by the sermon in the service was emphasized. You could be at least twenty minutes, and people listened. A canon of St Paul's who had been told that his sermon should be roughly that length wrote back a somewhat acid postcard: "I notice the time given to the music and that given to the Word of God." Cyril replied on another card simply saying: "It looks as if there has been some confusion."

At Evensong the psalms would be sung to plainsong with a variety of music for the canticles, and an anthem. I told Bill Lloyd-Webber that I would invent Christian words for "O Isis and Osiris" from *The Magic Flute*, as I thought it would make a wonderful anthem. He quite rightly said it would be too much of a stunt. On weekdays we sang the whole of Evensong to plainsong.

The church was packed to capacity every Sunday morning and evening. There were several reasons for this – the quality of the music and (we liked to think) of the preaching, the general boom in church-going towards the end of and after the war, and, by no means least important, the fact that petrol was still rationed so that people didn't go away at the weekend.

One Sunday morning some clever thieves siphoned off all the petrol in the cars outside the church while their owners were inside singing the praises of God. By coincidence a visiting preacher that morning had extolled the virtue of patience. You could see him in the street desperately trying to practise what he had preached, shouting out in an obvious fury to the other dismayed owners of cars: "It's not the end of the bloody. . . . It's not the end of the world. Let's keep a sense of proportion. What the hell does it matter. . . . I mean what does it matter if we get home late?" It was a sort of roaringly impatient patience which left you in perplexity about whether he was being really patient or not, on the same principle that the brave man is the person who does what makes him shake with fear.

We didn't have many visiting preachers ("They much prefer us," Cyril said with a great deal of truth), but of those we did have I remember a few in particular. There was Cyril's brother Herbert, a vicar in Hove, who for his text extracted two words from a verse in the first chapter of Acts – "But wait" – and told us how much happier we should all be if we had been willing to wait longer for everything. "Dull, pretentious and untrue," was Cyril's comment on his brother's efforts. Then there was Eric Abbott (at the time Dean of King's, London), who lectured us somewhat severely on the difference between the beauty of holiness and the holiness of beauty. "Well, at least, nobody ever thought I was beautiful," whispered Cyril, "which is more than can be said for Eric." A new vicar of St Alban's, Holborn, Father Startup, gave a Lent course and at dinner afterwards said how difficult this Lent was being for him as he was having to give three Lent courses. "But surely," said Cyril, "you can give the same addresses at each course, can't you?" "Oh no," said Startup, "you see, people follow me round." "But my dear Father," answered Cyril, "they don't follow you round to hear what you say but to gaze on your face." Cyril once invited an over-simple young priest who was extremely good-looking to preach at the High Mass "because, poor child, he has recently been in hospital for six weeks and it will cheer him up". He took as his theme the proposition that when in extremity people instinctively return to religion. And as evidence for this assertion he told us of a young man in the bed next to his in the hospital who every time they stuck a needle into him said "Christ Almighty". I forbore to tell Cyril that, like holiness, good looks were not enough.

When he thought it necessary he could be extremely critical of my own preaching. He taught me that if the members of a congregation cough, it is not their fault but the preacher's, since people only cough if they are bored. And once, when I had paid too much attention to style, he said to me: "You gave us quite a good meal this morning, but it was served in such elegant old silver as to be slightly cold. A miserable performance, my dear."

More interesting was something I didn't know until years later. One of the regular congregation was a psychiatrist (now very well known). He said to a colleague whose patient I was subsequently to become in Cambridge: "There is a young clergyman preaching at the church I go to in London who knows much more than he can take.

Sooner or later he will break down."

We did all we could to make the Sunday Theatre go as well as possible. It meant a great deal to a lot of people, as we were often told – by a nun, for instance, who was the matron of a home for the dying in Clapham, by a probation officer in Stepney, by men and women in the Forces on leave, by a clerk in the ticket office at Paddington, by the harassed headmaster of an elementary school in North London, by two medical students who one Sunday came to church in the white tie and tails they had worn for a ball the previous evening. That God should come to all sorts and conditions of people by means of beauty heard and seen had a profound and permanent effect on my theological thinking. For, although in this case the beauty was transmitted by means of a church service, obviously beauty could not be confined to things technically religious. I was on my way to seeing that if God was not a keen Christian, neither was He necessarily a churchman. Some years later the then Director of the Fitzwilliam Museum at Cambridge, Carl Winter, told me that he spent anything up to an hour a day in the quiet contemplation of some object of beauty in his museum. "I couldn't get through the chores without it," he said. It was impossible for me to believe that that wasn't what Christians would call prayer, though I knew that not a few clergymen would foam at the mouth at the idea.

Of course the Sunday Theatre at All Saints had its comic side. For instance, as well as the regulars, there was a shifting congregation which altered according to the music. Mozart on the whole brought in more women than men, Gounod more men than women, often looking extremely odd, especially if there was to be a procession, when they would arrive forty-five minutes early to get a seat next to the aisle.

All letters to the choirboys were opened and read by the headmaster. This was necessary as they used often to receive fan-mail with propositions about meeting in some teashop. It was difficult to discover how the writers of the letters got to know the names of this or the other boy. And the boys were warned not to talk to strangers. At this time Stanley Eley (later Bishop of Gibraltar but then Senior Chaplain to the Archbishop of Canterbury) lived in the house and officiated regularly in the church. He saw one of the boys in the Oxford Circus Underground and in an attempt to be friendly went up to him and asked him if he was going home for a day's holiday. The boy immediately replied in a stern voice: "I'm not allowed to talk to strange men," and ran away to the other end of the platform, leaving poor Stanley to endure the disapproving sneers and frowns of the people within earshot. He was not unnaturally furious and Cyril Tomkinson had to appease him by taking him out to dinner at his club.

Cyril, like Disraeli, had the ability to belong to and believe in an establishment which he could also stand outside and laugh at. In that sense he was a Catholic Protestant, to use Mme à Laurent's phrase from my childhood. When it was suggested that at the Midnight Mass of Christmas a practice of Father Mackay's day should be revived – a solo choirboy singing the first verse of "O come all ye faithful" immediately after the prayer of consecration – Cyril said he would agree if a collection were taken immediately afterwards. Once, as the choir was singing, he turned to me at the altar and said: "Don't stand there holding your hands like an Anglican bishop." He wasn't taken in by the religious goings-on. That meant that, like Hugh Worlledge, he was held in the greatest suspicion by those describing themselves as uncompromising Catholics. They thought he went on selling the pass left, right and centre.

❧‖5‖❧

ABOUT ONE THING Cyril Tomkinson was completely convinced: that whatever importance the Sunday Theatre might have, the real work of All Saints was done with individuals on weekdays, either in the confessional or in the less technical context of a tête-à-tête. There must, he said, always be a priest on the premises available day and night.

This fact became known and it brought in a considerable crowd with all sorts of problems and worries. It was the really interesting part of my work as it gave me contact with a very wide variety of people, old and young, men and women, rich and poor, educated and illiterate, most of them genuine, some of them thinking you were an easy touch.

Once a toothless man called at the house. He produced from his pocket a broken set of false teeth wrapped in a handkerchief saying that he was a shop assistant at Selfridges, that he had broken his teeth that afternoon, that he couldn't appear toothless the next day at Selfridges as the customers wouldn't like it, but that he knew a shop in the Tottenham Court Road where the teeth could be repaired overnight for a pound. Could I lend him the money as he had spent his week's wages but would be able to repay me the following Saturday? The story seemed to me so unlikely that it might be true. So I asked him where the shop was; he gave me the number, and I said I would meet him there at 8.45 the next morning and pay for the repair. I went to the number he said and found it was a newsagent's shop. When I asked whether they repaired broken false teeth they obviously thought I was mad. I thought that it was worth checking at the police station – not to report the man, but to enquire whether the police knew of any such establishment in the vicinity. They didn't. I walked home full of admiration for the imaginative powers of my caller the previous evening. On another day a man called and asked me to lend him £50 to set up a fruit barrow. When I answered (with truth) that I didn't possess such a sum of money, the man became abusive and kept shouting: "Is that what you call Christianity?" In the end I was able to get rid of him.

But most of the callers were, of course, those in genuine distress. By and large for obvious reasons people find it easier to go for advice to a church in central London where they and their families are unknown rather than to the local vicar, who in virtue of his office is part of the community to which they also belong. Eric Mascall used to pull our legs and say that people came to us through a confusion of ideas: because the music was superlatively good they thought that the advice must be as well.

Most people came with the sort of problems a priest is supposed to be of some help in sorting out. Sometimes people came who were clearly in need of medical and psychiatric treatment. Here we were lucky as a medically qualified psychiatrist was one of our regular congregation, and she was always ready to see without charge people we recommended to her.

Sometimes people needed legal advice, like the poor old man who had been in the chorus at Covent Garden and was being bullied and harried by neighbours who wanted his flat. Here again we were lucky, as a lawyer in the congregation was always ready to see anybody we sent him. It must be remembered that all this was before the days of the welfare state and the extension of the social services.

6

AS I HAVE NARRATED it this ministry to individuals sounds all very jolly and snug, as though as a priest I had all the answers and sent people away sorted out and satisfied. But, of course, the truth was very different. I suppose I was sometimes able to help some people a little – anybody who is prepared to listen does that – but I was in such a muddle myself that I imagine I probably did more harm than good.

My most serious defect as a pastor or confessor was that I didn't realize what a muddle I was in, or indeed that I was in a muddle at all. I had read a number of books about morals and moral theology and I had studied Christian doctrine in what would now be described as some depth. This gave me the illusion that everything had a Christian answer, and that, even if I didn't myself know what it was, I could in principle discover it from somebody more clued-up than I was. So I tended to put people and their difficulties into theoretical straitjackets. They became for me particular instances of general types, and for each general type I thought there were applicable specific rules which provided the ground-plan for the appropriate advice. I was unconsciously hiding from myself my own muddled state by having everything sorted out neatly on the intellectual level. The result was that I was no more than a lecturer in theology masquerading as a pastor, taking these two as "ideal" types.

To give an example of what I mean. A young man of about twenty-five called on me one morning and told me that he had made his confession to me the previous day. He asked me whether I would have given him absolution had I known what he was now going to tell me – that all the time he had no intention whatever of discontinuing to sleep with his boyfriend of the same age. The answer to his enquiry seemed to me quite clear. The books said that homosexual practices were wrong. If the young man had no intention at all of amendment of life in this respect, then he could not be given absolution. And that is what I told him. I now only hope that he disregarded everything I said. I had given no consideration whatever to the delicate, complicated, vulnerable humanity not only of my penitent but also of his friend, nor had I taken into account the fact that real genuine love, God's greatest gift making us only a little lower than the angels, can find expression in an infinite variety of ways, including those which any particular culture may find unacceptable.

The apparent security conferred by intellectual tidiness thus led me to treat people as if they were machines whose proper functioning was fully set out in the appropriate handbooks. In this sense it was by trying to dehumanize people that I tried to help them. It was, of course, a trick I had unknowingly first played upon myself.

It was combined with a faculty of which, for all practical purposes, I was also unaware: the ability to tell the majority what they wanted to hear because I had instinctively been able to probe their deepest prejudices.

Naturally, that is not how I thought of it. I thought of myself as expounding what I had now learned to call the Catholic Faith. It didn't mean that I prophesied only smooth things. There is a masochistic streak in most people which enjoys the occasional taste of bitter medicine (and indeed is apt to feel aggrieved if not given it) so long as their fundamental preconceptions are not upset so that they are not called in any radical sense to repentance. So I built up a little local reputation as a confessor, director and preacher by telling most people what they wanted to hear and confirming them in their prejudices. Some people even thought of me as a rising Anglo-Catholic star. It was gratifying to be hailed as a Nazarite, and it made me feel even more secure with my tidy definitions and hid still further from me the muddle that in fact I was in.

But the muddle wasn't entirely hidden. For the human being did sometimes growl at the lecturer in theology. The child within me did occasionally wake up from his anaesthesia.

Doubtless this happened in all kinds of ways of which I've remained permanently unaware. (The working of God's grace is seldom observable.) But as counsellor and confessor there were two issues which began to show me how much in the dark I was.

The first was rather specialized. Occasionally one or other member of the secret service would make his confession. The frame of reference in which their consciences were troubled inevitably hit for six any criteria to which I had given even intellectual consideration. No tidy answers were possible here, except perhaps to tell them to give up their jobs, which was not possible, and in any case it was not their jobs as such which gave them moral scruples. I had to rely on my intuition, fully realizing that what I said was hopelessly haphazard, too obviously inconsistent, uninformed, partial, unsatisfying, in short a hell of a mess. And it occasionally began to dawn on me that life in general might be more like the secret service than I had ever imagined; I had not yet read any of Graham Greene.

The other issue was a common one which was constantly coming up in the confessional. It was about the use by married couples of contraceptives.

The Lambeth Conference of 1958 gave its blessing to their use by the married, attaching to the permission the pious conditions and exhortations usual in such documents. But before this, opinion in the Anglican Church was divided, with the Anglo-Catholics (in their usual imitation of Rome) totally opposed.

Something of this Anglo-Catholic attitude had come to my notice in Pimlico. A High Church society with an office somewhere in Westminster (my informant was a priest who worked in the office) was financing the training of a married ordinand. Somehow or other it had slipped out to one of the trustees – a Religious (a monk) – that the couple were using contraceptives, and there was the most tremendous rumpus consuming literally hours of discussion. Eventually it was decided that unless the couple gave a solemn promise never to use contraceptives again, the financial grant would be withdrawn.

When I began hearing confessions at All Saints I discovered that a considerable number of husbands and wives felt extremely guilty about using contraceptives. They felt it put them on the wrong side of the church and hence cut them off from God. On the other hand it could be a matter of fundamental difficulty, perhaps even a danger to their marriage itself, to give up the practice.

I was myself unmarried and aged only twenty-seven. I thought it therefore essential to obtain advice from those I imagined most competent to give it. I wrote to two or three priests who were known as experienced confessors, including Raymond Raynes. In the nature of the case they were all Anglo-Catholics and they all gave the same reply: No artificial contraception could be allowed; it was against nature and so on. Raymond Raynes, I remember, said that he fully understood the difficulties which this prohibition might cause, but difficulties in life were the occasions of receiving the grace of God; and who knew what wonders of grace might be achieved by the endurance of these difficulties in marriage?

My opinions thus fortified, I went ahead in the confessional laying down the law. I was sure I could answer any question. I had it all taped.

But after six or nine months I began to be more and more severely shaken by what I increasingly considered to be the quite unnecessary frustration and misery and guilt caused by this relentless rule. And the moment came when I could no longer enforce or advocate it. It seemed to me exactly the kind of thing to which Jesus was referring when he said of the pharisees that they bound heavy burdens and grievous to be borne and laid them upon men's shoulders. Then, after a short time, I found that I was advocating the opposite of the rule in a quite positive manner. What I mean is that if a husband or wife felt a burden of guilt about this matter, I used to tell them that by mentioning it they had laid the responsibility squarely on my shoulders and could now go ahead with a clear conscience, and that, if I were mistaken, and artificial contraception was wrong after all, the guilt would be entirely on my head not theirs.

Now, thirty-five or so years later, and in view of the attitude taken by the Anglican communion since the Lambeth Conference of 1958, this must seem very much a storm in a tea-cup. But it certainly wasn't at the time, least of all for the couples concerned.

Today I should take the view that if people are silly enough to allow their conduct to be dictated by a bunch of clergymen, then they deserve whatever comes to them. If you opt for being a church mouse, you must be prepared to take the consequences. But at the time the issue made a very big dent in the armour of the professional priest and lecturer in theology I was trying to be, because the human being I also was, and the child within me, began to hint, and more than hint, that the clear-cut definitions in which I put so much trust might turn out to be broken reeds, and that the solid rock which was meant to keep people safe did, in fact, the opposite by crushing and destroying them.

Yet privately in my own self I felt wretchedly guilty at going against what was the received Catholic position. Was I luring people to their destruction by setting up my own private opinion against that of the church? It was sometimes not easy to live with this conflict of the spirit (my God-given humanity) against the flesh (my conditioned subconscious with its irrational guilts and phobias), especially as the flesh had very largely taken captive my intellect. For the mind, as Pascal said, is invariably the plaything of the heart.

There was a great deal of work in the confessional at All Saints. Sometimes, before Christmas and Easter, for instance, we were at it hours on end. It soon became impossible to remember who had said what, especially as everybody more or less said the same thing. I used to feel that if people must sin, they might think of something original and amusing. But they never did. That's the worst of sin – in the last resort it's so deadly boring.

One thing, however, interested me, and it has remained to this day something of a mystery.

Although everybody said more or less the same thing, some people drained you of vitality, being regular blood-suckers, while others with identical sins were life-giving and somehow renewed you. I discovered that this had nothing to do with age, sex, class, education, intelligence or anything else you could identify. People of all descriptions and kinds were blood-suckers or life-givers. I suppose it was something to do with the presence or absence in a person of some indefinable quality of outgoingness. In some deep, hidden, unknown place within, some people were what I can only call generous, while others weren't. This illustrated for me the apparent arbitrariness of God's grace. The generosity (if that is the right word) was a free gift of grace which some people had received and some hadn't, and in neither case was it a matter of desert. For both groups were equally sinners and, as far as in them lay, equally penitent.

THIS MYSTERY of grace as free, undeserved and apparently arbitrary was something I needed badly to apply to my own self. But instead I regarded it as a curiosity of the confessional which I couldn't properly understand. I kept it in fact at arm's length from myself because I wasn't yet ready to receive it. It was hardly strange that I wasn't, since all this time I was caught up in a contradiction which had become so much part and parcel of what I was that I was able ultimately to be delivered from it only at the cost of breakdown. And, after I had what is called recovered from the breakdown, in the sense that I was able once again to work and function normally, it took me seven or eight years before I was able emotionally and existentially to identify the contradiction and be delivered from it.

Any description of it will be flat and two-dimensional, and will appear to possess a clarity which poses clear-cut issues. In practice, of course, it wasn't like that at all. It was a muddle, a mess, not least because of the often all but insuperable difficulty of distinguishing between what was life-giving and good and what was death-dealing and evil.

Fundamentally, without being very much aware of the fact, I conceived my relationship with God to be one of contract. To put it crudely, my life was based on the tacit assumption that God would scratch my back on condition that I scratched His. I didn't think that God's scratching of my back would necessarily or even probably take the form of His giving me success or happiness. The history of Jesus hardly encouraged expectations of that kind. I thought of God's scratching my back in terms of His granting me fellowship with Himself, receiving me as His child like a good boy who had won His approval, even if His generosity meant that what I had done to win it was ludicrously inadequate.

If that was how I expected God to scratch my back, how was I to set about scratching His?

Here there entered into the story elements of trickery and false identity; of agents, if you like, taken to be on one side who were really on the other. It was a confusion which neither I nor any of my confessors (I had three during this period) even began to diagnose.

For the one God I thought I was serving had a double identity. He was partly Himself, the true God, and partly somebody I had projected upon the heavens from my subconscious, an idol by which I was no less taken in for being to a reasonable extent theologically sophisticated. My God was much more the idol than he was the true God.

It was with the idol that I conceived my relationship to be one of contract. Keeping his back scratched was not at all a labour of love. It had nothing about it of a free, loving, joyful obedience. It was a disagreeable and exhausting chore which made me in my heart of hearts hate the taskmaster who imposed it – that is God, my idol.

For my idol-God was a neurotic. How could he help being that? For a projection cannot be more healthy than the projecting agent. So my God felt unloved and insecure unless he was constantly the centre of attention. And when he felt insecure he would take it out of you by refusing to speak to you until you had formally apologized to him by going to confession, and sometimes not even then. So to prevent his feeling insecure you had to jabber at him at regular intervals. This jabbering consisted partly of what was called saying the offices, Matins and Evensong. If you wished to make him feel particularly good you added to Matins and Evensong a minor office or two like Prime and Compline. You also scratched his back by private prayer in your own words, and also by thinking about him in what was called meditation. Not least, you scratched his back by celebrating, or at least attending, Holy Communion every day.

All this was calculated – and I use the word literally – to keep God in a good mood as far as you were concerned. He might, it is true, unload a ton of bricks on your head or kill your dearest friend, but no matter, you had done your jabbering and had thus qualified yourself to be his blue-eyed boy.

What a relief it was to take a holiday from the slavery of being God's blue-eyed boy or – perhaps a better description – his lady companion. I remember the first summer after the war going to Ireland to join two friends for a holiday. As at Euston I got into the boat-train for Holyhead, put my suitcase on the rack and sat down in a corner seat, I murmured out loud: "Thank Christ." I was to be free from my idol for a whole fortnight. Yet I felt miserably guilty at my relief because I wasn't really free from him at all. He didn't allow holidays from obligations to him. I was simply being disobedient, that's all, and ungrateful as well. For wasn't it thanks to his benevolence that I was going on holiday at all?

BEING GOD'S LADY COMPANION was suffocatingly tedious, but it was far from the worst that my idol, my subconscious projected on to the heavens, could do. For this God of mine forbade me to be three-quarters of what I was. He demanded that whole areas of myself should be put in the deep freeze and left there frozen and, with luck, forgotten.

He demanded this of my sexual potential. The elimination of sex was one of the most important clauses in the contract I had made with him. I may have understood him differently as far as some of my penitents were concerned, but as regards myself the prohibition of sex was absolute. Even mildly attractive people God regarded as his sexual rivals. He was not a jealous God for nothing. And since sex and emotion are so closely bound up together, there were whole realms of feeling which were also frozen. God wanted me to be an emotional dwarf so that I might give my stunted heart wholly to him. And I used to tell him that my heart was stunted because I didn't love him as much as he deserved. How delighted he was by that admission. I could almost feel him patting me on the head.

All forms of self-assertion were similarly proscribed. God himself alone was the great I AM, and he didn't want any other I-ams about because they would be potential competitors. And since it is only by self-assertion, by a certain degree of aggression, that a man can discover who and what he is, I remained in self-ignorance. I didn't realize it, of course, as self-ignorance is ignorant of itself. It was, I thought, enough that I had a heart to praise my God, at least in intention a humble, lowly, contrite heart, believing, true, and clean, perfect and right and pure and good. That was my ideal.

And this meant that enjoying yourself too much was suspect. For God wanted you to enjoy him, and how could you enjoy him if you had too great a relish for gin or smoked salmon or Noël Coward or a long lie-in? Things of that kind had a tendency to make God seem awfully dull. So, although you could use them – theoretically the created order was a good thing – you had to be careful how you used them. If they became over-enjoyable, they might, like I-ams, become God's competitors and you would have to give them up as St Jerome gave up reading Cicero. In short, you could enjoy yourself safely as a duty, but it could be dangerous to enjoy yourself as a pleasure.

As I have described it in abstraction here this idol is all too obviously an idol, and his pathological parentage is unmistakable. But in actual experience things are not defined clearly in this way. They are not simply this or simply that. In actual life health and sickness are subtly entwined with each other and it's not easy to disentangle them. What is evil and death-dealing often looks good and life-giving and vice-versa. It is easy to mistake the true God for an idol and an idol for the true God.

It is clear to me now that around this time the true God began to reach out to me. But it's characteristic of Him to work by means of our humanity and not in spite of it. So the true God didn't deliver me from the idol by some miraculous intervention or sudden revelation. He did it by slowly fostering a revolt so that I gradually became less and less willing, and then less and less able, to knuckle under to the idol and its demands.

The conflict, however, was most dreadfully confused. For what was in fact a revolt against the idol looked and felt like a revolt against the true God. And it was as such that it was generally understood by my confessors, who thus played the part of the idol's advocates. They bade me subdue the revolt which was stirring within me and not give way to the devil. But the dynamic of the revolt increased irresistibly, however slow the process was. For nobody can fight successfully against the true God. But the burden of guilt engendered by the conflict steadily mounted. Wasn't I kicking God in the face, the God who was goodness and suffering love? – for no more than my confessors had I learnt to distinguish between the true God and the false. In the end the guilt became intolerable and I broke down completely. But that was not to be for another five or six years. Meanwhile the Anglo-Catholic fanciers continued to think I might become somebody of importance to them.

Their hope was illusory. For somewhere within me I was strongly aware of how ambiguous the church was. It was summed up for me in a remark by Reinhold Neibuhr reported to me at the time: "The church can be the anti-Christ; and when it denies that possibility, it is the anti-Christ." I suppose that without knowing it much consciously I apprehended that the church as a community, no less than myself as an individual member of it, worshipped the idol whose service is perfect slavery as well as the true God whose service is perfect freedom. But which was which and when? Who could tell?

WHILE I WAS AT ALL SAINTS two theological colleges offered me jobs on their staff. I visited each of them but didn't feel drawn to either. Religious establishments invariably give me the creeps. Their atmosphere chills and frightens me. Presumably it is something to do with my idol, or, more accurately, our idol, mine and theirs. I feel in these places that those who belong to them are so occupied with loving and serving God that they have left no natural warmth, no spontaneous care or affection, for human beings. I don't mean, of course, the human beings with whom they are supposed to be professionally concerned, like patients in hospital or meth-drinkers or down-and-outs or people with religious problems, but the ordinary common-or-garden human beings who live in the next house or the next room and are supposed not to have any difficulties. Towards human beings of that ordinary kind it is my experience that the more devout people are, the more callous they are, because their emotional energy is monopolized by what they consider the immediate worship and service of God. Perhaps I've been lucky in my experience of one set of people and unlucky in my experience of the other, but I've found that by and large agnostics care about you much more than professional Christians do. That sounds startling, but when I come to think of it, it's not saying anything more than the parable of the Good Samaritan.

At one of the theological colleges I visited something occurred which would have angered me if I had had any serious intention of going there. As it was, I found it amusing. I asked the Principal what my salary would be. "Oh," he said, "I can't tell you that. The procedure is that when you've accepted the job the college council will meet and decide how much you will be paid." I wasn't at all certain whether this was the sort of deal which a Christian ought to accept readily and with cheerfulness. Was I right to feel that I would have been angry had I been thinking of accepting the post? The question was academic since, as I've said, I was only amused, and if it was sinful amusement, well, that couldn't be helped.

PART THREE

Cambridge Don

SEVERAL MONTHS after this, Ken Carey was appointed Principal of Westcott House (a theological college in Cambridge), and began making enquiries about the possibility of my going there with him as chaplain. It so happened that at this time I was considering whether or not I ought to enter the Religious Life, or, in popular parlance, become a monk. Clearly, however much I liked All Saints. and enjoyed being with Cyril Tomkinson as his curate, it would soon be time for me to move on. And the alternatives seemed to be Westcott House or the Religious Life.

I spoke about it to Raymond Raynes. He listened to me for a quarter of an hour and then said: "Unless you enter the Religious Life you will be in mortal sin." This seemed to me one of the most extraordinary statements I had ever heard from somebody in a position of responsibility. How could he possibly be so absolutely certain? How on earth could he tell instantaneously that becoming a Religious would be for me pure white and going to Westcott pure black? It was, I thought, not only ridiculous but sinister. I had not yet learnt to recognize it as the expression of an infantile fantasy of omnipotence. But I did realize it was sick, and hence to be disregarded.

I was given some very valuable and mature advice by somebody who was then a Canon of Westminster. He said that if you were a Religious you were in danger of becoming a Personage, with old women of both sexes and all ages making a fuss of you. The Religious Life was a small pond in which small fish looked big. And because in that narrow context you looked big, you began to think you were. You developed an exaggerated sense of your own importance as a spiritual pundit. In Cambridge, on the other hand, it was impossible to feel important. There was too much beastly competition about. There would be scores of people very much cleverer and more able than you were, and hundreds who were your equal. You would know that it was out of the question to give yourself airs, even spiritual airs. You could grow only by keeping a due sense of proportion about yourself, and Cambridge would do that for you automatically – there would be no need for you to worry.

I am still profoundly grateful to Charles Smyth for this advice. It was some of the best I have ever had.

Ken Carey (whom I hadn't met) suggested that I had dinner with him at the United Universities Club, then still in its old premises. The evening included one of those awful moments of social calamity which still make one sweat to think about.

Ken's appointment as Principal of Westcott House had been controversial. This was partly due to the fatuity with which many dons imagine that a man's whole self is revealed by the class of degree he gets, and Ken, I think, had got a Third. But there was also some kind of Anglo-Catholic vendetta against him. I never quite knew what it was – Anglo-Catholic attitudes invariably pass my comprehension. Anyhow, the editor of the *Church Times*, Humphrey Beevor, had in a leader written a vitriolic attack upon Ken. And Humphrey lived at All Saints. I knew him well and liked him. When not on his newspaper he was an amusing companion, and endearing in the sense that he somehow aroused one's motherly instincts.

I realized at dinner how extremely sensitive Ken was and how any criticism or attack tortured him to the quick. He mentioned the *Church Times*, going pale as he did so, his hands quivering. I thought it wise and courageous of him to speak about it and clear it out of the way.

But cleared out of the way it wasn't. After dinner Ken led me down a long, narrow passage, perhaps we were going to the gents, I can't remember. I noticed that a figure was walking in the opposite direction, and as it came nearer

I saw to my horror that it was Humphrey Beevor. The passage was so narrow we couldn't help touching each other physically as we passed, let alone meeting. I think that now I should just have said hallo to Humphrey and walked on. But I was socially inexperienced, and had to make up my mind in a hurry. I decided that I should have to introduce Humphrey to Ken, but was terrified at the possible result. I seriously thought they might fight each other; Ken felt desperately wounded by Humphrey and Humphrey was extremely quick tempered and a bit of a swashbuckler. But to my relief all they did was to glare at each other and choke out the words "Good evening". It was, I'm still convinced, a narrow escape.

2

KEN CAREY was a supremely good Principal of Westcott House most of the time he was there, supremely good, that is, within limits. For if a young man was not particularly attractive physically and came from a lower-class background, then Ken was no use to him at all. It wasn't that he didn't try. He was immensely conscientious. But contact of any significant kind was an emotional imposs-ibility. For Ken a plain lower-middle-class young man was a brick wall.

His being oversensitive could also be a terrible nuisance. At times even the mildest criticism could make him stupidly stubborn precisely where wisdom suggested flexibility. A case in point was the rule that married men must sleep in college away from their wives for a certain period of their time at Westcott. (It was a rule, incidentally, that many of the married men only pretended to keep. I used to see them coming in early in the morning by a side door, and kept my mouth shut.) Charles Raven as Regius Professor of Divinity was chairman of the Westcott Council, and in a rather meaningful voice he once said on the terrace with a number of people around: "I'm sure, my dear Ken, with regard to married men sleeping in college, you wouldn't be guided by any rule of thumb." Ken felt this as a serious threat and spoke about it a great deal. He would not allow Raven to undermine his authority. So he became even more inflexible about this rule, which in my view was foolish, inhumane and asking for matrimonial trouble.

Also, when he joined in a public debate he was outraged when the people he hit hit back. He edited a book of controversial essays called *The Historic Episcopate*. When the other side slashed it, he took it as an attack on his personal integrity and honour.

I have mentioned these defects of Ken's qualities as Principal because on his death some of the eulogies on him were so exaggerated that they caused the kind of amused incredulity which lost sight altogether of his real great merits. As one bishop said to me: "*De mortuis nihil nisi bunkum.*"

If Ken's sensitivity could be a nuisance, it was also an invaluable asset in his understanding of people and it enabled him to be a spiritual counsellor of rare distinction. He was able almost always to go straight to the heart of a matter. He suffered a great deal because he was so thin-skinned, but his sufferings bore fruit in what they made it possible for him to do for others. In that sense he bore our griefs and carried our sorrows. He could give people the advice they desperately needed because he knew from the inside how they felt. When I was myself broken up and couldn't decide whether or not to embark on analysis (in those days most religious people were very suspicious indeed of psychoanalysis and psychiatry, especially the clergy), Ken was the only clergyman I knew who went straight to the point: "I expect an analysis will be painful and at times will deal violently with you. But that is the ministry to which for the time being God is calling you. 'For their sakes I consecrate myself'; that is how you must think of it." The comfort, in the proper sense of strength, which those words gave me is indescribable.

One of the marvellous things about him was that he

never forgot your birthday. A letter would arrive without fail. And since I came inside at Mirfield the letter would contain a pound note for me to buy cigarettes with. As you grow older being remembered like that means more and more to you.

I was lucky enough to stay with Ken at Kincraig (he had retired from being Bishop of Edinburgh) about a year before he died. He was a wonderful host. He made no religious demands on you at all and kept you in fits of laughter for much of the time.

Thinking it over I've come to the conclusion that the most valuable thing he did for ordinands was to make them *humanize* whatever it was they were concerned about, whether it was a cause or a theological idea or a moral principle or an ecclesiastical stance or a form of devotion. He would make them see what it meant in terms of their being human beings with other people being human beings as well. What did it do to their own and other people's humanity? He was fond of quoting a remark of B. K. Cunningham's: "The Supernatural, when divorced from the natural, soon becomes unnatural." I think that was what Anglicanism meant for Ken. And it was in that light that he understood the gospel. It was certainly what he gave to the men in his charge. Staying with him in Edinburgh, or in Kincraig on that last visit, we used naturally to talk of past members of Westcott we both knew. If a frown or a look of distress came on his face when I mentioned a particular person and asked if he had any news, I soon came to realize that it meant that the person concerned had become an extreme Evangelical or an extreme Anglo-Catholic or an extreme Charismatic or something else equally inhuman.

❦ 3 ❦

THERE WERE THREE of us on the staff at Westcott. The Vice-Principal was Alan Webster, now Dean of St Paul's, who was a tower of strength to Ken Carey and to whose kindness and efficiency we all owed an enormous amount.

My own job as chaplain was to teach the New Testament. But for a member of staff at a theological college his official work is generally the least of his duties. He is always on call, whatever time of day it is. Settling down at ten-fifteen in the evening for an hour's relaxation before going to bed, there might be a tap on the door heralding the arrival of a student troubled by doubts about the resurrection or by difficulties in prayer. Ken and Alan got much more of this than I did, but a share of it inevitably came my way.

I think that all three of us were slightly overawed by many of our charges. Most of them were veterans who had been colonels or majors in the war and who sometimes made me at least feel like the small man who puts his foot into it in a Bateman cartoon. This had its lighter, more hilarious moments, as when a retired regular naval commander commented with some asperity in an essay that the author of the First Epistle of St Peter was either the apostle himself or else he was a damned liar. Incidentally the commander preached his first sermon in the children's ward of the local hospital. When, on his return, I asked him how he had got on, he answered: "I think I did rather well. Only two of the children were sick."

It was not an easy time for these men. They had abandoned their wartime responsibilities to become students responsible for nothing. And they felt that the nature of their calling demanded that to a large extent they should cut themselves off from the social jollifications which their contemporaries were still enjoying. Their task, in fact, was to discover and make their own their new identity as clerics. And they were only too well aware that clerics were figures of fun. Underlying much of what they said and did was the determination not to be such clerics of caricature. Being at Westcott House, it was understood, meant that you weren't like that. But this perfectly natural and healthy resolution not to be ridiculous often became muddled up with class feelings. Nancy Mitford had not yet written about U and non-U, but not being a cleric of caricature came often to be interpreted as being U, that is, very upper class in your accent, expressions and attitudes, and making fun of people who weren't. Before the war, for instance, grapes were a rare luxury for the poorer classes. When some grapes were once brought into Westcott, one of the students made everybody laugh by looking at them and saying: "Ow, lovely gripes." One of the students wrote a play about the apostles. As it was to be in the open air I had to hear it being rehearsed outside my window. It began with an exaggeratedly upper class voice (it was a Marlburian – who else?) shouting: "Petah, can you come over heah for a moment?" This sort of pose occasionally caused a certain degree of resentment among men who, though very able, had no pretensions of coming from plush backgrounds. It made them try to throw their weight about in a way which Ken Carey regarded as uncooperative.

Yet it would be an extremely superficial estimate to describe Westcott House in those days as a snobbish place. It was rather a place which was doing its work in enabling its inmates to find their real identities by prayer and study and brushing up against each other. I wasn't aware of it at the time, but now I see that this process was much more frightening for those engaged in it than they realized, and that thus inevitably at times they clung to this or the other kind of false security, of which the upper class syndrome was merely one.

I suppose I taught the New Testament at Westcott with reasonable competence. Otherwise I was pretty useless. I can say this without shame as it wasn't my fault. I hadn't yet begun to find my own real self. Instead I clung to the false security of the image of myself as a "good Catholic". I made of an ecclesiastical stance a substitute for a personal identity. I thought that holiness consisted in knuckling under to my idol. Yet somewhere within me I knew darkly that I wasn't a "Catholic" at all and that the idol was the object of my hatred. I therefore felt particularly threatened when Ken Carey or Alan Webster disagreed with my High Church view of this or the other matter. And I was right to be upset, for their arguing against my views was as menacing as murder – the potential victim being my bogus non-self. Inevitably it made me feel frightened and miserable.

How, in such a state, could I be of any use to people who were taking the risk of discovering themselves? I was ignorant of what was happening to them. How could it be otherwise when I was ignorant of what was happening to myself? All I could do was to try to stuff them with High Church propaganda, and, to their credit, they refused to be stuffed!

A lot of the time I felt acutely lonely. I remember that when Wilfred Knox (he was a Fellow of Pembroke) died in 1950 I was filled with envy of him. He had finished his race on earth and the trumpets were now sounding for him on the other side. What a lucky man he was: he had died, and I was left in the wilderness of this world, forced often for appearances' sake to pretend to laugh at what I didn't consider at all funny and to commend a god whom in my heart of hearts I detested.

The students then at Westcott are now the leaders of the Church of England. Many of them are bishops – one is the Archbishop of Canterbury – and the most interesting of all, W. H. Vanstone, published a year or two ago one of the most vital pieces of Anglican theology written this century (*Love's Endeavour, Love's Expense*). I was lucky in this original contact, or rather, non-contact with these people, since in many cases it made possible my getting to know them properly at a later date after they had become more settled and I had at least begun to find myself. Certainly my life has been enriched by their friendship. So, looking back, I am very grateful to have been at Westcott for those three years, unhappy though I was.

But it wasn't by any means all doom and gloom. There were some heart-warmingly funny occasions. (Genuine laughter genuinely shared is, I believe, one of the things which best overcomes our separateness from one another.) The incident I remember with most amusement occurred in Stepney.

Each member of the staff used each year to take twelve to fourteen students to a parish for a week. One year I took my quota of students to St Dunstan's, Stepney, where the vicar, Peter Booth, had laid on an interesting and varied programme for us. It included a visit to Charrington's brewery. After being shown round the place and seeing the various processes which go to the making of beer, we were taken to the sampling room for some refreshment, and our conductor asked whether I would mind a photograph being taken of us for their local works magazine called the *Toby Times*. I saw no objection to this and a photograph was taken. Next morning it was blazoned on the front page of the *Daily Mirror* under the banner headline: PARSONS TO BE JUST DRINK IN KNOWLEDGE. And the copy read: "'This is a purely academic tour,' said Mr Williams as he finished his third pint of beer and tugged at his wilting clerical collar." Telling the story I always say I was afraid I should get the sack on my return to Westcott. In fact I knew that Ken Carey would be as amused about it as I was.

The Bursar at Westcott was a continual source of delight. He was a retired bank manager and the place owed a very great deal to him. He had decided views about what Westcott should or shouldn't be. When a student claimed to have a vision of the Virgin Mary the Bursar was extremely shocked, not on any theological grounds, but because that sort of thing wasn't done at Westcott. "I don't like using the word 'class'," he said to me, "let's use the word 'grades'. Some of these men, like the one in question, belong to a different grade to what is usual here."

He always knew who had committed an offence like spoiling part of the lawn or cracking a window. He used to describe the culprit in such detail that it was perfectly clear who it was, and then add: "No names, no packdrill." Winston Churchill used the phrase in a broadcast speech and Alan Webster said to me: "Did you hear Churchill quoting the Bursar last night?"

The Bursar was once asked to compliment one of

the cleaning women on her daughter's just having had a baby. He misunderstood the message and complimented the woman as though she herself had just given birth. "It's not me," the woman said, "it's my daughter." Intending to flatter her on her youthful appearance, he replied: "Well, having often seen you through my window during the past few months, it might well have been you." As he had several grandchildren of his own, he should have known better.

Talking of such things reminds me of a holiday I took at this time with two friends. One was a history don who was a Dr Somerset because he had a PhD. Though some years later he eventually got married, he was at this time extremely frightened of women and so shy in their company that he could scarcely speak. We stayed at an inn in a small mountain village in Savoy. One night we were woken up by a loud banging at the front door and cries of "*Docteur! docteur! Où est le médecin?*" We all got up to discover a party of villagers who were determined to take poor Dr Somerset by force and lead him to an *accouchement*. Bill Somerset went completely white with terror and was shaking as if in a permanent fit of epilepsy. The villagers simply wouldn't believe that he was only an historian and not a medical doctor. We eventually got rid of them, furious though they were at Somerset's refusal to help. The infant, we later learnt, was safely delivered and he and his mother both thriving. Somerset was then regarded with some awe by the villagers as possessing preternatural prognostic powers. He knew that mother and baby would be all right. That's why he didn't bother to come. Had it turned out otherwise, I think we should have had to leave the village.

❦‖4‖❦

During my last year at Westcott I had a nightmare whose fundamental significance eluded me for several years, though it scared the life out of me at the time. (I recounted it twelve years later in an open lecture laid on by the Divinity faculty at Cambridge.)

I was in a theatre watching a play. Something made me turn round, and at the back of the theatre I saw a human monster, horrific and merciless, who was savagely hypnotizing the players on the stage. The players, though they were dressed elegantly in eighteenth-century costume and speaking in sober civilized tones, were in fact no more than the servile creatures of the monstrous all-powerful hypnotist. All they said and did was at his brutal bidding. Watching him at work frightened me so much that I woke up in a cold sweat.

AFTER THREE YEARS at Westcott House I was offered a staff Fellowship at my own college, Trinity, as College Lecturer in theology. I had known for a week or two that the offer was in the wind, but I had been told that it was yet uncertain and that I musn't count my chickens before they were hatched. News that the offer was definite came to me around six o'clock one day, and that evening, according to previous plans, I went to an undergraduate production of *St Joan* at the Amateur Dramatic Club theatre. I remember the performance not only because I went to it immediately after hearing of my appointment, but even more because the girl in the title role – Jean Storey – some years later became the wife of our Trinity chaplain, Hugh Dickinson. Jean could be quick-witted when she wanted to be. I was walking down the Avenue at Trinity with her and Hugh when we met Mervyn Stockwood, then vicar of Great St Mary's. Hugh said: "I don't think you've met my fiancée, Jean Storey?" "Oh," said Mervyn, "are you one of the Suffolk Storeys?" "No," Jean answered, "I'm one of the tall Storeys." Hugh had been with us at Trinity for five years (a chaplain's usual stint) when he married Jean, and he left soon afterwards to become chaplain of Winchester. So I had no further opportunities of hearing examples of Jean's wit. Certainly on stage she was a more convincing Joan of Arc than my former young French nursemaid, Léonne.

Lonely as I had felt at Westcott House, I expected to be even lonelier at Trinity. I had forgotten how homely a place it was, and I was terrified by the great distinction and international reputation of many of the Fellows. They were world authorities on their particular line. Whatever would they think of me?

My estimate of the prospect couldn't have been more mistaken. I have never had such pleasant and congenial companions as I had during my eighteen years as a don. Trinity, of course, was large enough for fairly careful selection to be possible. There was no need to like or dislike quite a lot of people because one seldom saw them. But I found a largish number of kindred spirits. Trinity thus became my home, and in my feelings it always will be. Going back there is like going back home. This is not a romantic piece of self-delusion. Trinity was for me the scene of the most acute mental suffering it is possible for man to bear. My blood is mixed up with its stones, because it was there that I had to encounter the forces of destruction which I had either to fight and conquer or perish. It is also the place where I have been most happy and found the truest and most lasting friends. Henry VIII figures in my private Kalendar of saints, not because he founded the Church of England (though I think well enough of him for that) but because, under the influence of his sixth wife, Catherine Parr, he founded Trinity.

🦋|6|🦋

A LITTLE FURTHER ON I shall have to describe at some length and with a certain degree of intimacy how Trinity became my home because of the *agōn* or inner conflict to the death I had to wage there. But before I do that, I would like to describe some of the homely pleasures provided by its inhabitants.

One of the things I soon learnt from the Fellows is, I

suppose, obvious, but it seems as if you have to see it to believe it: the more really distinguished a scholar or scientist is the less concerned is he to impress anybody. Never less than at the Trinity High Table were you made to feel the weight of distinction. As a general rule (there were, naturally, exceptions) people didn't try to score over others in conversation, unless, that is, somebody was being pretentious. Pretension was the one thing which was never tolerated and always mercilessly shot down. I remember a scientist from another college bragging about his early and brilliant promise at school and how, even at thirteen, he had had the perception to ask the science master why a certain liquid turned green. The answer he got from Lord Adrian (the Master) was short: "And did he tell you to shut up?"

Adrian was the most attractive man I have ever met, and certainly the only one I have ever hero-worshipped. As well as being attractive he could also, when he chose, be extremely frightening. He had a numinous quality about him. He was a sort of *mysterium tremendum et fascinans*. He put certain people in a book of death, and when they appeared, or even when their name was mentioned, black rays emanated from him. This was even so when one of them had died and I had to go to Adrian and arrange with him a date for the memorial service. The black rays were the immediate reaction before he consulted his diary. On the other hand, he could be immensely kind. He certainly was to me when I broke down. I was able to speak to him quite candidly of my troubles and he helped me enormously by his dry matter-of-fact observations and advice. Later I sometimes went to him for advice about pupils in medical or psychological difficulties, and he always showed great interest and concern.

He was the last of the two-culture giants. A world-famous physiologist, he could quote reams of Greek plays in the original, thanks no doubt to his schooling at Westminster.

I suppose he would have called himself an agnostic.

He certainly wasn't an atheist. He knew too much, I think, to be too sure about anything. While Master of Trinity he became quite a proficient Bible scholar. As a matter of duty he always came to chapel on Sunday evening, and spent most of his time there studying the Bible. In chapel matters he was always most conscientious in his comments. Having admired the discourse of a visiting preacher, he commented to me as we came out: "A very good sermon – I should think."

One of the Fellows, before setting out on what he considered an extensive piece of travel, wrote his own memorial service and gave it to me in case he should die *en route*. (The service, incidentally, included the immortal rubric that a certain hymn was to be sung "to the tune that Burnaby dislikes", Burnaby being my predecessor as Dean of Chapel.) I couldn't resist the temptation of telling Adrian that this particular Fellow had written his own memorial service, to which Adrian immediately replied: "Was it a good service? I mean, shall we be disappointed if we can't use it?" We couldn't. The traveller returned safely.

Adrian gave a lecture in Athens in connection with some celebration there. For years afterwards he used to get every month a religious tract in abominable English from a pious Greek lady. The accompanying letter always began: "Dearly beloved brother in Christ Lord Adrian." The pious lady never put enough stamps on the letter. The porters would automatically accept it and Adrian had to pay a large postage-due bill every month for this exercise in piety. He came and asked me if I could do anything about it. I had to tell him that I had no control over the Christians in Trinity, let alone in Greece.

He was unable to disguise how repelled he was by what he took to be religiosity. Whenever he came to my room he used to give a furtive glance of dislike at the head of an adoring St Peter which hung on my wall – a reproduction of part of the Melozzo da Forlì fresco in the Vatican Museum. One day James Mitchell (my publisher, then only nineteen) was in my room dressed as a Franciscan friar when Adrian entered. Seeing James he looked absolutely horrified. I knew it was horror that one so young should be caught in the spider's web of religiosity. I explained that James was only rehearsing for a play and was really a Trinity undergraduate, at which Adrian immediately cheered up and laughed.

His physical agility was extraordinary. When over seventy he used to dart across Great Court like a streak of lightning. When he was elected Chancellor of the University the Trinity Boat Club rowed him to a dinner at the University Centre in Mill Lane. He acted as cox. At top speed the boat went through the very centre of the centre arch of Clare bridge. I assumed that Adrian had coxed as an undergraduate. Later he told me he hadn't. It was the first time he had ever done it.

He was a superb after-dinner speaker, always entertaining, and hitting exactly the right note for the occasion. At an old boys' dinner, for instance, for those who had been undergraduates just after the war when food was bad and scarce, he began his speech by saying: "I would like to congratulate all of you on the first square meal you've ever eaten in this Hall." It brought the house down. The clapping went on for two or three minutes. He lulled me into the illusion that after-dinner speeches were invariably entertaining. I seldom went to feasts at other colleges – most of the guests at Cambridge feasts were a stage army of diners – but once when I did I said to my neighbour, P. F. Strawson, that I didn't understand why people complained about speeches as they gave the sort of diversion welcome at that stage of the evening. Strawson disagreed with me. When the time came the Master of the college at which I was a guest made an appallingly clumsy, boring and lengthy speech. At the end of it Strawson turned to me with a satisfied smile: "You see what I mean?" he said.

At one thing Adrian was very bad, and that was being chairman of the college council – a sort of cabinet of the Master and twelve Fellows which met once a week in term. The discussions went on interminably. When it looked as if everybody had said everything they could say, Adrian would say something which started them off again. Sometimes he would carry on a conversation with himself about the matter in hand which was impossible to interpret. I remember once, for instance, his saying about the question under discussion: "Well, I suppose we could.... But then, of course they might.... It would perhaps be worth trying.... But no, even then it wouldn't be any good...." What he had in mind we never discovered.

A Presbyterian Divine shall have the last word on him. The Divine had preached in chapel and Adrian had entertained him charmingly at dinner and afterwards. When I was seeing the Divine out of the college at the end of the evening he said to me: "Lord Adrian is an agnostic. But – it may be wrong of me to say so, perhaps I shouldn't suggest it – but somehow I don't think heaven would be complete without him." It was a major theological concession. In my own bumbling Anglican way it had never occurred to me to doubt it.

7

ONE OF THE MORE noticeable Fellows of Trinity was an old clergyman called Simpson, an historian who by the early 1920s had published two volumes of a projected three-volume work on Louis Napoleon, and never wrote the third volume although living for another fifty years. He did, however, publish a chapter of it in the *English Historical Review* in honour of G. M. Trevelyan when Trevelyan died. Initially Simpson must have been against my appointment as he cut me dead for the first six months of my time at Trinity and then, by slow degrees, became extremely friendly. You could persuade him to preach about once every six years. Then for the next two or three years he would take the sermon round the various college chapels. His sermons showed me that preaching is a lost art. Not only did they read well when eventually they were printed, but his delivery of them was totally enthralling. Without a note, he would stand in the middle of the aisle as if transfigured. Light shone from his face.

He had an enormous amount of vanity, but very little pride. After preaching he used to receive fan-mail, and the most complimentary letters he would show round the common room. This angered some people and amused many more. I thought it had about it an almost childlike simplicity, though in most ways Simpson was very far from being childlike. He and Andrew Gow, the classical scholar, were enemies in an almost ritual dimension. The quarrel had started long before I arrived on the scene and I don't know what first sparked it off. It certainly led to some amusing examples of academic malice. Gow was arthritic and Simpson once said to me about him in a very sympathetic voice: "What we must remember about Gow is that he is always in pain." One night Gow was presiding in Hall and absent-mindedly said after dinner the grace which should be said before it. While the Hall was still silent, Simpson said to me in a loud stage-whisper: "Perhaps he thinks he hasn't had enough to eat." Gow gave as good as he got. Simpson had the habit of being run over in the street, but, curiously enough, he was never seriously injured. On one of these occasions Gow said to me: "Simpson has been run over, but it hasn't done him any good." Simpson was once injured slightly more than usual. The Vice-Master (at that time Patrick Duff), not, I think, unaware of the humorous possibilities of the situation, persuaded me that it was my duty as Dean of Chapel to suggest to Gow that for the time being he shared his manservant with the injured Simpson. Greatly daring I made the proposal to Gow. There was complete silence for a whole minute. Then Gow said dryly: "It's not a fate I would wish for my bitterest enemy." So that was that. In fact Gow, for all his erudition, his very bleak manner and capacity to crush with a phrase, was basically a most kind-hearted and lovable person. He always reminded me of a song from *Iolanthe*:

O amorous dove,
Type of Ovidius Naso,
This heart of mine
Is soft as thine
Although I dare not say so.

He told me that a former pupil, under the influence of the Moral Rearmament Movement, wrote to him some twenty years after going down and confessed that when he had said that his car had broken down it was untrue; he had in fact stayed on at a party in London. "I replied," said Gow, "and told him he needn't have taken the trouble to write as I never believed him in the first place."

Gow was a stoic, Simpson an epicurean. He was very much concerned with his own comfort and was once warned by a Vice-Master called Winstanley that he would have to rough it in heaven. He had a poacher's pocket made in his coat, and before coming to dinner in Hall used to fill it with various small screw-topped bottles containing various sorts of wine. These wines he would pour as he thought appropriate either into various glasses or over his plate of food. He had worked out the art of living to the minutest detail. He once said to me quite seriously – and I've never forgotten his advice and always followed it – "If ever you have to share an umbrella always share it with two people, then you can hold it over yourself." It was said that in the days when he still went to the theatre he always booked two seats, one for his coat and hat. He hated being even slightly too hot or too cold, and at meals in unfamiliar rooms he used to take off and put on clothes. Monsignor Alfred Gilbey, the Roman Catholic chaplain to the University, used each year to give a birthday dinner for Simpson at the chaplaincy, to which he kindly invited me. It was on these occasions that I was able to observe Simpson's sartorial performance. The soup would make him feel hot. So he would get up, take off his coat, remove a woollen waistcoat, put on his coat again and sit down. By half-way through dinner he would have cooled down. So he would get up again, take off his coat, put on his woollen waistcoat once more, then his coat again. The coffee might warm him up. If so, the performance would be repeated. The fascinating thing was the totally unselfconscious way in which he did this. It might have been everybody's common practice.

He was a great snipper. When out for a walk he always in a pocket carried secateurs, with which he used to snip at hedges, shrubs, branches of trees and so on, leaving the resultant mess on the ground for the gardeners to clean up. That was all right so long as he did it on Trinity property. But sometimes he couldn't resist the temptation to do it elsewhere, and there were occasional rumours of complaints. I was once interviewing a boy for entry to the college when the boy turned very pale. I was distressed by what I thought were his nerves, when he had the good sense to explain what was upsetting him. "There are some very odd-looking men outside your window," he said. I turned and found it was our garden committee examining the wisteria which used to grow on my wall. In front of the committee was Simpson gesticulating wildly with an umbrella he was holding by the spike at its base. It looked like an early silent film of a lunatic. I explained to the boy what was going on and he recovered quickly.

Simpson had bought some sort of patent clippers which enabled him to cut his own hair. We used to ask him how he did it, and were delighted if he answered (as he invariably did): "I take two or three snips every morning." He had two electric razors which he used at the same time. He said it made shaving quicker.

He combined his eccentricities with an extremely sharp mind. He was nobody's fool, and he could be a formidable adversary in debate. If the illness or misfortune of a Fellow or undergraduate touched his imagination he could be extraordinarily kind. He could also be very generous. When, after two years' novitiate, my books were sent up here from Cambridge, Simpson sent with them a dozen bottles of the best college port. I understand that he

financed the publication of an early book of poems by
Enoch Powell. He was very hospitable and, until he was in
his middle eighties, he used to give regular parties and
dinners for dons and undergraduates at which he was a
marvellous host.

He was (as I suppose most of us are) somewhat
selective in the Christianity he professed. He had no use at
all for the future life (perhaps it was the threat of having to
rough it), and altered the Pauline text so that it read: "If in
the *next* life only we have hope in Christ we are of all men
the most miserable." On his reading of the gospels he saw
Christ as somebody who never did an unselfish thing in his
life and who behaved abominably to other people,
especially to his mother. He disliked modern translations of
the New Testament on the grounds that St Paul was best
left incomprehensible. "The first Christians were the most
dreadful crowd of people," he once said to me, "but we
haven't made too bad a thing of it." What he particularly
abominated were visiting preachers who in their sermons
included what he described as "tripe about truth to please
the Master". Of Christian thinkers it was his view that St
Augustine took the worst of St Paul, and Calvin the worst
of St Augustine. There was no question that he was
sincerely devout. Like his rival, Andrew Gow, I found him
all in all a very lovable person.

❦❦‖8‖❦❦

AMONG THE RICH PERSONALITIES at Trinity during this time
were two mathematicians of very great distinction.

One was a Russian called Besicovitch. He had
escaped from Russia during the revolution, and in certain
moods would claim that at some point in the emergency he
had spent four days and nights in a canoe with Lenin's wife,
though I got the impression that he wasn't altogether
convinced by his own story. One hesitates to apply the
adjective "sweet" to anybody as it has become a nauseating
cliché. But no other word will do for Besicovitch. He was

the sweetest old man I have ever come across – mellow, gentle and benevolent. Although an atheist he had all the simplicity of the saint. When (this was years ago) there was a brouhaha about a girl being found at dawn in an undergraduate's rooms, Besicovitch turned to me conspiratorially in Hall and said: "Jel-oss-y, jel-oss-y, that's what eet ees, all thees fuss – jel-oss-y." It was hard not to agree with him. Although he had been in England for years he spoke English as if idiomatically it were Russian. This meant that he didn't use the definite or indefinite article. That was all right if, for instance, he asked: "Did you enjoy film?" But during my early days at the High Table he once confused me considerably by asking: "Can you pass water?" The Governing Body of all the Fellows once discussed whether some trees should be cut down. The issue was whether we should cut them down then and plant for posterity or enjoy them ourselves for another ten or fifteen years. Besicovitch made an impassioned speech for the trees to be left as they were, clinching his argument with the final words: "Posterity? – We are us." There wasn't a dry eye in the house. As he deserved, he was universally popular. He had no idea of his own goodness, but it was recognized immediately by everybody else.

The other mathematician was Littlewood. When over eighty he was still winning gold medals from the Royal Society for his work – very unusual for pure mathematicians who generally burn themselves out fairly quickly. He had several unusual notions, of which one was that vodka was de-intoxicating – not, of course, if you began by drinking it, but as an antidote to port. He once suggested to me that I could feel drunk in a new and delightful way by drinking madeira after port. He was quite right. He liked telling the story of how he had once mistaken somebody for a person said to be a strong Fellowship candidate. He had found this somebody what he called "a fluent ass" who talked with apparent competence about anything. How could a fluent ass possibly be academically able? Eventually he had the relief of discovering his mistake. The man who really was considered a strong candidate sat morosely in total silence. Littlewood was completely reassured. He used in the combination room to take snuff and then sneeze ten or twelve times so loudly that it brought all conversation to an end. After finishing this performance he would look pleased, indeed positively self-righteous, and say: "The addict longs to sneeze but can't." I used this in a radio talk (and still do in schools) for a description of hell: desperately wanting what you have made yourself incapable of getting. Littlewood was delighted when I told him that I had used him as an illustration of hell, or rather of what hell was not, though I don't think he took in the distinction. During the period when I was in very low water I passed him in the Avenue. He said nothing, but I could see at once from his glance and smile that he understood everything. He was an atheist. But from that moment I knew that at some time or other in some way or other he had been on the Damascus Road.

Because of his quiet kindliness and humour it is difficult not to mention the philosopher C. D. Broad. His humour was always warm and never wounding. He once asked me what I thought of Austin Farrer. I said that I thought he was the nearest thing to genius we had in the Church of England. "Well," said Broad, "that's not saying much." He once commented: "St Paul was rather red-brick, don't you think?" What he meant was obvious and undeniable. It was an abbreviation in modern idiom of Gibbon's words about St Augustine: "His erudition was too often borrowed, his arguments too often his own." To my successor as Dean of Chapel, John Robinson, Broad once said: "I want my memorial service to be Anglican but not Christian." In connection with a Fellow with a loud voice who was at the time away, he said: "Really it is so quiet here now, one could almost hear a bomb drop." One of the neatest things he said to me was when there were two candidates for a college office and he wanted me to second the candidate he was himself proposing, which I was happy to do as I was going to vote for him anyhow. He did not know this, so he introduced his proposal by saying to me of the other candidate: "I'm very fond of so and so, and all his faults are superficial...." It couldn't have been more damning.

The Director of the Fitzwilliam Museum, Carl Winter, was a Fellow of Trinity. I came to know him well (his younger son, John, was a pupil of mine) and used often to travel with him in Europe and North Africa. It is difficult to convey his attractiveness on paper as it depended on his vivacity and on the unconquerable spirit which kept him racing about everywhere after he had had more than one major operation and suffered from angina and heaven knows what else. He had a tremendous love of life which was contagious and always made his company the greatest fun. On our travels it was a relief that, as a professional, he had no inclination to cultural snobbery. While, for instance, after an hour looking at the mosaics at Monreale, the other two or three members of the party were still swooning over them with field-glasses, Carl came up to me and said: "I want a *gelata*." So we left them at it. What, I think, attracted me most to him was the fact that he overcame the world, the flesh and the devil by making fun of them. He was never their dupe. He knew them like old friends, saw through them, and laughed. And it made pious respectability look like the sham it is. I remember one of his remarks. A Fellow, who was an outstanding authority in his own line, had the stupid habit of talking a great deal about music when he had no knowledge of it at all. Carl and I were once sitting together at lunch in Hall when this Fellow, sitting opposite us, asked in all seriousness what we thought of the theory that Mozart was influenced by Rossini and Bellini. I didn't want (I don't know why) Carl to make the crushing joke I knew he would, so, to turn the conversation I immediately said: "How many operas did Bellini write?" Carl at once replied: "He wrote two operas. One was called *Norma*; the other *Abnorma*." He once brought a clergyman into Hall. I was sitting next to Broad, who turned to me and said: "I hope the fact that Winter has brought a clergyman into Hall doesn't indicate that he is about to take the veil." His illnesses eventually caught up with him and he died in the Evelyn Nursing Home after a dinner of asparagus and champagne. I saw him the day before. In spite of everything he was still his old self and kept me in fits of laughter during the whole of my visit. I came away feeling that I had been to the most enjoyable party. He was ready for Heaven if Dame Julian of Norwich can be trusted, and it is "right merry" there.

The late Vice-Master of Trinity, Jack Gallagher, was a contemporary of mine. His academic distinction earned him two chairs, the first at Oxford where he became a Fellow of Balliol and then at Cambridge when he came back to Trinity. What was rare about him is that he combined this academic ability with an immediate and profound understanding of people, what made them tick and grate, and often how to extricate them from the situations into which they had got themselves. It was an understanding I have seen in nobody who has not had several years of psychoanalysis. Jack, so to speak, was free born. In my experience of him he invariably used his understanding to prevent people being more wounded than they need be. If, for example, he saw that conversation was moving on to dangerous ground, he would cleverly change its direction. For this I have myself reason to be grateful to him on numberless occasions. He used to work all night and, if he were not lecturing, go to bed in the daytime – behaviour which prompted his bedmaker to remark: "Mr Gallagher is a funny man. He only gets up once a day." He was often very witty. There was a time when Lord Acton's remark in a letter to Bishop Mandell Creighton that power tends to corrupt and absolute power corrupts absolutely was being misquoted everywhere. (The most ridiculous version of it I saw was to the effect that all power corrupts absolutely.) At port one evening somebody misquoted Acton's statement, and Jack answered: "You've got it wrong, you know. What Acton actually said was: 'Everything corrupts and nothing corrupts absolutely'," which, as well as being a brilliant parody of the many misquotations, had the merit of possessing a great deal of theological truth in its own right. We were once moaning, as people invariably do, about our pay. "Pay?" Jack said, "Why, here they don't pay you enough to keep body and mistress together." And when there was some minor crisis in the bursary, he said: "The people in the bursary haven't had any sleep for days." The brighter undergraduates always adored him. It was the combination of learning, wit and humanity which drew them to him. He had to barricade himself against constant callers. It would have been worth being at Trinity simply to know him.

When I was Dean of Chapel I was very lucky to have Raymond Leppard as the Director of Music. It isn't necessary to say that he got the very best out of the undergraduate choir. And he wrote for us an Agnus, a Te Deum and an anthem version of Psalm 150. Working with him was always an exhilarating experience. We had to spend two or three days a year choosing choral exhibitioners and an organ scholar, co-operating with a group of other colleges. It would have been a dismally dreary chore without Raymond, but he made it into a kind of holiday I looked forward to. We agreed that choral exhibitioners (we elected four each year), as well as having good voices, must have interesting personalities. This made them easier for Raymond to train, and, from my point of view, it was a great asset. For interesting personalities have friends. The friends come to chapel to hear them sing, and they bring other friends, so that the chapel is invariably fairly full. It was a recipe which worked. What was its precise spiritual status was a question which, I fear, never worried me. Raymond was quite right to leave Cambridge. It became too cramping for a person of his great talents. He lived in the rooms above mine, and Janet Baker used sometimes to come and rehearse with him there. It isn't everywhere that you can hear Janet Baker's superb singing coming through the ceiling.

9

I WAS THIRTY-TWO when I returned to Trinity as a Fellow. There were a number of Fellows round about the same age as myself – add or (more often) subtract two or three years. Most of them were as yet unmarried and so living in college. One was an historian, another a physiologist, another an archaeologist, another a biochemist, and so on. We formed a vague sort of group in the sense that we often met, when the day's work was done, to drink and chat. We were convinced (as people of that age invariably are) that many of our elders were stupid and hidebound, and their latest absurdity would be reported for a good laugh. As far as politics, national and international, were concerned we had passed the age of innocence and nobody was sold on any political ideology of left or right. On matters of religion people's views were respected and given the serious hearing which alone can lead to valid criticism and discussion. Occasionally somebody who was expert in the field would tell us (in so far as it was possible to tell ignoramuses) how the mechanisms of colour vision operated in frogs, or what contributions Disraeli or Lord Salisbury had made to the subjugation of Africa, or opinions about Rousseau, commonly accepted as facts, which the evidence didn't support or positively disproved. The most intriguing thing I heard was from the biochemist, who explained how, if our constitution were the smallest fraction of a degree different from what it is, we should make our own alcohol, so that to feel cheerful all you would have needed to do was to walk briskly for a quarter of a mile. Somebody who was to become a well-known astronomer announced one night that he had solved the fuel crisis: "Dig up all the graves and burn the coffins and the remains inside them." It must be remembered that we had all had a heavy day's work in research, teaching or administration, and were now relaxing in an atmosphere where conversation was not necessarily wholly serious. The temptation was to stay up to all hours so that you felt like death the following morning.

Good resolutions to go to bed reasonably early were seldom kept. We enjoyed each other's company too much to break away from it.

After my rather bleak existence at Westcott House I found this friendly and congenial atmosphere almost painfully enjoyable. I realized it was something I had always wanted. Now I had it. But if that wasn't too good to be true (since it was a fact) it was often too true to be good. What I mean is that it often overexcited me. I found that my feelings became too hectic for them to be unwound properly. Worst of all it went on piling up on me an increasing load of guilt. The sort of pleasant life I was living wasn't the sort which my idol of a god could possibly approve of. On the contrary, he was furious about it because it left him for most of the time out in the cold. Rationally, of course, I didn't think that. I could have given a lecture on the theology of the created order. But my unconscious saw to it that the message came through somehow, more often than not as fits of apparently uncaused terror.

There was a further and very much more important factor. Up till then I had been able, as my god required, to ignore my sexuality by keeping it strictly under control and living as if it didn't exist. My god required this of me because by orientation I was homosexual, and therefore the licensed release of sexuality in marriage wasn't available to me.

In those days homosexual love (at least between men) was regarded by most people with a horror which was positively superstitious. (As a mother with three boys at Eton said, I believe, to Steven Runciman: "I don't know what I should do if a son of mine fell into the hands of one of those homo sapiens.") There may have been coteries where it was tolerated or even encouraged, like the Bloomsbury set or the King's College of conventional myth, but in general it was still the great unmentionable, whether in conversation, the Press or novels which weren't translations of Proust. Homosexual behaviour among adults in private was still a crime punishable by imprisonment, and the churches were the first to condemn it without qualification. It was sin personified; something, as St Paul said, for which the wrath of God descended upon the children of disobedience.

I remember about this time meeting an Anglican Franciscan in Trinity Street. His face had a particularly glowing and triumphant look about it. "I've separated them," he said to me. "I've separated them." I asked him what on earth he was talking about. It turned out to be two undergraduates in a neighbouring college who were in love with each other.

Thus it was that my deepest, most tender, and strongest feelings were felt by me to be monstrously horrible, something to be utterly condemned, as well as being, I felt, the legitimate target of ridicule deserving to bring down upon me the cackle of Cambridge. Had I not been in thrall to my idol I might have been able to liberate myself from these conventional estimates. But with the stranglehold upon me of the god the priests had encouraged me to believe in, even the smallest degree of liberation was quite impossible. I was little more than the puppet of the savage hypnotist I had dreamt about, little more then the dupe and slave of my own guilt-feelings.

But there was a part of me the hypnotist (the guilt-feelings which were my god) was unable to manipulate, a part free from his vicious tyranny. It must have been so. For I fell in love with a colleague; totally, hopelessly and catastrophically in love. The sexuality which the savage hypnotist had so far compelled me to ignore, at last exploded. It was, as I saw later, the victory of my humanity over the forces bent on destroying it, the victory of health over sickness, of good over evil, of the true God over the idol. But at the time it didn't feel like that, not in the slightest. How could it with my idol-god condemning me utterly? And in any case the first step (*le premier pas qui coûte*) towards humanity is invariably far less than fully human; the first step towards health is itself inevitably disease-ridden; when good begins to triumph there is still much evil about; and the true God manifests Himself only gradually, and, in the early stages especially, there is with the true much that is untrue and illusory.

The colleague I thus fell hopelessly for was called Stavros – his father was Greek but his mother was English, and he had been born and educated in England. He liked me. Indeed I think he was fond of me. But he had for me no sexual feelings of any kind. But he did give me the courage to tell him of my feelings for him, hesitatingly, of course, and apologetically. He wasn't at all shocked or even surprised. He was perfectly honest about his own feelings. He liked me a great deal, he said, but didn't love me. As might be expected, he was more cautious in future in his approaches to me, but he was as kind as his own nature allowed him to be. He told the others. That was quite natural and, in any case, I hadn't asked him not to. One of them said he was a hanging judge as far as homosexuality was concerned, but it was a bark with no bite at all, for he continued to be as friendly as ever. Most of them were understanding in a quiet way. One of them asked me whether I would care to bring my work to his rooms and do it there while he was getting on with his own. I particularly valued that sensitive gesture. I think that many of them were both amused and puzzled that I seemed to be making such heavy weather of it all. How could they realize that I was beginning to change gods, that my falling in love with Stavros was the first eruption of an earthquake, that I was being raised up from the unfeeling sleep of death to the severe pains and penalties, as well as the rewards, of life? They imagined that it was no more than a belated adolescent crush.

I was completely besotted by Stavros. With the best will in the world he couldn't begin to give me the overwhelming response for which I yearned with every ounce of what I was. That, of course, was a good thing. For my craving was sick in the sense that it was totally out of relation to reality. I didn't know it at the time, but I wanted

Stavros to be my father, mother, child, teacher, pupil, and heaven knows what else. I even had day-dreams of his discovering through my influence that he had a vocation to be a clergyman. No real person could have fulfilled all those roles. So Stavros' clear affirmation that he wasn't sexually interested in me was certainly a blessing, though at the time it was so heavily disguised that it felt like a curse. "If only, if only, if only," I used to think in my despair – the perennial song of those who remain emotionally infantile.

I would like to say here that Stavros and I eventually established a realistic relationship which has proved strong and lasting for over thirty years. His children are now almost the age he was when I first met him. My falling so obsessionally for him was the way in which the inner sickness of a lifetime eventually surfaced and insisted on being noticed. It was the poultice which drew out the hidden poison so that it could no longer be ignored. I was on the way to a severe breakdown, but my unrequited feelings for Stavros were only the occasion of it, not the cause. The cause, or causes, infinite in their complicated ramifications, spread back to the day I was born, perhaps earlier.

It was at All Saints, Margaret Street, that I first noticed that something was wrong with me. Cyril Tomkinson was still vicar there, and I used to go and assist him during part of my vacations. ("My dear," he said, "it will do you no harm for your name to appear in *The Times* as preaching here on Sunday.") On this visit, when I celebrated the Holy Communion the altar would sometimes heave itself up before me and then fall back into place. It was like being dead drunk. I used also sometimes to feel frightened and giddy standing at the altar, especially with the drop behind me of three or four steps. On my return to Cambridge I had a medical checkup which showed there was nothing wrong with me. So I went to see a priest in a neighbouring college known to be a good Anglican Catholic (he celebrated every Sunday morning at Little St Mary's church), who claimed to have some sort of expert knowledge of psychology. I don't want to speak much about him as he was fundamentally a man of great kindness and compassion. Raymond Raynes told me how lucky I was to be able to obtain psychological assistance from so good a churchman, meaning it would be ecclesiastically safe and not lead me into sin. In fact (though I didn't see it at the time) the personality of this priest was in process of disintegration. He was stubborn and aggressive, extremely doctrinaire in what he claimed was the pure milk of Freudian orthodoxy, though he had had very little training and certainly no qualifications for psychiatric or analytic work, and could do little else but transmit his own neuroses to those who became his patients. Yet, as I said, he was at heart a good and generous man in so far as his sickness allowed him to be, and if I had emphasized the harm he did, it is to make the point that if you are in psychological difficulty, then go to a psychiatrist and not to a priest, just as you would go to a surgeon and not a priest if you had a poisoned appendix. The priest, as priest, is no more capable of coping with your psychological difficulties than he is of removing an appendix, though not a few priests suffer from the illusion that they are, at least after hearing a lecture or two and reading three or four paperbacks. And a psychiatrist should be chosen because he is a skilled psychiatrist and not because he is a good Catholic or reads the Bible every morning. I have a lasting suspicion of people who are known as a *Christian* dentist or a *Christian* doctor or a *Christian* psychiatrist or a *Christian* chiropodist. Invariably it means that they are bad at their craft. God is honoured by a dentist being a good dentist, not by his singing hymns.

I suppose it could be said that this priest opened me up psychologically. That certainly needed doing. But it could have been done more gently and gradually, with temporary stitches here and there to leave the wound less gapingly open.

Be that as it may, I became more and more the victim of terror – terror of things which, rationally considered, were not terrifying at all. I was soon unable to go to dinner in Hall because of the intolerable panic it brought on. I used sometimes to steal myself for the supreme ordeal of going to a nearby Indian restaurant for a meal, but eventually that became too much for me. I had to eat alone in my rooms. The next vacation I went home. When I sat down to dinner with my parents – there were only the three of us – it was too much for me, and I had to leave the table after the first course to go for a walk. My parents were very tactful and asked no questions. After that I ate by myself, before or after they did.

Travelling by public transport became a torture, whether it was bus or train. It was all but unendurably terrifying. In London, travelling by Underground was out of the question. When I am now on an escalator, I still remember the days before I had given up forcing myself to do it and was certain I shouldn't get to the top or bottom, as I shook visibly as if with St Vitus' Dance. I couldn't go to the theatre or cinema as some trifling detail on stage or screen would bring on a terror so intense that I had to rush out. In time I couldn't trust myself to go into a shop. I remember my shoes were completely worn out and I needed new ones. Friends used to ask me why I didn't buy any (I wasn't short of money). They couldn't believe it was too frightening. I was far too terrified to attend a church service, let alone to take one or to preach. I often ached all over physically with what the doctor called fibrositis. And all this meant that inevitably I was cut away from the society of others and had to lead a solitary existence. When I knew that some interesting guest was expected in Hall (one evening, I remember, it was Father D'Arcy) I used to feel particularly miserable. Stavros, I was sure, would be there, scintillating. I used to turn out my light so that I couldn't be seen, and stand at the window to catch a glimpse of him as he went from Hall to his rooms. Sometimes I was cheered simply by the knowledge that he was in residence, and then discover that after all he wasn't. The light I thought I saw in his room was in fact only the reflection upon his windowpane of the lamplight in the court. Sometimes I would hear his footsteps coming towards my rooms (he was kind in visiting me) and then pass them. It was somebody else he was going to see.

Meanwhile my phobias increased to such an extent that I became unable to walk outside, and then, scarcely across my room. I had lost the use of my legs.

The priest whose patient I was kept on telling me that all this was perfectly in order and, indeed, to be expected, and that the last thing I should do was to seek further professional advice. That, he said, would be to evade the problem I had to face.

But by this time it was clear even to me that something must be done. So I telephoned my G.P., who came to see me and arranged for a properly qualified psychiatric consultant to visit me immediately. The consultant had me at once transferred to the Evelyn Nursing Home and put me under narcosis, a drugged state of less than semi–consciousness.

When I came to after four days the first thing I was told was that Adrian had called to enquire how I was – a very characteristic action. The consultant, no doubt wisely, forbade any professionally religious person to come and see me. And since after coming out of the narcosis I was unable to sleep at all at night he allowed me injections of morphia on five successive evenings. It was unbelievably comforting to know that at 11 p.m. sharp one would unfailingly lose consciousness and not regain it again until 5 a.m. I was interested to notice that the morphia acted always with the precision of a punctual train. Its effect ceased every morning at 5 o'clock exactly. It tended for the first few hours after I had regained consciousness to put my eyes out of focus, so that I could read only with difficulty.

One of the penalties of having what is convention-ally called a nervous breakdown is that your nurses tend to treat you either as if you were a small child in the nursery or with barely concealed hostility because they think you aren't really ill. (I suppose most of us do that to the old as well.) It is humiliating, to say the least.

I was kept three weeks in the Evelyn, and the only bright spot of my stay I remember was a visit from Jack Gallagher, who entered my room, looked round it for half a second, and said: "Well, it's nice to see how the rich live."

When I returned to my rooms in Trinity I was still unable to eat in company or to walk abroad without terror. I still pined agonizingly for Stavros, and used often by myself to get absolutely furious with him, boiling with rage at the bad things I projected upon him. In this fantasy portrait he was cruel, callous, narcissistic, a flirt, a cock-tease, not caring a damn how much he made people suffer, and so on. I went by taxi to the consultant at his house three times a week. Some people assumed that after coming out of the Evelyn I should recover steadily as one does from a routine operation. I myself knew in my bones that it wouldn't be like that. It would, I was certain, be a very uneven process, going backwards as well as forwards, and, withal, a very long haul.

What intrigues me and now amuses me is the behaviour of the clergy towards me. (In what I'm about to say I except Ken Carey – I've spoken before of his invaluable advice – and also John Burnaby, who was a very wise person and in big things very sensitive and perceptive. To the great loss of the Church of England he was its last "lay" clergyman. He was ordained on his Fellowship and never went to a theological college.) The clergy felt that they must be able to do something for me. So they wheeled out various pieces of ecclesiastical apparatus with the intention of using them for my good. They wanted to choke me with Holy Communion, to persuade me to make a good confession, to have me anointed with oil. When the clergy had tried out all these devices and saw that the effect was nil, they began to get shirty, writing me stern letters accusing me of malingering and exhorting me to pull up my socks and show some sign of a stiff upper lip. This upset me a great deal at the time. But now I see that they felt their inability to do anything for me as a threat to themselves, and took their revenge accordingly. And this now seems to me rather funny.

I was anointed with oil by the Bishop of Ely, Edward Wynn, one of the gentlest and most compassionate of men. He kindly had me to stay for the night at his house in Ely. After dinner I made my confession to him, and the next morning I was anointed by him in his private chapel, after which he celebrated the Holy Communion. Everybody who knew him will know how consistently benevolent he always was. But all I got from this combined operation was severe earache. The house was an old one. My bedroom had a door at each end, which meant that I was in the middle of a strong draught all night.

In the nature of the case the healing couldn't work. For there was in myself too great a confusion between the true God and my persecuting idol. Consciously I was doubtless asking my loving Father in heaven for forgiveness and healing, and doing so with the greatest possible conscious sincerity. But unconsciously what I was doing was knuckling under once again to the savage hypnotist from whose wicked domination I needed to be set free if I were ever to get well. In other words, what I did at Ely was to assuage my irrational and destructive guilt-feelings so that their power over me was maintained if not increased. It was like trying to cast out devils by Beelzebub. For what counts with each of us (to use Cardinal Newman's well-known distinction) are not the beliefs to which we give notional assent but those to which we give real assent. And these two are by no means always the same. At Ely notionally I considered myself the child of God's love. In terms of real assent I was still the slave of a monster who was crushing and destroying me, and to whom I was once again bowing the knee.

I suppose that I allowed the clergy to go ahead with their idea of asking the Bishop to anoint me because of the confusion I've just described. But it wasn't only that. If you are being destroyed by irrational guilt-feelings, it isn't strange that you do in fact feel very guilty. You feel you are a criminal, and your chief crime is to exist at all. In these circumstances you naturally look round for allies, and to obtain allies you have to ingratiate yourself with people. The clergy were my most obvious allies, and my agreeing to be anointed was part of the ingratiating process. This was recognized by a devout Christian, who, in reply to my request for his prayers, wrote: "I will certainly pray for you on Wednesday morning when you are to be anointed with oil, I had almost said grease." But it was a disturbing statement, all the circumstances considered.

Those who come into contact with people overwhelmed by neurotic illness are often by the contact made uncomfortably aware of their own hidden and repressed neuroses, and take defensive action accordingly. This is generally in forms which are less than kind, though occasionally they have the mercy of being funny, as when a clergyman from London, preaching one Sunday evening at a neighbouring college, kindly came to see me on Monday morning. He stayed for half an hour, during which in a loud voice he three times volunteered the information: "I am not myself a neurotic." The third time I asked him who was visiting whom. He shook his head sadly. Obviously I was in a very bad way.

I often used to storm with rage that it was possible for anybody to suffer so overwhelmingly as I was doing. It seemed an outrage, an obscenity, this paralysing terror always waiting to spring out at me at any moment; my consequent inability to concentrate on anything or enjoy anything; the inevitable isolation – my being left for hours and days on end with nobody but my own damned self; the suspicion I saw (or thought I saw) in the eyes of those who did visit me that I was a criminal who had at last been found out; the hopelessness of my passion for Stavros, my fantasied saviour and ruin whom I loved and hated with demonic intensity; the prayers which were answered by nothing but the cruelty of an empty echo, so that I began to pray like the old waiter in Hemingway's short story: "Our Nothing which art in nothing, Nothing be thy nothing;

Thy nothing nothing." For that was all this sound and fury finally signified – at least as felt by me – nothing, and that was the last and greatest outrage of all. I hurled a tumbler at the wall so that it shattered in a thousand fragments. But all that did for me was to remind me of a remark Jack Gallagher had made to me half in jest some nine months before: "Harry, what a poseur you are." I had drawn Nothing again.

10

I WAS LEFT a great deal of the time with only the enveloping pain, but not all the time. There was something, perhaps a great deal, to put on the other side of the balance sheet.

To begin with, there was my former tutor, Patrick Duff, who, with characteristically unostentatious goodness, used to telephone me at about ten o'clock every evening he was in residence and invite me round for a cup of tea. His rooms were close to mine and I could crawl there all right. He used to tell me all the news and gossip of the day, and often there would be one or two other Fellows with him. Patrick was able (it was, I suppose, his goodness) to create an atmosphere which didn't terrify me. And this contact in his rooms with the outside world every night week after week did an enormous amount to put me on my feet again. I don't think he ever knew how much it did for me or how grateful I was. He isn't the sort of man to whom you can tell that sort of thing. But his regular and gentle hospitality was healing if anything was. I used often to arrive het-up and in despair and leave calm and reasonably cheerful. And it was in his rooms that I was to make what was perhaps the most important and was certainly the most beneficial discovery in my life. But that I shall describe in a moment.

Among the people who used to come and see me was John Wisdom, the philosopher. I particularly valued his visits, for in the past he had himself had certain psychological difficulties, and (as his published work makes clear) he possessed considerable experience of psychoanalysis. It is, however, the earliest of his visits that I remember with special gratitude because it was the first time since I had gone under that I was deeply and delightedly amused. The occasion showed me that what counts, what hits you in a personal contact, is not what the person says but his underlying intention and attitude, conscious or unconscious. John told me of a friend of his or it may have been a relative – I can't remember – and said to me about him: "He was in a dreadful state psychologically. Like you he was hospitalized for three weeks. He came home from hospital and stayed there two or three months. Then they had to take him to a mental hospital, where he has now been for twenty years, and it's obvious that he will never come out again." The ineptitude of that remark to somebody in my circumstances seemed to me profoundly funny. There was behind it no aggression, no fear, certainly no malice. It came straight from the good heart of a holy innocent. If ever I loved John Wisdom it was that evening. I laughed every time I thought of what he said, and I still laugh about it now. He wished to be of help to me and his wish was granted him, though not, I suspect, quite in the way he imagined.

I remember another example of goodheartedness which amused me. There was a Fellow much loved and respected in the college who was heavy in build and with a voice somewhat stentorian. (When King Faisal II of Iraq dined in Hall with his suite this Fellow was much in attendance upon them, which prompted Simpson to say to me of him: "He'll probably be given a decoration – Elephant of Jordan, Third Class.") He often used to take me for a stroll in the afternoon, when I had recovered enough to walk abroad without too much terror, relieving me of the effort of talking by talking most of the time himself. We often walked by the river and he would discourse about the winning of the initiative by the House of Commons in the Tudor and Jacobean age, or the state of religion in the Victorian era, or what he imagined was Bergson's philosophy, or how left-wing historians inevitably got their history all wrong. He obviously thought (rightly) that my feelings needed educating so that I might acquire confidence. One afternoon some swans glided by as he was describing how biased J.L. and Barbara Hammond were in their descriptions of village and town labourers. Seeing the swans, however, he stopped his criticism of the Hammonds, stood still, and said to me in the nearest approach to an actor's voice he was capable of: "Ah, look at those swans. How nice it would be if they could turn into undergraduates and dance for us." There have been lessons in the art of living more subtly given, but the very clumsiness here was attractive because amusing, and the lasting impression was of a great and generous heart.

I I

AFTER A TERM OFF I was able to teach again. Teaching didn't frighten me at all, at least as far as most undergraduates were concerned. But at this time it so happened that four or five extreme Evangelicals decided to read theology, and they were all to a man rigid fundamentalists. They were friendly enough and always courteous, but they scared the daylights out of me and I couldn't then make out why. I later realized that they were (at least at that time) the slaves of the savage tyrant from whose clutches I was myself trying to get free. In their case the tyrant insisted that they believed, contrary to all evidence and reason, that the Bible was historically and scientifically true in every detail. What else the tyrant required of them I wasn't in a position to know; though I gather that he forbade all alcohol except cider (why he exempted cider I never discovered) and certainly the theatre and cinema. (After I'd got to know these men one of them asked me my opinion of what he described by the intriguing euphemism of "unhelpful films".) When a pupil disagrees with you in a supervision (tutorial), it is generally the best thing that can happen as it livens things up and enables a useful discussion of the topic concerned. But these fundamentalists regarded you not only as mistaken in the line you were taking, they regarded your taking it as clear proof that you were wicked. And this, of course, aroused and stimulated my guilt-feelings. And hence my terror. They were extraordinarily and often amusingly funny in their defence of literal historicity. I once pointed out to one of them that in Genesis there were three stories that looked very much alike. In one story Abraham passes his wife off as his sister to Pharaoh, in another he does the same to Abimelech King of Gerar, and in the third Isaac does the same to Abimelech. Didn't these three stories look like three different versions in different traditions of the same story? "Not at all," answered my pupil; "it was a favourite joke of Abraham's and his son shared his sense of humour." Of course on one level I found it funny and repeated it as such to friends and colleagues. But deeper down I felt the iron grip of my old slave-master, and found myself trying to placate him, embodied as he was for me in these particular pupils, by giving expression for their benefit to pious sentiments in a pious voice, and often passing over critical issues which should have been faced. For one dreadful afternoon a week I had three of them in a row for an hour each. You couldn't offer them any sherry since, as I've said, alcohol was forbidden them. So I used to keep a bottle of gin in my lavatory where I could go in and take a swig to repair my ravaged nerves, and then pull the chain. To such a pass was I reduced by religious zeal on the rampage.

In ordinary circumstances I enjoyed teaching. In prospect it was a bore and you would far rather not do it. But afterwards you felt more alive. Obviously you had received as well as given.

At this time my duties were entirely academic. After getting over the first awfulness of breakdown, I was able to return to them with relief and pleasure. But religion, both private and institutional, was too tainted for me to touch for at least eighteen months. I stayed away from church and chapel entirely, and said no prayers. I had had enough of God for the time being. It was an indescribable relief not to have this ghastly figure breathing with disapproval down my neck, and to tell him instead to fuck off. It was the idol I was disposing of. But I wasn't at all clear about that at the time. And in any case the idol and the true God were so hopelessly mixed up in my feelings that I couldn't tell which was which. So I had to empty the baby with the bathwater. And if that was so much the worse for the baby, it was, I felt, so much the better for me. At last I had the first glimmerings of freedom. It was not until years later that I came across Yeats's line: "Hatred of God may bring the soul to God." But that, I think, is what was happening to me. For the true God will never fuck off, however much you tell him to, while in the end the idol does, even if he remains in the wings and returns every now and then with his filthy magic.

If I never went to church or said any prayers, there remained in me none the less a Christian insight without which I don't think I could have passed through the worst period of pain, when everything was a black nothing.

While Michael Ramsey was still Regius Professor of Divinity at Cambridge I had discussed a project with him for which he advised me to read three sermons on sacrifice by Scott Holland published in his *Logic and Life*. It was the third sermon, called "The Sacrifice of the Redeemed", which remained with me. In it Scott Holland (using a nauseatingly flowery and melodramatic style belonging to his day) made the point that it is the nature of human privations and sufferings of all kinds to feel like dead-ends. But human suffering, the more of a dead-end it feels like, the more is it an invitation to join in Christ's sufferings, and in Him to help bring life and light and healing and liberty to mankind. So the cruelly destructive and negative nature of suffering can be seen, if only in a glass very darkly, as charged with positive and creative possibilities. Of course it isn't calculable. It's a mystery, which means it's too real for precise definition. When I was so terrified that I couldn't remain at my parents' dinner table and went for a walk, I remembered Scott Holland's sermon. I was in Baynards Park (it is on the Surrey/Sussex border). The ground in front of me sloped upwards to the big house. And it came to me with overpowering force: "I am now eating Christ's broken Body and drinking his outpoured Blood. The service of Holy Communion in church is only a rehearsal, like military manoeuvres. But this I am going through now, this is for real." The vision soon faded as all visions must. And I found myself once more afraid and out in the cold with nothing. But I had had a glimpse, however momentary, of the true God, who, far from being a tyrant, was prepared to suffer in order to create, and called men to share his suffering so that in the end they too might look on what had been made and find it very good. If, as I said, the vision faded completely and left me as I was before, yet somehow it remained potentially within me. It came again for a brief moment the next Christmas Eve as I was listening to the carols from King's on the radio: "And he leads his children on, To the place where he has gone." As I heard the well-known words I began to shake with sobs. The lines were not, of course, speaking of a conventional heaven, but of where perfect fulfilment is found by means of a love which is willing to suffer to the uttermost for the sake of others. That was Christmas. That was how we partook of the divine nature. That was how suffering was used.

But I was soon left alone again, out in the cold with nothing – except for clergymen worried (I think in fact they were cross) because I didn't go to church, and the terror which was always waiting to pounce and make life insupportable.

Meanwhile I was going to the psychiatric consultant three times a week. As I've said, he was highly qualified and had had a great deal of experience. I knew personally people who were enormously grateful to him, and patients were certainly queuing to see him. But it became more and more evident to me that we were not on the same wavelength and hence were getting nowhere. In some important way we didn't click.

Previously I stressed the importance, if you are in psychological difficulties, of consulting a qualified psychiatrist who is experienced. I now want to stress that as well as that essential condition, there must be some sort of personal equation between the psychiatrist and yourself. In my experience this personal factor is of vital importance. If the therapy is to work there must be a certain preliminary degree of empathy between psychiatrist and patient. If that doesn't exist it is no discredit to either of them. Everybody is limited with regard to the type of person he is able to respond to. But if there is no element of mutual response, the therapy isn't going to get very far.

I wasn't then able to see this clearly. I was only worried because my visits increasingly seemed a waste of time as the contact between us appeared to decrease.

Patrick Duff had a cousin (her nickname was Dodo) who was medically qualified and at that time was working at the mental hospital at Fulbourn. I met her often in Patrick's rooms and inevitably talked to her of my problems. One day she said to me: "There's a psychiatric consultant who comes to Fulbourn. He's called Christopher Scott. I think you'll get on well with him. I know he has a private practice in Cambridge and London as well as working in the psychiatric department of Addenbrooke's Hospital. Why don't you see him?"

I took Dodo's advice. The original consultant was extremely helpful and undertook to send my papers to Dr Scott, and, as far as I can remember, arranged the preliminary appointment with him.

This was a turning-point in my existence. Dodo's suggestion, made in Patrick Duff's rooms, was the discovery of a lifetime.

❧⟦12⟧❧

THE SCOTTS lived in Storey's Way. Where Churchill College now stands there were then only fields. Mrs Scott (as I later learnt she was) opened the front door and left me to wait in the dining-room. I found the atmosphere of the house reassuring. The dining-room furniture was old, good and unostentatious. There was about the room a quiet and unselfconscious grace. It seemed to assure me that the Scotts were authentic people who would have nothing gimmicky about them. In about ten minutes Dr Scott himself appeared and led me to his consulting room. I realized when the hour was over that we were going to hit it off. We had already made contact.

I was Christopher Scott's patient for fourteen years. For the first three years I went to him three times a week. Then I went twice a week; and for the last year once a week. It can be no surprise that I came to know him and his wife, Ursula, extremely well. Ursula used to have a short gossip with me after letting me in. Later I learnt that she used to give Christopher her unprofessional but I have no doubt extremely shrewd estimate of his patients. I think she regarded analysis as a bit of a joke, though she never said so explicitly. Certainly she was (and is – Christopher died in 1977) a very warm person and her humour is always enlivening, not deflating. Once when Christopher was in bed with 'flu I telephoned her to ask how he was. "He's all right," she said, "but he's feeling suicidal, and the trouble is that Christopher isn't used to feeling suicidal." It wasn't the sort of report you would have been given by a psychiatrist's receptionist.

Cambridge is a small world, and I recognized the voice of the man who was let out of the front door after his session while I was waiting in the dining-room for mine. By this time I didn't mind in the slightest if anybody knew I was being analysed. But I was aware that many people were sensitive about it and liked to keep it as dark as possible. I used often to meet the man whose voice I recognized, but said nothing about it to him. After a time we were both at a party and had had several drinks when he came up to me and said: "You go to Christopher Scott on Mondays, Wednesdays and Fridays at ten o'clock." He in his turn had recognized my voice gossiping with Ursula. It was like the *dénouement* of a farce, and we both laughed.

In fact I slowly discovered that a number of Oxbridge dons went to Christopher. He was singularly intelligent in a deeply intuitive way. He had done his homework all right in the sense that he had all the Freudian and post-Freudian theories and techniques at his fingertips, as also the various kinds of Jungian insights. But he refused to put people in the straitjacket of any particular analytical system. We should not, he used to say, become the victims of Freud's genius or Jung's. So he used to listen and interpret material according to the particular patient's psychic constitution and needs. Thus, for instance, if, after listening a great deal, he thought that a person's religious faith was fundamental to him (however much it may have become diseased and perverted) he was certain that that person couldn't understand or come to terms with himself unless his self-knowledge and self-acceptance included a religious dimension.

There was one way in which I was able to check Christopher's interpretation of material, and that was with regard to dreams. His interpretation of a dream invariably reminded me of an event or state of mind which I had entirely forgotten and about which he couldn't possibly have known. Incidentally, it needed three years' analysis before I was confident enough to remember that nightmare of such central significance about the savage monster hypnotizing the actors on the stage.

Of course, we had tiffs, sometimes quite violent ones. The analysis wouldn't have worked without going through phases of negative transference when the patient unloads upon the analyst the resentments and grudges he has been storing up within himself for a lifetime. Yet Christopher's absolute integrity was so transparently obvious, and with all his insight and skill he was so totally unassuming, and his real and enormous authority was so quiet and unparaded, that it was impossible to be angry with him for long because you saw through the projections you were foisting on him.

It was obvious that he used to think a great deal about patients' problems between sessions, especially when on holiday in Cornwall (they had a cottage at Constantine Bay). For he used every now and then to write me long letters from there putting forward some point of view he thought I needed to consider. It strikes me now as fantastically generous that he should do this on his holiday.

He wasn't a Christian, at least in any formal sense. Certainly he never went to church. And he wouldn't allow himself in his consulting room to become involved in any theological matter. "I'll stick to my last," he would say. "I'm a doctor." But once, after going to a feast at Magdalene and sitting opposite a very eminent ecclesiastic, he broke through his customary reticence and said: "I can see now what you're up against."

Without doubt he was a man of profound spiritual perception. And, after the analysis had finished and I had come here to Mirfield, it became clear to me that he was a mystic. He had penetrated to and was in communion with Reality. I think he spent a great deal of his leisure and holiday time in what would now be called contemplation. But there was nothing phoney or artificially induced about it. In any case it wasn't at that time in fashion. He did it as something which came naturally.

The aim of an analysis is psychotherapy in the sense that elements of the personality that have been repressed and locked away out of sight in a dark room, or put into a deep-freeze, are brought out into the open and unfrozen, so that you may see and feel them, accept them, absorb them into the main stream of what you are, and thus achieve a more comprehensive integration of your personality. This means that the psychotherapy can't be a matter of gradual but steady improvement as physiotherapy is if it is working properly. For the success of psychotherapy will often consist in your being ready to face an aspect of yourself you have hitherto evaded. And the facing of it is generally a matter of storm and stress, of anger, depression and tantrums. So the analytic process is, in the way I've described, extremely uneven. Something unexpected may blow up at any time, and apparent calm in no way necessarily indicates that the cure is working. It may merely indicate that issues are being side-stepped.

I am more grateful than I can possibly say to somebody who has long been one of my closest friends. He is now over fifty and I am godfather to the eldest of his sons. After leaving school he did his national service in the Brigade of Guards, going into action in some trouble spot abroad. He then came up to Trinity, stayed the usual three years, and took a degree. After I had been in analysis about two years he returned to Cambridge to do some postgraduate work. Soon after his return I found myself in the middle of a violent analytic storm. I projected a great deal of it on to this friend of mine. This made me go round to his lodgings one afternoon when I knew he would be out, and break up as much of the contents of his room as I could. On his return he knew immediately that it was I who had done it, and he never breathed a word about it to a single soul. Could charity, not to mention friendship, go further? I've recorded this partly to mark my profound gratitude to him, and partly because it was the most violent of the analytic storms I passed through. I telephoned Christopher Scott and had an extra session with him that evening. On my return to Trinity it was snowing, and as I approached my rooms a muffled figure came towards me. It was Jim Butler, then the Vice-Master. He said a cordial goodnight to which I replied with equal cordiality, but I thought: "Jesus, if he knew what I'd done."

The fits of terror (I think the technical name for them is phobic anxiety) took a long time to diminish and never completely cleared up. In time I forced myself to go into Hall, though the prospect of it frightened me to death. I never knew how bad it would be until I had sat down at the table. Sometimes it wouldn't be too bad. Sometimes it would be almost unendurable. Only once did I dash out in panic after gulping down my soup. Adrian told me that quite a number of the Fellows had had difficulty about

eating in Hall, adding wistfully: "I've only been bored."
The hall at Trinity has two High Tables. The top table for
some reason was for me the less alarming of the two, and
facing down the hall was much less alarming than having
my back to it. Luckily you could sit where you liked, so it
was possible for me to place myself in the position where
there was least strain. After three or four years the terror
became less frequent, and, when it did pounce on me, less
intense. In the end it faded away almost completely.

It faded away almost completely, but not quite. For,
although terror or phobic anxiety can and does diminish, it
diminishes chiefly by your being less and less taken in by it.
To begin with, when you feel the first stirrings of terror
you are certain that it must grow and build itself up in a
crescendo which reaches a point where it becomes
unendurable. You are also certain that because it happened
yesterday, it must happen again today. It is as if you were
mesmerized by the (false) analogy of physical disease. In
point of fact when terror looks in at your window, it isn't
at all inevitable that it should come in the front door and
take possession of the whole house. To the degree in which
you are able to disregard it (something not always possible)
it will slink away and cease to trouble you. A crescendo
following the first stirrings of terror is by no means
necessary or inevitable. And, by the same token, because
terror gave you a bad time yesterday, it doesn't follow that
it must do the same today.

I had to accept this first on faith from Christopher.
Then I proved it in my own experience. On the other hand,
I could never guarantee to myself that on any occasion I
should necessarily be able to disregard terror when it
looked in at the window. It might well invade and take
charge of me.

Christopher was always stressing that the self of
which we are aware is only a very small fraction of our
total self, the mere top of a huge submerged iceberg. This
unknown total self included what we had been forced by
adverse circumstances to repress, to lock up out of sight in

the dark room within us – all those feelings which had been subconscious*ed* because we couldn't bear the strain of entertaining them. In a rough and ready way it corresponded, at least to some small extent, with the Freudian id. But the most important and (to use the unavoidable spatial metaphor) infinitely larger part of the submerged iceberg was that unknown self which is the fount of all that is good, lovely and creative in what we are and do. The unknown self in this sense corresponded largely with the Jungian Unconscious. When terror threatened it was on this unknown self that one had to rely, since it transcended the injured and shop-soiled self of which one was aware and also the region of the subconscious*ed*, where things in themselves good and natural became diseased because shut away in the dark.

The full metaphysical and religious implications of this scheme (which for me was no mere scheme since I had tried it out in practice and knew it from first-hand experience) didn't dawn on me until I'd been here at Mirfield for several years, though I was obviously working my way towards it in my essay in *The God I Want* published in 1967. Here at Mirfield what I've described has provided me with the basis of a faith by which to live. But I shall speak of that later at the appropriate point.

As well as forcing myself to go into Hall, I had to force myself to go out for a walk. Some years previously I had been given a walking stick, and this now became my strength and stay on my walks, though it was often also, alas, no more than a broken reed. For I often wondered whether, in spite of my walking stick, I should be able to make it to the next lamp post. It was a great triumph when I first got from Trinity Great Court to the Senate House and back. As in Hall, and in the same way, I slowly acquired more confidence and in time was able to walk to Storey's Way and even to Coton. Certain places had a special terror for me. One was the pavement beneath the high brick wall which stretches from the entrance to Sidney Sussex College round into Jesus Lane. It was much easier for me the other side of the two roads.

After I was able to walk abroad with fairly reasonable confidence a friend suggested that we should go for a holiday together to Porlock Weir in Somerset. The friend was Graham Storey, then senior tutor and later Vice-Master of Trinity Hall (the college next to Trinity) and the editor of Dickens's letters. I knew him well and realized I couldn't have a better companion; also we would drive there in his car. So I accepted his invitation, but viewed the prospect with absolute dread. The very name, Porlock Weir (I hadn't been there before), began to acquire for me the most sinister significance. In my sick imagination it became a monstrous place of torture which would imprison and eat me up. But I had enough confidence in Graham to go in spite of these fantasies. And I didn't tell him of them, as I thought that if I did he might quite justifiably consider me as stark staring mad.

In the event it was a very successful ten days. The hotel we stayed at was excellent. I was very grateful to the woman at the reception desk for smiling and welcoming me instead of shuddering with unconcealable disgust and disapproval. I was able to sit at our small table in the dining-room without too much or too frequent distress. The weather was kind to us, and we walked quite a lot on Exmoor. We also went on various sightseeing expeditions in the car, including one to Dunster Castle, where the Luttrells kindly invited us to lunch, and I found that I could once again be a guest without causing an embarrassing scene. Altogether it was for me a very rewarding ten days. It was the first of a great number of travels I did with Graham Storey, the last being in 1968, the year before I came inside here at Mirfield, when for a month we toured Iran together.

As well as Hall and walking abroad, there was still church and chapel, and these were by far and away the toughest nuts to crack, and in fact I never fully cracked them.

By fits and starts I found religion slightly less

nauseating than I had done. A great deal of it was still nauseating, and there were times when the whole of it was, without exception But there were other times when some aspects of it were profoundly meaningful.

I began forcing myself to go to chapel, at least on Sunday evening, though I never went to church in the vacations. I certainly said no regular prayers, but at times there was one petition I was able to repeat with sincerity: "O my God, I hope in Thee for grace and for glory." In this context grace meant the ability to give myself away to others, if need be at cost to myself, and glory the capacity to do this fully and thereby to find life and joy. I could use this petition because, as I said, I felt that I did sincerely at least hope for those two things.

In general I was out to kill the god who soaked you in guilt-feelings and demanded continual self-abasement, confession, atonement, absolution, and so on. (I say I was out to kill him as he was still very much alive inside me.) And I was finding my way towards the God who was prepared to suffer anything in order to create His universe and give Himself to it.

But such specifically religious beliefs and feelings were by definition conscious. My worst enemy was the terror which sprang upon me apparently from nowhere, and with much greater violence in chapel or church than anywhere else. Sitting in chapel on Sunday evening was often an all but unbearable ordeal. And it was made worse by the fact that there was only one door out of the chapel – the main door at the west end – so that a hurried exit in the middle of a service would be a melodramatic gesture which could not but be seen by everybody present.

Suffering in this way Sunday after Sunday often made me absolutely furious with God for allowing it, and the fury sometimes took the form of protesting to myself that religion was a lot of bloody nonsense. One evening the protest became vocal – I slightly altered the verse of a well-known hymn and sang it very loudly:

> "The healing of his seamless dress
> Is by our beds of pain;
> We touch him in life's throng and press,
> And we're *not* whole again."

John Burnaby noticed. He looked up from his hymn book and towards me across the aisle. But he was forbearing enough not to say anything about it afterwards.

But as in Hall and out walking, the terror became less frequent and less intense, though in chapel it took much longer to diminish and was far more likely suddenly to recur in its old violence.

After not being able to preach in chapel for two years, I thought I had better force myself to start again. So John Burnaby put me down for a Sunday. I took sleeping pills the night before. When I woke up in the morning I was trembling with fright. The worst of it was that the service didn't take place until 6.45 in the evening, so I had the whole day to get through before the fearful ordeal started. I had, of course, fully written out the sermon. It was all ready. What terrified me was the prospect of delivering it. I didn't know how to make the time pass. Grabbing my stick I went out for a walk. I was cheered and made to feel more human by the luck of meeting C. D. Broad. "Good heavens," he said, "what are you doing out here on a Sunday morning? When does God get his look-in?" I assured him that God would get his look-in in the evening, and we parted laughing. Getting back to my rooms there was endless waiting. I couldn't concentrate enough to read the newspapers, let alone a book. I've never known time to go so slowly. At last there came the horrifying sound of the deep chapel bell, notifying me that my hour had arrived. I put on my surplice and hood and seized my square, carrying my manuscript in the same hand. I crawled to the chapel and into the preacher's seat, almost paralysed with fear. Then I had a further agonizing wait while what seemed an endless service took its course. Fits of terror kept on sweeping over me like breakers in a rough sea sweeping over a man bathing and knocking him down. The lessons were short – I'd been allowed to choose them and had seen to that. But the intercessions went on interminably. We seemed to pray for everything on earth except dogs and cats. Had the chaplain no imagination, no mercy at all? At long last the hymn before the sermon was announced and begun. This was it. I had now to go in. The hymn ended. I heard myself saying: "In the Name of the Father and of the Son and of the Holy Ghost Amen." The congregation sat down and looked at me. I started my sermon and preached it to the end. As I did so the waves of terror were constantly sweeping over me. At last, thank God and all the holy angels, it was over and the final hymn was announced.

There is no point in not being honest. I discovered that the congregation had been spellbound by the sermon. It was subsequently published in *The True Wilderness* under the title "Life Abundant or Life Resisting?"

But the terror in chapel continued, though it was easier at some times than at others. I began going again to Holy Communion on Sunday morning. In general conventional terms I was "well" enough by the summer of 1956 to accept an invitation to go to Moscow and Leningrad on an Anglican delegation to the Russian Orthodox church led by Michael Ramsey, who was then Archbishop of York. (There is no point in describing it, as a full report was published by the Faith Press in 1957, edited by Herbert Waddams under the title *Anglo-Russian Theological Conference*.) And in 1958 I was able to take on additional responsibilities. One was as Dean of Chapel, that is, vicar of the college with two chaplains assisting. It involved appointing the chaplains (they only stayed five years), and looking after the appointment of incumbents in the thirty-two parishes of which the college is patron. The other responsibility was becoming a tutor in the Cambridge sense with about 180 pupils and some 60 vacancies each year for undergraduates reading any subject.

Although now in a conventional sense I was "well" I continued with the analysis because it was leading me into a wholeness and integrity I had lacked before. And it was giving me on the side an insight into my Christianity, showing me what in it was diseased and to be discarded and what was of the highest permanent value.

The content of this re-evaluation was collected in *The True Wilderness*. This was not published until 1965, but it consisted of sermons preached over the past ten years in Trinity chapel. I had had no idea at all of publishing them, but James Mitchell, then working at Constable, asked me to send him all my old sermons. From these he selected twenty-one, and asked me to write an introduction. The book became the only bestseller I've written. After selling for a time in hardback, it became a Pelican and then a Fontana. Some seventeen years after publication it still sells, even in hardback. I now feel rather depressed when people praise it: I would like them to enthuse about some subsequent publications! – though these have sold well enough.

In chapel the terror came to focus on two occasions. The first was at Evensong on Sunday when at the end of the service I had to take a long, lonely walk through the empty sanctuary and up to the altar to give the final blessing. Invariably I did it in fear and trembling, wondering whether I should make it, though I always did. I tried to change the way in which the service ended – saying "The grace of our Lord Jesus Christ, etc." from my stall. But the chapel committee (who knew nothing whatever of my distress) were insistent that they wanted a blessing. So I had to restore it.

The other occasion was the celebration on Sunday morning of the Holy Communion. It was a service with hymns and a short address, and in those days we had on average seventy to eighty communicants. There was a vague tradition that the Dean celebrated on Sunday, and I kept to it rigidly because I knew that once I asked a chaplain to celebrate, I should go on asking him and never steel myself to do it. I found it particularly difficult to stand in front of the altar with my back to the congregation and with three or four steps going down behind me. Luckily ecclesiastical fashion now came to my aid. For it was just about this time that the avant-garde began to celebrate from behind the altar facing the people. I found this position much more reassuring, and I was able to sell it as the church's *dernier cri*. Even so, right up to near the end of my time at Trinity I took the precaution of going to bed early on Saturday evening, taking a double dose of sleeping pills, and some strong tranquillizers with my morning tea and biscuits. Thus fortified I was able to conduct the Lord's own service on the Lord's own day. In my last year I was able to dispense with both the sleeping pills and the tranquillizers. It was all right except for one Sunday. I haven't the slightest idea why, but that Sunday I unexpectedly got into an absolute panic in the middle of the service and it continued until the service was over. I didn't, however, want to revert to the drugs, so the following Sunday I chanced my arm and nothing nasty happened.

13

THE EVENTS I've just recorded could be described as a chronicle of breakdown and recovery. That would be a true description within its own narrow limits. But it would be far indeed from the full truth. More adequate would be the image of death and resurrection: death to a narrowly based life lived in slavish subservience to a tyrannical idol and resurrection to a richness of being which consisted of freedom to discover who and what I was combined with the ability at least to begin to become it. Another image for the same thing would be that of birth pangs and delivery: "A woman when she is in travail hath sorrow, because her hour is come: but as soon as she is delivered of the child, she remembereth no more the anguish, for joy that a man is born into the world."

These images could be used to express what was a deeply personal experience of my own. But with the experience came the recognition that what here was personal wasn't simply individual, existing in isolation by itself. I recognized that in my personal experience something universal was being articulated, that what had hit me personally was part of some sort of comprehensive reality. For didn't the whole creation groan and travail in pain together in order to bring forth what was new (as Teilhard de Chardin later described the process of evolution)? And wasn't what was true of the whole creation true also of God Himself? For wasn't that the way I had now come to understand the meaning of Christ crucified? I could no longer separate what Christians call redemption from the whole comprehensive work of creation. And Christ crucified said now to me that in order to create the universe in all its infinitely varied loveliness and splendour, God Himself was prepared to suffer to the uttermost. And, as I've indicated, I saw that I was called upon to accept my own personal sufferings, in so far as they were unavoidable, as my particular share in the cost to God of His creative work, and that this was true even of the terror from which I was rightly doing all in my power to liberate myself.

This vision, and the new life of resurrection which brought it to me, had some practical consequences which I must now describe.

I suppose that every curate sometimes dreams of preferment. And if he is moderately able, he wonders whether his dream will come true. I was no exception to this rule. I was too lazy, not too virtuous, to press myself forward. But I occasionally wondered whether something nice might one day be thrown into my lap.

But now I had to reckon with my terror or phobic anxiety; as my analysis proceeded it decreased (as I've described) almost, but not quite, to the point of non-existence. The little that remained of it left me free in all areas except one. The one exception was the area of church ritual. I was generally free from it even there, but I could never be certain. It might return now and again. And my bet was that if I were exposed to fairly constant bouts of church ritual, I would probably have to meet my phobic anxiety with increasing frequency.

In fact no preferment was ever offered me. I'm glad now it wasn't, as in some euphoric mood I might have been foolish enough to accept it.

Ceasing to be a career clergyman brought very great advantages. To begin with, there was formerly a contradiction which kept on nagging at me and which now was disposed of. I didn't see how God could be a career, at least not the God alleged to have been revealed in Christ crucified. I came to believe (and still do) that the ordained ministry with its hierarchical structure is no more than a sociological phenomenon, a necessary organization of convenience common to almost all civilizations, since most people in all ages seem to need their deepest feelings and yearnings organized for them, or at least explained to them, by authority, and it is to the interest of the authority to see that they are thus organized and explained in an acceptable way. The sacred canopy (to use Peter Berger's phrase) held over the organizing authority seemed to me more and more ambiguous to the point where, frankly, it began, in its Christian no less than in its other forms, to look bogus. The true priest, I came to believe, is anybody who is the channel to others of God's love, and is willing to share something of the cost of that love; and whose eyes are open to perceive God's presence everywhere and in everybody. Priesthood, I believed, and still believe, has nothing to do with entering a special divinely ordained caste. Hence if I had my time over again and could take to it my experience of this present round, I certainly shouldn't become a clergyman, though I might well become a Religious or monk.

Another advantage of no longer being a career clergyman was that I no longer felt any obligation to accept Christian orthodoxy as a package deal. It wasn't so much that I no longer had to protect my professional future (though I suppose that that element was present – there is nothing like the smell of preferment to make a man orthodox), but that I felt free from the responsibility to conform, since conforming was for me no longer a required virtue. The rejection of Christian orthodoxy as a package deal meant that I could examine every item of it and accept or reject it as it seemed true or false to my experience – an experience, by the way, which was fully aware of how much we have always to depend upon the experience and beliefs of others to check and amplify our own. If in time the result was that traditional Christian orthodoxy looked less and less like a stately cathedral and more and more like a half demolished railway terminus – well, that made God more important to me as doctrines about Him grew less important. I was much impressed by Jung's statement in his Terry Lectures that religions exist to protect men from religion. The ultimate Mystery must be reduced to neat little doctrinal brown paper parcels so that it becomes acceptable because no longer threatening.

❦ 14 ❦

TWO OCCASIONS in particular during this period showed me how scared many conventional churchmen were when sleeping dogs were thus no longer allowed to lie. These occasions were both television programmes of forty minutes in which I unfolded my beliefs to Ludovic Kennedy, a very expert and probing interviewer. The first was on an Easter evening and was about the resurrection of Christ. The second, some ten or twelve months later, was about Christian morals. I received a quantity of abusive (as well as grateful) letters in both cases, and in the second case the church press went to town about it.

As it happened, after the programme on Christian morals the episcopal chairman of what was then still called the Church of England Moral Welfare Council wrote me a letter in his own hand thanking me for the programme and saying that he was sure it would be an enormous help to many people. Three days later a stranger appeared in my rooms who turned out to be a reporter for the London *Evening Standard*. He was concerned to discover what my reaction was to the attack made upon me that morning in the *Church Times*. I told him that I wasn't aware of the attack as I never read the church press. So he left. I then hurriedly went to our common room to see what the *Church Times* had in fact said. It was the leading headline on the front page – HURT AND SCANDAL OF TELEVISION PROGRAMME, and it was followed by the publication of a number of letters of the Disgusted Tunbridge Wells variety. I became very tired of the cliché that the writers were "shocked and disgusted". In private letters, if not in the church press, an additional argument against me was that I was a claret-drinking don and as such totally disqualified from having any religious opinions at all. (Orthodox pundits were allowed their claret without protest.) The charge in my case was totally false. I never drank claret in the combination room as I preferred port or madeira.

Very few of the Fellows of Trinity read the *Church Times*. Those who did used subsequently to grin at me and say: "How's the viper?"

What I had said in the programme was that it was always everywhere wrong to exploit other people, whether the exploitation were economic, racial, personal or sexual. It was always wrong to use other people as mere means to my own ends of convenience, pleasure or power. This led me to say that it was possible for exploitation to exist within marriage as it was possible for a man and woman to live together in the full sense without exploiting each other; and that where this was indeed the case there was nothing wrong in their cohabitation without benefit of marriage. The fanatical fury which this statement aroused in the early 1960s among church people is almost unbelievable today.

The reaction to the two programmes in terms not only of abuse but also of gratitude showed me how urgently Christian orthodoxy in the realms both of faith and morals needed to be dismantled, examined and rebuilt.

This has to some extent been attempted since then, but the attempts have invariably caused storms of protest in the Church Assembly or the Synod, whose members seem to consider the safeguarding of their own sense of security as their top priority, however much it may shut up the kingdom of heaven against men and prevent those who are entering from going in. Of course those thus prevented are stupid to take any notice of what the Synod says, and I suppose that because of their stupidity there is a sense in which they deserve what they get. But then, as Benjamin Jowett remarked, what is truth compared with an *esprit de corps*?

Doubtless I am here falling into self-righteousness, as there was one central area of my life when in effect I told all babbling churchmen to go to hell.

I hoped when I began analysis that I might discover some heterosexual potential within me which the analysis would enable to grow. I did, near the beginning, have a promising dream. It was of a very painted, tarty-looking woman. She scared, not attracted, me. And I said to her: "I'm not ready for you yet. Not ready." But the promise of the dream was illusory. Nothing like it recurred, and after fourteen years' analysis I still had no heterosexual feeling. I enjoyed the company of women and got on well with them. I liked them to be good-looking and well dressed. But they stirred in me no genital response.

It wasn't surprising really. When I was six or seven and we were still living in France, I had my only two pre-adolescent erotic dreams, at least the only two I can remember. I felt a warm, glowing and delightful love in the first dream for a *sergent-de-ville* who used to be on point duty not far from our house, and in the second for a conductor on a tram we used sometimes to take. Thus in my case homosexual feeling preceded puberty by a number of years.

Among the questions I had to face now I was beginning to be born anew, or raised from the dead, was what to do about sex. I believe, and still believe, that it is always wrong to exploit people. But it became less and less obvious to me that sleeping with somebody, which for me meant another man, was necessarily in itself to exploit him. It might, on the contrary, be the occasion of a mutual self-giving and enrichment. And I became more and more aware that what was holding me back was no longer any sort of moral scruple, but sheer funk. I became more and more convinced that if I was to achieve any sort of personal integrity I must have the courage to sleep with somebody.

During the next years I slept with several men, in each case fairly regularly. They were all of them friends. Cynics, of course, will smile, but I have seldom felt more like thanking God than when thus having sex. I used in bed to praise Him there and then for the joy I was receiving and giving. We cannot be whole unless our bodies are accepted, and the mutual acceptance of each other's bodies in sex is one of the most glorious things in human life. That is a platitude, a commonplace, where conventional hetero-sexual activity in marriage is concerned. But it can also be most wonderfully true when it is two men who are sleeping together. Those people who consider it vicious have either never had any experience of it, or it has been an experience in the context of exploitation or destructive guilt-feelings rather than of mutuality and freedom.

It is difficult for many moralists to understand what I am saying because in their experience of life they have mostly started at a point exactly opposite to the point from which I started and have travelled in exactly the opposite direction. They can't therefore understand that what for some people is self-indulgence is for others a summons to integrity. The integrity may require an initial act of courage, but afterwards it is built up by pleasure, happiness, joy and fun. The fun is important. Laughter in bed echoes the laughter of the universe.

It has been my experience that sleeping with somebody creates with him a bond which is permanent. The bond has remained years after we have given up having sex with each other. We know each other with a particular intimacy which is quite undramatic, and feel at home in each other's company in a special way. Few people realize how true this can be of homosexuals.

In this whole matter I feel rather like the man born blind in St John's Gospel. When the man was confronted by the pharisees with theological and ethical objections against his healer, he made a simple statement: "Whether he be a sinner or no, I know not: one thing I know, that, whereas I was blind, now I can see." Similarly I'm not trying to construct an ethical or religious theory. I'm simply recounting my experience. I was once in the misery of bondage and then became free. And in the achievement of that freedom sex played its not inconsiderable part.

A mutual fondness and respect are necessary if sleeping together is to be fulfilling. You needn't be deeply in love. But if you have been and cease to be, then it is better to stop having sex.

I fell deeply in love twice more after Stavros. In both cases it was related to reality in a way in which with Stavros it never was because now there was about it a mutuality which previously was absent. It brought me untold happiness in spite of the inevitable quarrels which occasionally blew up with their consequent hurt feelings. There were also moments of the intensest misery, as there usually are in such circumstances. But the happiness outweighed several times over the incidental misery, not least because the happiness lasted while the misery didn't.

In each case we stopped sleeping together when the other person ceased to be in love with me. Naturally I didn't find that an easy change. But fundamentally, in a part of me deeper than the unavoidable wound, I was grateful for the other person's honesty. For love can't exist on a basis of pretence or fraud. And after the storms of transition from being in love to loving, came serenity. Serenity comes, in fact, the moment you realize, not merely intellectually (that's easy and no help at all) but emotionally, if you like existentially, that however much John, Peter, George, whoever it is, may fall in love with somebody else or sleep around, you still have in the harem of his heart a place which nobody else can fill.

As far as I myself and these two people are concerned we have now for each other in both cases, with all passion spent, a love which I think would bear it out even to the edge of doom. And what more can anybody ask for than that?

❧ 15 ❧

HAPPINESS IS SO MANY-COLOURED that it is difficult to compare one state of happiness with another or to say that you were happier at one happy time than at another. But I can at least say that my last twelve years at Trinity were for me a very happy time indeed.

I had recovered from my breakdown and was deeply aware of the great kindness towards me of many of my colleagues. In terms of its Master and Fellows the college had seen me through an extremely sticky patch and had elicited from me an affection which extended to its very bricks and mortar.

As tutor and Dean of Chapel I had been given responsibilities which stretched me, but it was work I enjoyed and I wasn't therefore stretched too much. During this time at Cambridge there was a great deal of theological ferment in which I was involved, and that made life exciting. I was able to travel abroad each spring and summer with close and congenial friends. And, to crown it all, Rab and Mollie Butler arrived to take possession of the Master's Lodge. It was as if, after years of desolating pain and depressing greyness, some genie had pulled aside a curtain and announced to me: "Prince, your time has come." But it was, of course, the change within myself that enabled me to enjoy the good things which now came my way. The idol whose slave I had been was being rung out, the true God was being rung in. And in place of my former narrow and destructive moralism I had begun a search for integrity, something which is often costly, always risk-laden, and certainly fatal to any form of complacency or self-righteousness, but is, on the other hand, never without at least some particle of glory and often ablaze with it. I understood a little what St Peter meant when he blurted out: "It is good for us to be here."

16

A TUTOR IN THE CAMBRIDGE SENSE is in general charge of his pupils. In those days at Trinity he had fifty to sixty vacancies a year which he could fill as he thought fit with people wanting to read any subject. This involved a great deal of interviewing, which was laborious work. And you had slowly to discover to what extent you could trust the reports sent to you from the various schools. You had, for instance, to take into account that the too-clever-by-half sort of schoolmaster might send you the kind of report he thought you would like to hear. So, to take an example, if a housemaster at Eton wrote of a boy that "he is not at all a typical Etonian", it might well be a sign that you had to treat his report with considerable reserve. On the other hand you had also to take into account that some masters at smaller schools were not skilled or experienced in writing reports to tutors and might show off the boys they were recommending to considerably less than full advantage. Nor did results in A-level, or even the college scholarship exam, necessarily tell you anything like the full truth. Some schools tended to rev boys up to an artificial academic level for A-level and scholarship exams so that they had already prematurely reached their peak, and their academic future was therefore one of inevitable decline. An entrance award of course guaranteed a boy entry to the college, but it was not by any means an assurance that he was academically able. His performance in the scholarship exam might be a maximum beyond which he was unable to climb, and it was sad for him slowly to discover, as he continued to work hard, what was in fact his natural and real level. The only exception here was mathematics. The college mathematical examiners were infallible in their judgement, since mathematics seems to be a thing you either can or can't do. A mathematical examiner would often say to me: "This boy's papers are hopeless. But that is because he has obviously been badly taught. He has talent in spite of his doing so badly." And they were invariably right. In other subjects estimates were more fallible. It would sometimes happen that an examiner would guarantee a boy a place by giving him an entrance award, then a year or so later complain to me that I had admitted somebody academically worthless.

Apart from those who gained entrance awards, the decision whether or not to admit somebody to the college lay entirely with the tutor. This was both a good and a bad system. It was a good system in that it personalized a boy's relationship with the college: it was the same person, his tutor, whom he initially approached, who interviewed him, admitted him to the college, and subsequently looked after him during his college career. It was a bad system in that the members of the college staff, who would be responsible for teaching him, had no decisive say in whether or not he should be admitted. The system has now been rectified so that the members of the college staff have this decisive voice – a very much more healthy state of affairs.

At the end of each term reports on a man's work would be sent by the person teaching him to the tutor. Thus, if a man had been lazy, it was the tutor's duty to reprimand him. I remember that on one occasion when I had to do this I said to the man concerned in as severe a voice as I could muster: "I hope you'll work very much harder next term"; to which he replied: "I hope so too." It was too engaging an answer not to laugh. But then my theological studies came to my aid and I was able to explain that we can't hope for something which it is in our power to control. A more effective reproof came from an enraged parent whose son had done very badly in his first-year exams. The father telephoned me and said: "I've told him that unless next year he gets at least a high Second I shall put him in the army." The boy was so terrified by the threat that he got a First.

In general, however, the function of a tutor was to be a man's advocate, not his judge. So if a man got into a scrape it was his tutor's job to get him out of it. When a miscreant came to see me I never had the courage to say what I was longing to, a quote from *The Importance of being Earnest*: "Produce your explanation, and pray make it improbable." The vitally important thing was somehow, if you could, to convey to your pupil that, even when you ticked him off severely, you were fundamentally on his side, a feat which even God doesn't do all that well. One thing you had always to remember was that a certain type of undergraduate would show his shyness and nervousness by a silence which a fool would mistake for vacancy or sulks, while another type of undergraduate would show the same shyness and nervousness by an attempted display of social competence which a fool would mistake for conceit or arrogance.

What helped here was hospitality. This required some care, since for people to unwind you had to choose the right mix of guests and the right sort of entertainment: some people would find a dinner party relaxing while others would find it an ordeal, so that for these latter you had to think of something else, a buffet supper or something of that sort. Another important thing was consistently to smile at pupils when you met them, showing that you were glad to see them. This was not at all the trivial or governessy thing it might sound. It made undergraduates feel that you approved of them; they were too young and inexperienced to realize that when you cut people or scowl at them it generally isn't because you disapprove of or dislike them but because your income tax demand arrived that morning.

One of the touching things about undergraduates is their naïve honesty. My favourite example was a bread-and-butter letter which read: "Thank you so much for dinner last night. I should have enjoyed it immensely had I not had a bad cold." Another example was the remark of a man who had to spend five or six weeks in the mental hospital at Fulbourn. When he was better the doctors sent him to a convalescent home in Cambridge, where I continued to visit him. At that stage he said to me: "I took your book to Fulbourn and I thought it was marvellous. Now I'm better I don't think it's so good" – this, of course, without the slightest suggestion of wanting to be aggressive or rude.

But it wasn't only undergraduates who could be naïvely honest in this way. Parents could sometimes be as well. The son of a crusty old admiral went down with pneumonia, and the doctor had him transferred to the Evelyn Nursing Home. I telephoned the admiral – he lived in Scotland – and told him that the boy wasn't in any way dangerously ill but that he'd contracted pneumonia. The admiral's immediate reaction was simple and direct: "The bloody fool."

Here I would like to say that people of under-graduate age can be seriously ill mentally and then recover completely and for good. I have known several under-graduates sent to the mental hospital at Fulbourn and kept there sometimes as long as three months who have got well, taken good degrees, settled into responsible jobs, got happily married, had children, and in general been in perfect health. These people are now in the middle forties.

Cambridge is particularly lucky in the psychiatric facilities immediately available to undergraduates. A team of first-rate consultants has been built up as a branch of Addenbrooke's hospital, and a tutor can send a pupil there directly if he thinks there is need.

There were occasionally the most shattering trage-dies – motor accidents in which undergraduates were killed and, very rarely, a suicide. Perhaps the worst thing about being young is that you have no experience of disaster survived (the phrase, I believe, is E. M. Forster's) when, that is, your girl gives you up or everything at the moment is as black as pitch. I don't want to dwell on catastrophes of this sort, though their impact, naturally, was savage. But one incident I must record as it showed me most vividly how goodness will out. An undergraduate was killed in a motor accident. His friend, the driver, was drunk. The driver wasn't killed and was in hospital with only minor injuries. By chance I happened to know the family of the dead man. His father was the black sheep of the family who had gone off the rails in this and the other way and was very much in disgrace. He came immediately to Cambridge. When he arrived at my room he said: "I'm afraid I'm later than I meant to be. The hospital was further away than I thought." He saw I looked puzzled and said: "Oh, I've been to the mortuary and identified Tony's body. But I had to go and see the driver, didn't I, and do for him whatever little I could?" It brought home to me in the most moving way possible what Jesus meant when he said: "Many that are first shall be last and the last first."

Gratitude here compels me to mention the best secretary a person could ever be blessed with: Maureen Ely, now Mrs Russell. She was (and is) the only person in the world who can read my writing. She was marvellously efficient. She kept confidentiality completely. Nothing was too much trouble for her. There was a great number of my letters she could herself compose. And with her great kindness she combined the most delicious sense of humour. She knew not only what was what, but also who was what. Her remarks about the undergraduates and some of the younger Fellows are probably best not repeated here, but they were extremely funny. I once stopped dictating a letter to gaze through the window at some very glamorous-looking passers-by, and she said to me: "We shall have to buy you a telescope." I did my letters in a room immediately under the Master's study. The Butlers hadn't been in residence for more than two months when Mollie asked me: "What do you and your secretary laugh about so much every morning?" Maureen was (is) the best sort of Christian. One of a large family, she was the daughter of a Baptist minister.

17

AS DEAN OF CHAPEL I was never entirely certain what my position was in terms of ecclesiastical or canon law. But I took the not unreasonable view that I wasn't under the jurisdiction of any bishop, my Ordinary being the Master and Fellows of the college, from whom the appeal was to our Visitor, that is the Crown. Whether or not I was altogether right in regarding Trinity chapel as in some sense a Royal Peculiar, it was certainly a very convenient doctrine.

The college council gave me permission to revise the service of Holy Communion in the Book of Common Prayer. This was a number of years before the revisions, dismally known as Series One to Four, started issuing from church headquarters. I wasn't insensate enough to throw Cranmer's magnificent liturgical prose into the dustbin. I merely rearranged and added to it a little. So, for instance, I expanded the prayer of intercession to make it more comprehensive and allow opportunities for topical allusions, which I personally dislike, but which the young regard as the hallmark of sincerity. I put the Prayer of Humble Access before the Sursum Corda, and I added a short phrase to the consecration prayer: "Almighty God, our heavenly Father, who of thy tender mercy didst give thine only Son *to take our nature upon him* and to suffer death upon the Cross for our redemption." And after the words of institution I added what Cranmer had written in his first Prayer Book of 1549. I asked one of the chaplains, Hugh Dickinson, to write rubrics, explanations and devotional notes. The whole thing was then superbly set out, printed and bound by Will Carter, the craftsman printer. I think we had a hundred copies made. It survived all my time at Trinity, but was inevitably and rightly later discarded for the church's own revisions – clumsy constructions in flat, tired English made from assorted pieces of doctrinal Meccano.

Much more difficult than making slight adjustments

to Cranmer was the composition of memorial services for Fellows. It was the tradition at Trinity that these should be tailor-made. It involved searching the Scriptures with considerable ingenuity to find psalms and lessons suitable for, let us say, a Reader in Morbid Histology who happened to be an atheist. Ecclesiasticus and the Wisdom (not the Song) of Solomon were here invaluable. As the services were always printed, you could omit verses and combine them from different chapters, and the same could be done with the psalms. What you had to be careful about was not to include some dreadful *double entendre* which hinted at an uncomplimentary truth about the deceased. Then there was the proofreading, at which I'm always bad. I just spotted in time, at my third reading of the proof, that in Vaughan Williams's memorial service (he was an honorary Fellow) we were praying that he might remain in the city of God's everlasting damnation, instead of dominion.

I once spent an idle evening drawing up, while he was still very much alive, a spoof memorial service for Bertrand Russell, who was a Fellow, but during this period never visited the college. I've now forgotten a great deal of it, but I remember it included the hymn: "I vow to thee, my country, all earthly things above / Entire and whole and perfect, the service of my love." The psalm was: "The fool hath said in his heart: There is no God," and the lesson was the passage in St Mark where Jesus is told the story of the woman who had seven husbands and is asked whose wife she will be in the resurrection of the dead.

I only met Russell once. It was while I was on a visit to Trinity when a curate in London. He asked me whether Christians were required to believe in the devil. I answered that many of them would regard disbelief in him as evidence of his existence. Russell was amused at this answer. It was hard to understand the very considerable hostility with which the older Fellows regarded him. It couldn't have been his pacifism in the First World War as this was precisely the generation who, after their return from the front, insisted on his being reinstated in his college office. I suspected that it was his success with the ladies, because, of the various kinds of success, that is always the hardest to forgive.

What I'm particularly proud of is that in the memorial service for a devout Roman Catholic Fellow, the choir sang an anthem to Our Lady – the first sung in the chapel since the time of Mary Tudor, who gave it to us.

We had once to have a special service for somebody whose relatives came to discuss it with me first. "There's a special hymn we would like," they said, "which is in the Eton hymn book, but you may well not know it or be able to get hold of a copy." I asked them if they could remember the hymn's first line. "Oh yes," they said, "it's 'Praise to the Holiest in the height'."

Once a year at the Commemoration of Benefactors I had to read out in chapel the names of the major benefactors to the college and what they had given. Even at breakneck speed this took at least forty minutes. The first time I did it I made a mistake I didn't notice. The list of benefactors begins with Edward the Second. I, apparently, said Edward the Seventh, which prompted Jack Gallagher to say to me later: "After that, I thought you were going to say that the chapel was given by Lily Langtry."

Choosing preachers for Sunday evening was quite a business. The undergraduates preferred us locals because, I imagine, we knew their wavelength. As well as the chaplains, John Burnaby, and myself, it was sometimes possible to persuade a lay Fellow to preach and this was invariably very popular. One lay Fellow, who was known to be rather long-winded, once, to everybody's surprise, not to say relief, finished his sermon in just under fifteen minutes. Or so it appeared. But it was a false dawn. For after a minute of silence he said: "And now let us consider St Paul." An audible groan went round the chapel.

I invited the first woman preacher. She was Ruth Robinson (John Robinson's wife). Simpson was dreadfully perturbed at the idea. He came to my room just before Hall on the Saturday evening and asked me whether, as a woman was preaching, we might, immediately after the sermon, have the hymn: "Jesu, Lover of my soul, Let me to thy bosom fly." I had to tell him that the choir had already practised the music and no alterations were possible. In the event, Ruth preached so superb a sermon that she won everybody over to her, including Simpson himself.

Her great success encouraged me to invite another woman to preach who shall be nameless. This was a complete disaster. I told her she could be fifteen to twenty minutes. But she forgot where she was and was still holding forth after forty minutes. It was particularly unfortunate that evening, since, as used to be the custom, the Judge of Assize and the High Sheriff with their entourage were dining in Hall and had been invited to drinks at the Master's Lodge before dinner. Dinner was at eight, and I heard the college clock strike eight while the preacher was still holding forth. I had already, hoping she would see it, taken off my watch and waved it in the air, but to no effect whatever. Finally, when she paused for breath, I got up and shouted: "The service is now over and we will all leave the chapel immediately." I must say that Rab took it all with immense patience and serenity. (I thought of the black rays which would, quite justifiably, have emanated from Adrian's face and thanked my lucky stars for Rab.) As in those days women couldn't, officially at any rate, sleep in the college, the Butlers very kindly put her up in the Lodge. The following day I received a letter from Mollie Butler about something else which ended: "I thought so-and-so (the preacher) was rather a sad person. She wears men's pyjamas." It was the final exit of any woman preacher in Trinity chapel while I was Dean. Enough, as they say, is enough.

I remember two other events in chapel because of the amusement they gave me.

An undergraduate, after reading a lesson, looked very surprised at the titters which went round the building as he left the lectern. Without being aware of it, he had concluded his reading with the announcement: "Here endeth the second eleven." It showed me that cricket should always be included in any study of comparative religion.

The other event takes more explaining.

I had one summer been touring Greece with two other people, one of whom was Simon Phipps (now Bishop of Lincoln), who had recently been our chaplain but had by then left us for work in Coventry. We had spent a week on Mykonos, from which we made the usual day trip to Delos. On our return to Mykonos we stopped for a drink at a café. For about a quarter of an hour Simon was silent as he wrote something on the back of a handbill. He then read us what he had written:

> "I saw Apollo's torso
> And a portion of his *morceaux*
> Which they'd hidden most discreetly in the grass.
> But the rest was rather bitty
> As his legs are in the Pitti
> While Lord Elgin had carried off his arse."

I knew that Adrian would be amused by these verses, and so recited them to him as we were waiting in the ante-chapel together before Sunday Evensong. I had to raise my voice as the organ was playing rather loudly. Then without the slightest warning the undergraduate organist suddenly stopped playing, and in the complete silence my voice was heard right through the chapel shouting: "Lord Elgin carried off his arse," followed by Adrian's laughter. The congregation gave us some very curious looks when we eventually processed in.

Once a term the Holy Communion was followed by breakfast for everybody in Hall. On that Sunday two girls from Girton kindly came to my room so that undergraduates and Fellows with small children could deposit them there and come with their wives to the service. I was the first to return to my room afterwards and always found the children perfectly contented. Trouble, however, invariably began when the first parents to arrive took away their children, as this made those left feel abandoned. If parents gossiped with friends a bit before coming to fetch their children, the children by then would almost certainly be screaming their heads off, partly in fear and partly in anger at being forsaken by mum and dad and left waifs and strays. But they soon cheered up once the parents had arrived. The legacy these crèches left behind them in my room consisted partly of toys hidden deep in chair cushions, but much more the smell of wet nappies which continued for days, however long one opened all the windows. It amused me when subsequently visitors – say, a security man come to vet an applicant for the Foreign Office – noticed the smell. You could see he did from his embarrassment. When he then sat in a chair and felt a hard lump which turned out to be a toy horse, the scene reached the proportions of farce as he asked with a grave face: "Is so-and-so in your experience of him a trustworthy and sober person? Is his life in any way irregular?", by which time a small doll would have dropped off the sofa, and I would have begun trying to suppress giggles.

Most of the work for the chapel was done by the two chaplains, who were always highly valued members of the community, working all day and half the night getting to know undergraduates and helping them to sort out their problems. The three of us used to meet each Saturday morning in term to discuss policy and make arrangements. All the best initiatives came from the chaplains and all the most successful ideas. But in these matters they were extraordinarily self-effacing. Their deep and quite genuine modesty often made me feel the most awful fraud. Yet I was immensely grateful for their loyalty and tact. Trinity could never be the same without its chaplains.

Another solid standby was our chapel clerk, Mr Hutchinson. You could always rely on him to have everything in perfect order both for an ordinary service and any special occasion. Towards the end of my time I invited him to preach. He took as his theme Samuel's prayer: "Speak Lord, for thy servant heareth," and told us that too often our own prayers consisted of the opposite petition: "Hear Lord, for thy servant speaketh." It was a deep and notable sermon. Prince Charles, I remember, read one of the lessons.

With regard to undergraduates and their religion I think there are various mistakes which have to be avoided.

One is to allow, or even encourage, a bunch of desperately unattractive zealots to take possession of the chapel and choke everybody else off.

Another is, when a man comes to chapel, to try to rope him in for something or other. A number of people want to attend chapel without being roped in for anything.

Another is to make a man feel that you are more interested in making him religious than you are in him himself.

Another is to kick him with God when he is down.

Another is to try to persuade him not to give up religion. He may need to for the time being in order to grow.

Another is to imagine that God has only the three years of a man's university career in which to save his soul, when in fact He has all the time of eternity.

Another is to give young people the spiritual equivalent of hormone treatment (they aren't at a theological college) so that their spiritual growth is much too fast and they outgrow their strength.

Another is to imagine that one's attempt to cope with one's own insecurities is a desire to bring people to God. Pastoral lust is the most insidious form of lust because it is the one most easily disguised as virtue.

Another is to mix only with young people where, as an adult, you are always at an advantage.

Another is to confuse bringing people to chapel with bringing them to God. For a dean or chaplain a full chapel is often an ego-trip.

It belongs to students to be searchers. Their métier is

to travel hopefully, not to arrive prematurely. But that, of course, is true of all of us.

❧‖18‖❧

ABOUT THE THEOLOGICAL FERMENT in Cambridge at this time there is no need to say much, as Alec Vidler has described it better than I could in his own autobiography, *Scenes from Clerical Life*.

My particular contribution to it was not always understood. I see now that this was due chiefly to my failure to state clearly what I was trying to do, the result of course of not being entirely clear about it in my own mind. To many people I gave the impression that I was attempting to criticize the traditional dogmas of Christianity by means of what had become the traditional dogmas of Freudian psychology. It was thought that I was opposing two systems of ideas to each other and invariably claiming that the Freudian system showed that much of the Christian system was untrue. If this had indeed been my intention, then the protests against it, it is hardly necessary to say, would have been entirely justified. Christian doctrine cannot retain its integrity if it concedes to Freud an unconditional surrender as though the *Future of an Illusion* could replace the Fourth Gospel. And, almost worse, such a surrender would have shown a monstrous insensitivity to the infinite subtleties of ultimate truth, an intellectual and spiritual philistinism of the most revolting kind.

But in fact it was something different I was finding my way towards and trying to aim at. As a result of being analysed I had, to some extent at least, grown in self-awareness. I knew myself as I hadn't done before. I had begun to apprehend my own personal identity. I was disillusioned with thinking as a purely cerebral activity, a mere accumulation of ideas and a juggling with them. For such mental gymnastics had brought me nothing and nowhere. Under the intellectual veneer of traditional Catholic orthodoxy it had left me in the clutches of guilt-feelings which were pathological because unrelated to reality, and which were personified in my dream of the sadistic monster who hypnotized the actors on the stage. I had imagined that I was ransomed, healed, restored, forgiven, because Christian doctrine as intellectual theory asserted that I was. But in actual fact I was sick unto death and little more than a slave. This contrast (which I was now perceiving) between intellectual conviction on the one hand and on the other my basic orientation and fundamental commitment led me to see that Christian truth, to be really possessed, must become part and parcel of what I was. A doctrine, to be fully appropriated, had to be knit into my personal identity. I saw that I could not truly say "I believe," unless it was another way of saying "I am." And the "I" here was the total me, which included the unconscious self as well as the conscious.

This was the point I tried to put over in my contribution to *Soundings* (1962), but its impact was weakened by my attempt to be too cerebral. It came over more clearly in the open lecture I gave, "Psychological Objections to Christian Belief" (1963). Certainly the audience seemed to understand what I was affirming, and so too, after its publication, did the reviewer in *Encounter*.

But the best medium for putting the point over was the sermon. For here "I believe" as another form of "I am" could be exemplified by a particular Christian truth like the fall of man or losing your life to save it or God within who is the Holy Spirit. I saw more distinctly what I was doing and was able to articulate it with greater clarity when in 1965 I prepared an Introduction for *The True Wilderness*. I wrote:

"Although I have been psychoanalysed and have read many of the works of Freud and Jung, learning a great deal from them, I could not propagate their opinions like a new gospel based on a fundamentalist acceptance of what they wrote. What was withheld from me was the ability to transmit second-hand convictions whatever their source. All I could speak of were those things which I had proved true in my own experience by living them and thus knowing them at first hand. It may comfort some people to label this procedure existentialism. But although I have read Heidegger and Sartre, I am not aware of being one of their disciples. What I have been forced to attempt is something different – to describe only those places where I have lived and belonged."

That is also a description of anything I have subsequently written.

Because theological enquiry is conducted by human beings it is never without humorous potential. To begin with, to speak at all about God, who by definition is ineffable, has about it a kind of *Alice in Wonderland* quality which, when you stop to think what you are doing, can often seem very funny. That is why the more dogmatic a person is the funnier he can look. Yet, on the other hand, to dramatize one's speechlessness before the Almighty can also frequently be comic. Canon Charles Raven, for example, used often to speak of himself as enjoying "a timeless moment with the ineffable", and it made me wish I were a Max Beerbohm and could draw a cartoon of Raven undergoing such an experience. Perhaps the best thing in the end is to be blatantly anthropomorphic, like the Australian bishop I heard preaching in our college chapel one Trinity Sunday. He told us that the unity of the Trinity could be compared to three things: the unity of a rowing eight, the unity of a lover and his lass in the moonlight, and the inner unity of well-being which could be described as that Kruschen feeling. But no doubt Dogberry does it best, because most simply, when he says: "God's a good man." In an ideal world the rest would be silence.

Silence, however, wasn't the characteristic trait of a professor of philosophy at Cambridge who, somewhat to the sound of trumpets, became a Christian and was baptized. As a preliminary he sent a long statement of belief to the Bishop of Ely, who found it frankly unintelligible. The bishop sent the statement to a Christian philosopher, Dorothy Emmet, at that time a professor at Manchester. Rumour had it that after reading the statement Professor Emmet sent the bishop a telegram of three words: "Baptize him. Emmet." I like to think that that was true, but in any case the Cambridge professor was duly baptized. Alec Vidler, who initiated, organized and encouraged the group which subsequently produced *Soundings*, invited the Cambridge professor to one of our meetings to tell us about his becoming a Christian. The professor spoke fluently without so much as pausing for breath. At length, after about ninety minutes, one of the group interrupted him with a loud voice and asked: "Can you tell us what difference becoming a Christian has made to you?" The professor paused for less than half a minute and answered: "Well, I suppose it has made me talk less," and then continued speaking as before for about another hour. It left us wondering how many words a minute he was capable of in his pre-Christian days.

After *Soundings* had been published the group met to discuss the reviews it had been given. We spent a great deal of time going through the review in *The Times Literary Supplement*, which, according to the practice in those days, was unsigned. Such was the prestige of the paper that every point made in the review was considered with great seriousness. We were like research students poring over the examiners' report. My occasional giggle was no doubt charitably ascribed by the others to my nervous disposition. In fact it was due to my knowing who the reviewer was. He had told me at the price of swearing me to secrecy, at least for the time being. He was Hugh Dickinson, one of our two chaplains at Trinity, who, intelligent though he was, was hardly a theological heavyweight compared with people like John Burnaby, George Woods and Alec Vidler himself. I have now divulged the secret because by this time it can have no interest at all for anybody, apart from the humorous situation it engendered.

When Alec Vidler left Cambridge, Dennis Nineham, then Regius Professor of Divinity, organized a similar group, but included in it representatives of some other disciplines – a lawyer, a professor of English (L. C. Knights), a philosopher of science, an historian, and a psychoanalyst and lecturer in psychology. Our concern was hermeneutics – how to interpret Christian doctrine and what it could mean for people living in the contemporary world. I think I learnt more at these seminars than I have anywhere else. Dennis Nineham's questions were, as always, extremely penetrating, and their power to stimulate came from the obvious fact that he was himself very much a seeker and would be content with nothing less than the truth. He was never comforted by the comforting half-truths made possible by applying a telescope to your blind eye. One of the group was Maurice Wiles. He belonged at this time very much to the traditional orthodox persuasion, and I thought of him as little more than an immensely learned expounder of patristic thought. When, therefore, he left for a chair in London (before becoming Regius Professor at Oxford) I was surprised to receive from him a most generous letter thanking me for making him think again about this and that. Gratitude here compels me to mention how much I learnt from L. C. Knights. He showed me that the critical study and appreciation of literature is one of the best – probably one of the indispensable – partners of theology. I remember particularly his indignation when somebody repeated a customary peice of theological cant: "But King Lear never existed." "Never existed?" he answered; "What about me? And you? And all of us?" That statement taught me more than I had ever learnt about Jesus Christ and the historical obscurity in which he must always remain hidden. "Jesus Christ the same yesterday, today, and for ever." Was that statement true the day he was born? What L. C. Knights said about King Lear suggested that it was.

I cannot omit to mention (since they belong to this period) the four lectures published as *Objections to Christian*

Belief (I contributed psychological objections). The lectures were of a routine kind in the sense that every Lent term the Faculty Board of Divinity laid on a series of open lectures for anybody interested. They were held that year in the old Examination Schools (now pulled down). Each time the place was packed out. It wasn't a case of standing room only. From five minutes before the lectures were due to begin there wasn't even standing room. The first lecture on Moral Objections was given by Donald Mackinnon. None of us had anticipated that there would be such a crush, and, although I arrived to hear Mackinnon some eight or nine minutes before the starting time, I was hardly able to get in. In the end by dint of pushing and shoving I was able to squeeze myself between a wall and a girl from Girton. She managed somehow, by holding her arms high, to find room for a notebook and pen, and stood poised to take down what Mackinnon had to tell us. But the lecture began and she wrote nothing. Then, after Mackinnon had been prophesying for some forty minutes, she wrote something down very briefly, and afterwards wrote nothing more. This made me curious to know what she had thought worth recording. At the end of the lecture I was able for a moment to see. The blank page of her notebook contained one word: contraception. I found this amusing and also very touching. What particular personal issue was it, I wondered, that she was concerned with and how did she resolve it?

❧❧❧ 19 ❧❧❧

IT WAS DURING this time (in 1965 to be precise) that Rab Butler was appointed Master of Trinity in succession to Lord Adrian.

Rab Butler's first wife, Sydney, and Mollie Courtauld's first husband, Augustine, had both died, and Rab and Mollie were married in 1959. Mollie's eldest son, Christopher, was a pupil of mine at Trinity, and in the summer of 1958 he kindly drove me over to Spencers in

Essex to dine with his mother and to meet his father, who, although obviously in the final stages of illness, generously saw me for a few minutes and welcomed me to his home. We were a largish number at dinner and the party included Rab, who was then Home Secretary. I remember that after dinner the gentlemen strolled for a few minutes in the garden before rejoining the ladies. As we were all relieving nature I suddenly saw an extremely sinister-looking man (or so it seemed to me) staring at us over the hedge. I thought I had better draw Rab's attention to him. Rab laughed and said: "Don't worry. That's my detective." It was the first of my few fleeting contacts with the big world.

In 1963 Chris Courtauld came back to Trinity as one of our chaplains. At the time (he was a curate in Oldham) he had been offered another interesting job, and I was afraid he would accept it instead of coming to us. But in the end we were lucky. Comparisons (Dogberry again I think) are odorous, but I can at least say that in my experience from 1938 to 1968 Trinity never had a better chaplain than Chris. When he was moving in I went round to his rooms to see how he was getting on and found Mollie, with carpet sweeper in hand, making an attack on the sitting-room floor. She looked so devoted to her work that I thought it best to disappear with reasonable speed.

Two years later I was dining with friends in London one evening, and we turned on the television news. A picture of Trinity Great Gate appeared on the screen. I couldn't imagine what it was about as I had left Cambridge only after lunch that day. It turned out to be the announcement of Rab's appointment as Master. I got back to Trinity round about one and found the lights in Raymond Leppard's rooms, above mine, still on. I went up immediately to see him. He had recently got to know an old lady who had only two reactions to everything. She always said either "Such fun," or "So sad," whichever she considered more suitable to the occasion. Raymond could imitate her perfectly. "You've heard the news?" I asked him somewhat breathlessly. He put on the old lady's face and kept me in suspense. Eventually he said: "Such fun," and we both laughed.

Nobody in the college had the slightest inkling of the appointment until it was announced that Sunday. Rab later told me that Harold Wilson had appointed him against the advice of his patronage secretary. "Rab's going to Trinity," he said bluntly. For that at least he deserves our unqualified gratitude.

The next morning Chris Courtauld came round to my room and, very characteristically, offered to resign. He said he thought it might be awkward for a chaplain's mother and stepfather to be in the Master's Lodge. I hadn't myself thought of that at all, but it occurred to me that Chris might possibly have his own reasons for wanting in the circumstances to leave. It soon became clear to me that (as I should have known) he wasn't thinking at all of himself, but of the college. I said that I thought that, far from being awkward, his being the Master's step-son would be a help in his work and that, much more important, it would add considerably to the gaiety of nations. It was a great relief when he said he would stay on.

If you have never before known a distinguished political leader and public figure, you can't help looking at him with considerable curiosity. On his arrival in your midst you examine him as a zoologist examines a member of a rare and little known species. His belonging to a much larger world than your own can even be felt as a bit of a threat. At the very least it challenges the assumption that the scene to which you yourself belong is superior to all others. It makes you feel less smug than you did. And in reaction you may defend yourself by stressing that you are as good as the newly arrived celebrity, and indeed, according to any proper scale of values, much better.

Feelings of that kind were not altogether absent among a few of the Fellows, not to mention their wives, when Rab first arrived at Trinity. Some of them tended to regard him as members of the Chinese Celestial Court in the early nineteenth century regarded the silly ridiculous man who claimed to come from a place called Europe. It was an attitude which Rab soon dispelled by his friendliness and the total absence of any kind of ostentation. And, of course, he very quickly learnt the ropes. But he didn't by any means always let on that he had. Playing the incompetent appealed to his sense of humour, and the unperceptive were often taken in. When the drawing-room of the Lodge was full of Fellows and their guests, he would sometimes sit in a chair by himself looking extremely comatose. "Poor thing," some people would say either in irritation or sympathy, "he's past it." In fact he was taking in everything and everybody and not missing a single trick.

What I found most intriguing about him was his immense subtlety of mind and manoeuvre. He never wore his policies on his sleeve. If sometimes he appeared to, it was only to draw you out so as to enlarge his knowledge of college opinion. He was a democrat to his fingertips in the sense that on any issue he took as many soundings as possible and then advocated the line most likely to succeed because he knew it had the most popular support. That is how he practised the art of the possible. It meant that he was never defeated. But this wasn't a matter of personal vanity as though he were engaged in a continuous and successful attempt to save his own skin. It was how he thought things ought to be managed. It was an exercise in politics as he considered they should be. One of his political heroes was Stanley Baldwin. Even on the miniature stage of college affairs it was easy to see how he was Baldwin's disciple. His aim was not to lead crusades, but to maintain and increase harmony. He was, I think, haunted by the knowledge that a house divided against itself cannot stand. (Hence his pursuit as a Tory minister of consensus politics – what journalists christened Butskellism.) Not that Trinity was a house divided. Far from it. But Rab saw that an existing harmony couldn't be maintained by its own momentum. It had, all the time, to be kept in repair.

It goes without saying that he was a superb chairman. He showed me what an extremely skilled craft chairmanship is. Under him the college council got through its business much more briskly than before. Yet there was never any sense of hurry. Everybody was given ample opportunity to state his views. At times there was a certain poignancy in Rab's being chairman: when, for instance, an endless description was being given of handbasins which were about to be fitted into certain rooms. Was it for this, I used to think, that he had once been responsible for the fate of nations? Yet the only sign of impatience he ever showed was to clip his nails. Once, just before a council meeting began, he looked at the metal inkpot in front of him and said: "What we need is a large inkpot made of ala*bas*ter" (pronouncing "-bas-" to rhyme with "ass"). Few people noticed the remark. He was, I imagine, thinking of Lord Curzon.

One of the areas where Rab's skill as a statesman was most useful was in his dealing with undergraduate agitators. He was always ready to see them. And, far from giving them the impression that they were a nuisance, he made them feel that their complaints were a valuable contribution to the life of the college and that he was grateful for the opportunity given him of fitting their complaints into the comprehensive picture of college problems as a whole. The undergraduates concerned were invariably disarmed by the courtesy and seriousness with which Rab listened to what they had to say. They were flattered by his appearing to need their help in seeing how the redress of their grievances could be grafted on to the general setup of the place, and went away happy and reconciled when in fact nothing at all had been either done or promised.

In the second half of the 1960s there was in Cambridge a wave of undergraduate unrest from which Trinity wasn't and couldn't be immune. Rab called a general meeting one evening in Hall which could be attended by any Trinity undergraduate. The hall was packed tight. On the dais sat Rab accompanied by twenty to twenty-five Fellows. Rab looked as calm and unperturbed as though he were presiding over a routine board meeting of Barclay's Bank. The rest of us were feeling extremely apprehensive. Was the calling of this open meeting a wise move? Wouldn't it end in catastrophe? We showed our jitters by nervously tapping our feet while some of us looked slightly seasick. I can't remember in any detail the actual motions proposed, but I do vividly remember the gist of them and I shall describe it by way of slight caricature. With an absolutely poker-face Rab opened the meeting by saying: "I believe Mr Smith has a motion to propose." An undergraduate then raised his hand and said: "Yes. I wish to propose that the college be burnt down." Rab: "Mr Smith proposes that the college be burnt down. Will anybody second that motion?" Another undergraduate put up his hand – "Yes. I second it." Rab: "Mr Jones seconds the motion. We shall now put it to the vote. Mr Smith proposes and Mr Jones seconds that the college be burnt down. Those in favour please raise their hands." A gallant but rather small number of hands went up. "Will those against please raise their hands?" A whole army of hands went up. Rab (still absolutely poker-faced): "The motion is lost." And so it went on for the entire evening. Every revolutionary proposal was voted down, Rab looking all the time as if the undergraduates were deciding whether they wanted tea or coffee for breakfast. It was a masterpiece of management.

Rab's sense of humour could be as subtle as his diplomacy. But you had to know him well to understand what he was up to. I once attended Sunday lunch at the Lodge when the Bruces (Bruce was then American ambassador in London) were there. We were drinking port after the ladies had left the table when Bruce, in order to make conversation, said how odd it was that pub port made you ill while vintage port didn't. "You would have thought," he added, "that it would be the other way round. After all vintage port is very much richer than pub port." The remark was in the form of a question. Rab considered it for a moment and then gave it a perfect parliamentary answer in the sense that what he said gave nothing whatever away. "There is no doubt," he replied, "that there is a great difference between pub port and vintage port." Sometimes there was a mischievous flavour to his humour. At dinner at the Lodge I was once sitting next to a woman who was herself sitting next to Rab. She was excruciatingly boring as only conceited people can be, and like all conceited and boring people she was totally unclued up. "How many children have you?" she asked Rab. With the faintest suggestion of a smile he answered: "Well, between us we have ten." For once the woman looked puzzled and nonplussed. I didn't think it was for me to spoil the fun by explaining the situation. On one occasion my somewhat pseudo-interest in a painting of a sea coast in the small drawing-room in the Lodge drew from Rab a chuckle with the words: "It's a Crome. We remember that by saying it's a view of Cromer."

But my favourite memory of Rab as Master is something which he wouldn't have remembered. It was his spontaneous reaction to the Passion story in St John's Gospel, which, with intervals of appropriate music, was read as a whole on the last Sunday of his first Lent term. As we came out of chapel he said to me with an obvious lump in his throat: "Terribly sad story that." After having had to fill my head with what Westcott, Loisy, Hoskyns, Dodd and Bultmann had written about the Fourth Gospel it was refreshing and moving to hear Rab's immediate, instinctive reaction to it.

So far I have spoken only of Rab himself, but the half and more has not yet been told. For I have said nothing about Mollie, and for many of us during that time Mollie practically was Trinity.

Not that she interfered in the slightest with college business. But she took a tremendous interest in everybody and everything and made us all feel that we were important and interesting and lovable, dons and undergraduates alike.

She had the *savoir-faire* of an experienced London hostess. But that in itself wasn't the secret of her magic. The secret was her dedication. She never once spoke about it. In fact she was herself probably unaware of it. But to those with eyes to see it was obvious that she used her social expertise as the practical expression of her Christian faith. She wanted her guests to feel at home and enjoy themselves because that was her way of loving her neighbour, though I think she would have laughed if anybody had told her so. She was tireless in her efforts to entertain people, thinking out ways of doing so like musical evenings or a quiet lunch for an elderly don where he was the only guest. She spent every ounce of energy she had. But you would never have guessed it. Her entertaining seemed quite effortless. Rab used sometimes to complain in the half-serious half-comic manner which was a speciality of his. "Mollie does far too much," he would say as we waited in the ante-chapel for Sunday evensong to begin. "We had fifteen undergraduates to lunch today, and quite frankly I've told her it's ridiculous. It's too exhausting. She will have to stop it." His grumbling had a sort of counterpoint to it which conveyed that he was very proud of her, though clearly he knew what all this self-giving cost her.

Eloquence is hardly a characteristic anybody would have ascribed to a very shy and dull young man from a neighbouring town who was staying with us here at Mirfield a few years ago and helped me one day to wash up lunch. Yet he gave to Mollie one of the most eloquent testimonials I have heard because it was so entirely natural and spontaneous. I discovered that he was a third-year Trinity undergraduate. He was obviously unaware that I knew the Butlers. Eventually through the hissing and groaning of the washing-up machine I was able through the steam to get him talking. After a bit he said: "Lady Butler is a wonderful person." "Oh," I answered somewhat curtly, "why?" "Well," he said, "I went to a party at the Master's Lodge my first year. Then last term I went again. And, do you know, Lady Butler remembered that I was reading physics and chemistry?" Naturally he had no notion of the careful work which lay behind that knowledge. Nor was he meant to. And it must be seen in the context of the numbers at Trinity. With Fellows, research students and undergraduates it topped a thousand, and most of these moved on after three years and were succeeded by others.

There is a great deal more I would like to say in praise of Rab and Mollie. But I don't want to abuse their admitting me into the intimacy of their family circle by recounting what might be embarrassing. But there is one incident I can tell because it occurred in public and was so thoroughly characteristic of the Rab–Mollie partnership. After a dinner party one evening Rab was sitting on a sofa in the drawing-room next to a female don. Neither of them was speaking. Seeing their silence, Mollie crept up behind the sofa and whispered in Rab's ear: "Speak to her, darling." "She won't speak to me," answered Rab. "Try harder, darling, try harder," Mollie replied. What the consequence was I can't say since I had to move to another part of the room for fear that the cause of my laughter would be too obvious.

20

OTHER PEOPLE'S HOLIDAYS are boring even without home movies. But at this time the holidays I was able to take contributed a great deal to the richness of life, and therefore I can't pass over them completely in silence.

I used to travel abroad in the Easter vacation and also again in the summer. What made these holidays special were the kindred spirits with whom I was lucky enough to travel. There were fourteen of us in all, but we never travelled all fourteen together. Three or four people within the group would arrange a particular holiday as they were able to get away. What made the fourteen of us aware of our solidarity was the name given us by Osbert Lancaster. He came across a group of us on two occasions, both times unexpectedly – once on a Greek island, where he arrived in a yacht (we had come by steamer a week before), and once

– it wasn't the same group – turning a corner among the royal tombs at the Escorial. Perhaps it was the ecclesiastical atmosphere of Philip II's prison palace which led Osbert there and then to baptize us as the Church of England Ramblers Association. The name stuck, and it was to the Ramblers that I dedicated *True Resurrection*. Some readers of the book imagined that the name Church of England Ramblers was to be interpreted allegorically, and wrote to tell me that they too were only spiritual ramblers and so on. It was a reasonable inference. But it is universally true that anybody not in the know because not in the club is good for a laugh.

In 1962 (before the Jewish war) four of the Ramblers went to Israel and then on to Jordan. On the hills above Nablus we witnessed the slaying of the Passover lambs by the Samaritans. It was more gruesome than we imagined it would be seeing these vivacious young animals having their throats slit as their killers furiously chanted some religious dirge. ("Little lamb who made thee? Dost thou know who made thee?" became at the time the cruellest of satires.) The Samaritan High Priest had previously tried to sell us a scroll of the Pentateuch he claimed to have been written by Moses himself, declaring it to be "the oldest book in the world".

One day we drove from what was then Jordanian Jerusalem to Bethlehem. After a visit to the church of the Nativity we were driven to some fields nearby and it was clear that our guide expected us to get out of the car. We wondered what he was going to show us. He beckoned us to stand together, and in his very slow drawling English began to tell us the purpose of our visit: "The night that Christ was born there were shepherds" – but he got no further. Mervyn Stockwood cut him short by saying hurriedly but very firmly, if not indeed with a slight note of exasperation: "Yes, yes, we know that." So we all immediately got back again into the car and drove off.

In Israeli Jerusalem we were most generously entertained. Among others we met a state official who was responsible for the welfare of visiting ecclesiastical dignitaries. He was a man of some humour who obviously found considerable amusement in the various ecclesiastical quirks of his charges. "Earlier this week," he told us, "I was very worried by the arrival here of an Eastern Orthodox potentate, because at this holy time of year he was not allowed to eat meat, fish, eggs or cheese. But in the end I solved the problem by having some asparagus flown here for him from Rhodesia."

I wasn't disillusioned by the holy places. The gospels had led me to expect that each would be a den of thieves. Their commercialization, therefore, far from being a shock, seemed to link them in unbroken continuity to the days of Jesus. But the hills and lake of Galilee were, in those days at least, entirely unspoilt. Mervyn celebrated the Holy Communion on the shore of the lake with a picnic table as an altar. That, I think, was for us all the supreme moment of our tour, because it was there that we were most conscious of standing on holy ground.

People renewed, as we were after that simple service of Holy Communion, are people most ready to laugh. On our drive back to Jerusalem we became immensely hilarious as a result of an item of news we heard on our car radio. "The Bishop of Southwark," it was announced, "is now touring Israel with Lady Elizabeth Cavendish, his lady-in-waiting." Elizabeth is a lady-in-waiting to Princess Margaret, and the Israeli newscasters had somehow got their facts slightly muddled.

There are some other incidents on the Ramblers' travels which are worth recording.

Four of us were touring Spain one summer. We didn't reserve rooms at Salamanca, as we remembered from previous years that there was a big hotel there in which rooms were invariably available. What we didn't know was that our arrival coincided with the town's annual fiesta, with the result that all the rooms in the hotel were booked. It was too late to drive another five or six hours in the dark to the next town, so the four of us, Graham Storey,

Elizabeth Cavendish, Simon Phipps and myself, stood in the square outside the hotel looking as if we had just been condemned to a painful death. Then relief arrived in the form of cards handed to us by a youth advertising what called itself the Hospederia Oxford. The name was encouraging. The youth offered to lead us there. And we gratefully followed. The place certainly looked a bit dirty, but at least there were four rooms. So we thankfully booked in, and then went out for the rest of the evening. On our return about 1 a.m. the Hospederia Oxford was obviously quite busy. We went to our rooms, but none of us slept much as there was continuous noise the entire night – voices and footsteps both sounding rather furtive, constant movement up and down the passages, and doors opening and shutting with considerable frequency. Comparing notes the next morning we discovered that it had soon become clear to each of us that the Hospederia Oxford (why Oxford we never learnt) was a knocking shop. No matter. It was giving us shelter for the night and, like King Edward VII, none of us wished to be an arbiter of morals, especially abroad. The next morning, however, the madame presented us with a bill in which we were charged five times the amount charged at the big hotel. At this we protested, but the madame was firm. That was the usual price. Indeed she had made a reduction as we had come in a group of four. But why, we asked, were her prices so very much higher than those at the big hotel? With a combination of pity and the strongest possible moral indignation the madame explained that the service at the Hospederia Oxford was infinitely better than that at the big hotel. It was difficult to know what to answer, but we were determined not to pay prices higher than those at the Ritz Hotel in Madrid. Eventually we threatened to take our grievance to the Spanish tourist office in Salamanca. At that the madame changed her tactics. She ceased to be indignant and affected instead a pose of injured nobility, very much the great lady whose obligation it was to remind the riff-raff of their moral duty. "You must pay me," she said, "what your conscience dictates." By this time we were so cowed that we paid her what we would have paid for one of the best rooms at the big hotel. Clearly she had won. "At least," said Simon, "it wasn't the Hospederia Cambridge."

After I had joined the Community at Mirfield another Rambler, Simon Stuart, was generously my host (as he has been many times since) in a tour of the Pyrenees. In the course of our travels we stayed for a night or two at the French town of La Preste, and decided to go straight from there to Barcelona. At this point, for reasons which I needn't describe, we were reduced to only one car. So it was decided that Simon Stuart and I should drive to Barcelona, taking everybody's luggage with us, while the rest of the party went by train. When Simon and I arrived at the Spanish frontier something happened which our limited imaginations had entirely failed to anticipate. As a matter of routine the two customs officials asked us to open the boot and pointed, without interest, to a suitcase which they asked us to open. It turned out to belong to Elizabeth Cavendish, and contained, naturally enough, brassières, panties, dresses and an outfit of cosmetics. The two customs officials gave us both severely old-fashioned looks and called over two policemen to examine the haberdashery. It was in vain that after a few minutes we collected our wits and explained that the suitcase belonged to a friend. Did we think they were going to be taken in by that tale? It looked for a time as if they would forbid us entry into Spain. At last they allowed us to continue our journey, but not before they had put on a show half of resignation and half of disgust. "It only remains," I said to Simon, "for me to tell them that I'm a monk." But we thought it wiser not to.

One of the Ramblers was John Betjeman. The marvellous thing about travelling with him is that, without being in the slightest degree didactic, he enables you to see with his eyes a building which at first sight looked very ordinary. They were never the buildings given a star by Baedeker, but those whose architectural glories were hidden until he almost miraculously revealed them.

Walking with him down a street in a small unknown town was a voyage of discovery as he shared with you his own delight with a terrace of houses or a display of ceramic decoration on the walls of a town hall. He also had an infallible nose for outstandingly good but extremely dim-looking restaurants, whether at St Jean de Luz, León or Palermo. In one of the restaurants he discovered in a town in Calabria the padrone was so pleased at our obvious appreciation of his food that he brought John a book to sign. John wrote not his name but that we were members of the Church of England Ramblers Association. The padrone took the book to the local lawyer, who was lunching at a table near to ours, hoping he would be able to decipher it. There was much mystification and shaking of heads and arguments, and we left before the riddle had been solved. Presumably it never was.

Travelling by car in Italy John had an unfailing recipe for dealing with things like punctures. Seeing our distress a car would stop and its occupants get out and come over to us. John would then say in the charmingly persuasive and ingratiating voice which none of the rest of us could imitate: "Siamo Inglese, molto stupidi. Tutti Italiani intelligenti." This was invariably greeted with loud protests of "No, no, *Inglese* intelligenti," and before we knew where we were they had changed the wheel for us.

The Ramblers travelled in Scandinavia, Turkey, Iran and Morocco, but this isn't a travel book and to describe these journeys wouldn't further its general purpose. In any case others have described much better than I could the journey, for instance, from Marrakesh over the Atlas mountains to Taroudant and so to the Barbary Coast, or the mosques at Bursa, the Ottoman capital before the capture of Constantinople, which are a surprise because their architecture is uninfluenced by Santa Sophia.

But I must mention the storytellers to be found each day in the Jael Fnar (the great square) in Marrakesh. The storyteller would be squatting on the ground forming a circle with his listeners – a group of thirty to forty men with a few boys. What was remarkable was the complete and absolute attention paid to the storyteller by his audience. Their eyes were glued on him, popping out of their heads. Sometimes they would jump with fright, or look agonizingly anxious, or show signs of relief, or burst out laughing. They were all miles from the Jael Fnar, totally caught up and overwhelmed by what they were listening to. It was frustrating knowing no Arabic and not being able to follow the story, but it was fascinating to realize that it was precisely in this way that the stories in our Old Testament were first told, handed on, and gradually beaten into the shape in which we have them on the printed page. It was thus that Rebecca was first brought as his bride to Isaac, and Esau was cheated out of his inheritance by Jacob, and Balaam's ass was goaded by his master's obtuseness into human speech. One was transported back three thousand years, and it made one hope that in Marrakesh the cinema and television would not soon triumph and spoil it all.

And I cannot end this chapter without singing at least one or two songs of Araby and tales of old Tangier – that is, Tangier before the package tours had arrived and it was still an international zone with every small consulate dignified with the title of a Legation.

In the mosque in the Kasbah there was perpetual intercession. News of people needing prayer (those, for instance, involved in motor accidents) was brought in from time to time. One evening I was allowed to enter the mosque and was struck at once by its atmosphere of prayer. That in itself was hardly odd, but it reminded me of somewhere else and I couldn't, to begin with, remember where. Then it occurred to me that it was of course the Sacré Coeur in Paris, where there is also perpetual intercession. As nothing else could, it demonstrated to me how prayer transcends religious boundaries, and if prayer, then the God to whom it is addressed.

And so does human kindness and love, and the God who in all places is their source.

An Englishman in his late sixties lived in the Arab quarter of the town in a small room with a mud floor. Years before he had taken up with and adopted an Arab boy, and when the boy was the right age had had him trained as a carpenter. The Englishman had since lost most of his money. The Arab boy was now nearly forty, married with five children. As a carpenter he earned a reasonable income, and was now keeping the old Englishman and looking after him, giving him the best room in the house. We called one morning and it was obvious how fond and proud the Arab was of his former protector. He brought in mint tea and cakes for our refreshment, going about the business with the unobtrusive skill only found in servants who love and respect their masters. And the Englishman, on his side, radiated happiness. After a bit he confided in us, chuckling like a schoolboy. "Do you know," he said, "that twenty years ago Ahmed and I had VD together?" It was clap and soon cured. There in that Arab house there was no mistaking the goodness of God, whatever verdict upon it would have been passed by the suburban Jehovah.

Social barriers were less divisive in Tangier than in many other places. A young Moroccan – he was in his early twenties and spoke French – who was head waiter at the most popular restaurant in the town used often to come up to our house for a drink and a chat after his day's work was done. He was very proud of the small Volkswagen he had saved up enough money to buy and always kept it in mint condition, regarding it more as a trinket than as something useful. He spoke a great deal of the frustration he felt at the small town life he had been compelled so far to live, and longed to emigrate to London. (Some years later he did.) He was an interesting combination of shrewdness and naïvety, and was able to be open and friendly as those people are whose dreams may yet come true. I once gave him a holiday shirt of mine which he had much admired. Next time I went to the restaurant I found that he had managed to combine wearing it with his waiter's uniform. He kept the neck wide open so that the label was clearly visible:

Arthur Shepherd, Cambridge (and then in Indian ink), H. A. Williams. As well as being very pleased, my reaction to this was a royal one – *Honi soit qui mal y pense.*

It wasn't in fact very relevant, since the last thing which could be said about members of the English colony in those days was that they were at all censorious. They had no need of those fantasies about other people's lives with which pharisees the world over compensate themselves for the brittle emptiness of their own. Indeed the English colony as a whole had about it an unmistakable air of *quia multum amavit.* It was their total freedom from moral and spiritual pretensions which reminded me of the publicans and sinners whom Jesus loved. And if his words can be trusted (perhaps we can't trust them) these people would enter the kingdom of God before many pious churchmen. For these latter, whatever their liturgical protestations, often consider themselves fundamentally meritorious, while the English Tangerines knew *ex animo* that they weren't. Yet they looked after each other with great kindness and generosity, and they were certainly given to hospitality as we were grateful to discover.

One of them, taking us up to the flat roof of his house, was describing to us in what direction Gibraltar lay. He pointed with his hand across the beach and out to sea. "You see that buoy?" he asked, and to make his meaning perfectly clear he spelt the word for us: "b-*u*-o-y". Only a Tangerine would have done that.

PART FOUR

Puzzled
Pilgrim

PLATO, I think, was right in his suspicion of the arts. They distort life by simplifying its immense complexity. Perhaps novelists of the highest calibre are able to some extent to avoid this trap. But most writers impose a consistency upon the raw materials of human existence, which conceals how mixed up and contradictory those raw materials invariably are. This, I believe, is particularly true when somebody is writing his autobiography. He has to marshal his life and feelings into an artificial symmetry, abstracting and emphasizing some things while ignoring others. For if, with his limited talent, he tries to tell too much at the same time his narrative becomes not merely clumsy but unintelligible.

Yet as he reads through what he has written he becomes more and more dissatisfied with it as it becomes increasingly clear to him that less than half the tale has been told.

What, then, can he do?

The least he can do is to change his glasses and look at what he has been describing through a different pair. In other words, he can examine levels of his life less obvious but maybe more important than those with which he was formerly concerned. And thus, perhaps, he can suggest that living is not the tidy business he has represented it as being, but consists of the continual building up of adjustments and the continual undermining of them as the various forces within him struggle for recognition and dominance; and that, further, an adjustment can both be built up and undermined simultaneously. Hence the disorderliness of life as lived, with many more than two ignorant armies clashing by night.

I have described the happiness of my last twelve years at Cambridge. It was certainly quite genuine. I was a slave who had been set free, a sick man who had been made whole. I was glad to be alive and immensely grateful not only for the good things which came my way, but, even more, for my ability to receive them with thanksgiving. I had been given the garment of praise for the spirit of heaviness.

Or had I?

For mixed up with my happiness were contrary feelings at war with it. As far as I know, these had little or nothing to do with my former persecuting moralism. For the savage hypnotist, that old deceiver, had by this time been robbed of most of his power. What was now emerging within me was more like a sense of emptiness, an ultimate dissatisfaction. It was as if an important part of me was uninhabited. I had taken possession of my house, but had so far failed to live in some of its main rooms.

At first it seemed stupid to pay any attention to feelings of this kind. I had so much to enjoy; why allow introspection to spoil it? After all, a sure recipe for gloom is to sit down and think about yourself. Wasn't the wisest thing to ignore the emptiness and get on with living? Shouldn't common sense be given its due?

That, for a time, was possible. For the emptiness as yet was nothing sharp or immediate. It was only a dull ache in the background. But it didn't go away. On the contrary, it forced itself forward. The more I ignored it the more it demanded my attention. In the end its persistence forced me to reckon with it. What, I had to ask myself, did the emptiness spring from? What caused it? There was, I discovered, no single answer.

2

ITS MOST OBVIOUS CAUSE was humiliating because it consisted of failing where most people succeed. I longed desperately to share my life with another human person, which for me had to mean another man. I had (as I've described) a number of intimate and affectionate friends, and between us there was much giving and receiving on every level, including the physical. For this I continued from my heart to thank God. I was accepted, body and all. The thing that was missing was the single unique relationship with another, and my inability to form or maintain such a relationship was something I had to acknowledge to myself. I had failed in one of the primary challenges of life. Maybe I began too late. I was nearer forty than thirty by the time I had finally rejected the conventional and ecclesiastical estimate of homosexuality (I was nearer fifty when homosexual acts ceased to be a criminal offence). It is difficult in middle age to begin a race which most people begin when they are eighteen or twenty, especially when society at large is often hostile, or, at best, certainly gives no help.

But *qui s'excuse s'accuse*. I had failed in the task (sometimes it seemed more like the necessity) of sharing my life deeply and comprehensively with one other individual. The resultant loneliness became increasingly difficult to bear because of its obvious finality. There was nobody, when I returned to base, to ask how this or the other enterprise had gone. When I got back to my rooms they were in exactly the same condition as when I left them – the same newspaper at exactly the same angle, the same chair-cushion dented in exactly the same way. That is all right as a temporary arrangement which is to last until ... but for me it was until I died. Days and weeks and years would have to be spent fundamentally alone. It began to give me a grudge against life. I saw myself becoming querulous and disagreeable, set to destroy affection by insisting on it, and taking too much to the bottle.

Clearly this sort of emptiness was intolerable. I had to do something about it. But what, for Christ's sake?

I envied those who could find solace by immersing themselves in a homosexual ghetto. But the gay party or pub had no attraction for me. Many people find there at least a certain degree of authentic contact and communion. But I couldn't. I was temperamentally disbarred and made to feel lonelier than ever so that I became irritated and angry. But at least I didn't deceive myself into thinking that the anger at my disability was a form of moral indignation. In the out-goingness of people to each other and the genuine exchange thereby brought about I was aware of God's goodness. But it wasn't for me. I had to return to my record-player and my brandy, an unwilling prisoner of respectability.

It must look as if I was fool enough to imagine that marriage *per se* was always wonderfully fulfilling. I was, however, aware that there was no need to look very far to find evidence to the contrary. There were, I knew, marriages where nothing remained but the bare bones of the legal institution, with husbands and wives feeling as alone as I did. But in my experience these were in the minority. A married couple might for years look as if they gave very little to each other. But when one of them died the other's sense of grievous loss showed how much it had in fact been. For what is involved here is not only love but belonging. We all need, it seems, to belong to somebody, even if it brings its own pains and penalties with it. To belong to nobody is to be dispossessed. "It is not good that the man should be alone."

But, I was shown, there are degrees of dispossession.

At this time Frances Cornford was living in Cambridge. As you would expect from her poetry she was a woman of great charm and warmth and sensibility. She told me (she was a widow) how immensely happy her marriage had been and how she and her husband had complemented each other. She went on thinking out loud about him. It was obvious how fond of each other they had been. Then she added: "He always felt most dreadfully alone." I didn't take much notice of this at the time. But her remark stuck with me, and in due course it began to grow in my mind like a plant. Could it be that the dispossession of which I felt myself the victim had to it more than the inability to belong to somebody? Had it also a larger dimension? The plant continued to grow.

A few months later I remembered something which

had happened to me years before when I was a curate in London. It was a winter's day and show had fallen. Fuel was scarce (it was soon after the end of the war) and I thought I would warm myself up by going for a walk. So I made for Regent's Park. It was about teatime and the sun was just beginning to set. There was in the air the unaccustomed stillness which snow brings. The park was looking supremely beautiful. The trees with their leafless branches thinly covered with snow looked like the ethereal guardians of some sublime secret. The grass was white with patches of green here and there as though it rejoiced in the snow without being overwhelmed by it. The shrubs were bursting through their white covering as if delightedly playing a game. And the sun – a combination now of gold and red – suffused the air and gave its colour to everything. It was impossible to conceive of anything more glorious than what lay around me. It was overpowering without losing any of its gentleness. It was blessedness and love.

Or it should have been. But it wasn't.

For it aroused in me a sharp sense of anguish as if sentence of death had been passed on me, reducing me to despair. I wanted to enter the glory around and become part of it, to become the beauty I saw so that I could share its bliss. I wanted that winter scene in Regent's Park to take me to itself and cover me with its identity. But that was impossible. Between me and what I saw there was a great gulf fixed so that it couldn't pass to me or I to it. I was, I felt, permanently excluded from its surpassing loveliness. I could never become what I saw. I must remain a stranger to it, an outsider. It was as if I was both in Eden and also exiled from it, and the exile was much the more bitter by reason of its ambience. To see and not be able to enter, to behold without being able to become, makes a man feel a thousand times more isolated than he was before. And so I felt as I walked home that day from Regent's Park.

I now remembered the experience as a possible clue to the emptiness I felt growing within me, the dispossession. Had it some sort of cosmic context? Should I ever come to grips with it if I restricted my attention exclusively to my failure to find a partner?

The question came back at me now and again because I sometimes had an experience the exact opposite of the one I had that day in Regent's Park. It was never so strong or sharp, but it happened more than once.

Bathing in the sea, especially in the blue sunlit waters of the Mediterranean (as yet unpolluted), tended to dissipate my sense of exclusion and make me feel I belonged to the element I was swimming in. It was an experience of union with the glory of the natural world. I remember in particular an occasion at Lacona on Elba when as I swam I felt perfectly at one with my surroundings, shore as well as sea, and said to myself: "Whatever life holds for you, nothing can take away the bliss of this moment."

It led me afterwards to ask myself whether my feelings that morning could be explained in any way. It seemed to me that they could, and along several lines.

There was, first, what might be called the evolutionary explanation. All living species came originally out of the sea. We still had something of our primordial existence latent within us, and this it was which rejoiced to find itself once again in its original home.

Or there was the psychological explanation according to which immersion in the sea was a fantasy return to the security of the womb; or, in more fundamentalist Freudian terms, to jump into the sea was to insert the penis into the vagina.

Or you could take the mystical view that the encompassing sea was an analogy for, or, better, a sacrament of, the encompassing mystery of Godhead in which – though we were seldom aware of it – we lived and moved and had our being.

There seemed to me no need to choose between these various explanations. To insist that any one of them excluded the other two seemed sheer bigotry. Why shouldn't all three be right? This wasn't the lazy assumption that there is some truth in everything so that there is no

need to be discriminating. It was – I was beginning to see –
an insight into the interrelatedness of existence which lay
behind its complexity. For all thought and language depend
upon the possibility of describing one thing in terms of
another. And that possibility itself depends upon the
perceived correspondence between one thing and another.
Thus our existence in the womb doubtless has about it
much that corresponds to our primordial existence in the
sea. And both have something which corresponds to the
mystic's awareness of the God who encompasses him.
While as for the penis in the vagina, it is notorious that
treatises on the higher levels of prayer are often couched in
markedly erotic language. Of this the chief literary
monument in Western culture is, of course, the Song of
Songs, while one of its most arresting visual representations
is Bernini's Ecstasy of St Teresa in the church of Santa
Maria della Vittoria in Rome, where the face of the angel
holding the dart has about it an expression which combines
the disclosure of the holy and other-worldly with the
anticipation of immediate sexual pleasure. Clearly Bernini
had understood how in some important way the two
correspond with each other.

What happened to me in Regent's Park and later at
Lacona brought home to me how difficult it is to interpret
one's feelings with any degree of fullness. Most obviously
my sense of dispossession was due to my inability to share
my life with somebody else. But this fact was linked, subtly
but indissolubly, with other things which were wrapped up
with it and might in the end turn out to be even more
important. I wanted evidently to belong not only to
somebody else but also in some important way to the
natural order. And nature, it appeared, sometimes shut the
door in my face and sometimes welcomed me inside.

But, so stated, that obviously wouldn't do. For
nature neither rejected nor accepted. Regent's Park was just
Regent's Park and the sea at Lacona was just the sea at
Lacona. To describe them as saying "No" or "Yes" was
fantasy, the projection upon them of my own state of mind.

Yet that, too, was considerably less than the full truth. For to say that the park was just the park and the sea the sea was to regard them as isolated units or clusters of matter existing in a vacuum, and failed to explain why these units evoked me while others didn't. I didn't feel accepted or rejected by an underground train or Whewell's Court at Trinity or Central Hall, Westminster. If what I experienced was no more than the projection of my own mind upon an object in itself lifeless and neutral, why was I so particular about the object chosen for this purpose, especially as the choice wasn't a conscious or deliberate one, but just seemed to happen willy-nilly?

I was driven to the conclusion that the model of projection was a mistaken one which led nowhere. A more fruitful model was that of meeting. What I had experienced was a meeting between myself and some other which was alive, an other which in the park had somehow refused to welcome me, while in the sea it had greeted me with open arms. But this other which was alive couldn't be merely earth, vegetation and salt water. These things, I became convinced, were rather the transmitters of a living reality which they embodied and revealed, but which they didn't monopolize, since the reality stretched infinitely beyond them. The glory I found in them was theirs, it is true, but it was also infinitely more than theirs, as the sun is more than its radiance upon a garden.

But if, as I now believed, this was indeed the case, then it was in relation to the living reality which park and sea embodied that my sense of exclusion or inclusion had to be understood.

This didn't mean that I had abandoned my conviction that for any state of affairs there were a number of explanations, each valid within its own limits. It simply meant that those various limits had to be assessed and a scale of values worked out accordingly. It was, for instance, doubtless true that the sea charmed and comforted me, because it re-enacted for me the security of the womb. But this didn't exclude the more important truth that the sea was also the sacrament of God's encompassing presence. And the two things were related. For if in the womb we were formed and made, so were we also in God, even if it be to an infinitely fuller extent. The lesser truth reflected the greater while the greater gave to the lesser its full significance.

It was by a long way round that I had been brought to an elementary insight. But the prolonged journey was necessary since it is only the truth that you discover for yourself which has the power of truth. To be told something is seldom to know it, however numerous the instructors. And in any case there is always the lurking suspicion that people are merely grinding their own axes or repeating conventional statements from which all life has long since been drained away. And, further, the more earnest they are, the less convincing. For ardent dogmatists always seem to me much more concerned with persuading themselves than those they are addressing, however little they realize it.

So my journey was necessary, even if it brought me no further than a pulpit commonplace. I had recognized within myself an emptiness or dissatisfaction. This was most obviously due to my inability to share my life with somebody else so that I belonged to nobody. But it had also other and more ultimate causes which could be summarized as my failure to recognize or come to terms with the mystery in which I blindly lived and had my being, the encompassing mystery of Godhead. It revealed itself to me as a living mystery because it refused to leave me alone. Of its refusal to let me be, of, if you like, its interference with me, I have given two of the most vivid examples as representative of others: one when it showed me the utter misery of my alienation from it, and one where it filled me with the surpassing joy of union with it. And in both cases it spoke to me by means of quite ordinary things, no more than a walk in one case and a bathe in the other.

Evidently an extended crisis of discernment had been encountered and passed through. I was now, from one point of view, on the farther side of it, even if, from another, I also lingered still where I had long been. For few of the important breaks in life are clean.

In so far as I had passed through the crisis of discernment, the mystery of encompassing Godhead, or in more conventional language, God's glory, now tended to break out on me. And when it did so it took me into union with itself so that I was covered by it. No longer did it refuse and exclude me.

I knew from books I'd read that what happened to me on these occasions was a fairly common experience and had been given a variety of names by those on whom it had fallen. But my knowing that it had occurred to many others and been given a variety of labels didn't diminish its overwhelming reality for myself. What, however, I think my reading did do was to prevent me from overestimating the experience or entertaining any inflated notions about it. To be on occasions aware of what, for want of a better description, I have called the encompassing mystery of Godhead seemed best understood as a form of sensibility comparable to having an ear for music or an eye for painting slightly more susceptible than the average. Like the Garter, there was no damned merit about it. Indeed the sheer gratuitousness of the disclosures partly puzzled and partly amused me. They seemed to take no account whatever of worthiness or desert. For they came to somebody who seldom, if ever, said his prayers, who was nauseated by pious practices and bored to fits by the company of pious people, who preferred Henry Miller to the Bible and Noël Coward to *Hymns Ancient and Modern*, somebody, moreover, who was always ready selfishly to snatch at a bit of fun and was growing bitchy because he thought not enough fun came his way.

Nor did there now seem any accounting for the occasions on which I became aware of God's glory enveloping me.

Regent's Park in the snow (when as a conscientious and God-fearing clergyman I knew myself alienated from the glory) and the sea around Elba (when I knew myself at one with it) could be regarded as more or less conventional settings. But the experience now began to come in the most unlikely places without any apparent rhyme or reason.

It came more strongly than ever before when some four years after Elba I was in Trinidad and travelling on a bus from San Fernando to Port of Spain. The journey took about two hours, but I was unaware of the time passing since I was caught up in a bliss which it is impossible to describe. It was an experience of the ultimate reconciliation of all things as Love, a living presence, flooded over me and swept me into its own radiance, combining in itself an infinite grandeur with a tender personal intimacy. I didn't notice when we had arrived at Port of Spain. The bus conductor tapped me on the shoulder and asked me whether I was all right. I saw that the bus was empty, thanked him, and got out. Before attending to the business for which I'd made the journey, I wandered aimlessly round the streets for about half an hour to recover from what I'd seen.

Awareness of God's encompassing glory never came to me again as strongly as it did on that bus in Trinidad. But the fit came now and then in a lesser degree. Sometimes the awareness was evoked through the medium of specifically Christian imagery. So once, in a crowded cafeteria on Waterloo station, it came to me with the force of a revelation that the place was Emmaus. The tea and buns being consumed by the crowd was the broken bread in the midst of which Christ's presence was revealed; and I had once again the immediate certainty of some ultimate reconciliation in which everybody was caught up because they were all filled and alive with God's homely but surpassing glory.

The infinitely rich reality of redemption – that "all shall be well and all manner of things shall be well" – was often at the heart of these fits of awareness. This fact linked them with the earlier experiences I had had, first in Baynards Park, when I was aware that in my pain I was being allowed to eat Christ's broken Body and drink his outpoured Blood; and then listening to the carols from King's on the radio, when I realized overpoweringly how and in what way Christ led his children on to the place where he had gone.

But the awareness of redemption was now wider than it had been then in the sense that its light tended now to shine for me (as it did on Waterloo station) upon others as well as upon myself. It was as if their ultimate destiny could be foreseen and anticipated as a living reality in the present.

This awareness came to me with particular frequency on my visits to Tangier, which thus became holy ground for me, to the amusement of the more mature among the clergymen of the Cambridge establishment and the pious horror of the others. I couldn't explain to them – or at least I didn't – that the people I met in Tangier seemed from time to time to be radiant with God's glory so that in their company I knew myself to be in the very house of God and gate of heaven.

It was indeed a somewhat bewildering experience. It came willy-nilly, but it left me with the necessity of puzzling it out. Could I make any sort of sense of it? As a rational being I had for my own peace of mind to put it into some sort of explanatory framework.

Could it, then (I asked myself), have anything to do with the fact that the English colony in Tangier was by and large composed of people who refused to put up with the shams and hypocrisies of conventional respectability and insisted on something better and more real? Even if one supposed that they had failed to find it in any satisfying degree, at least they had had the courage to look for it at the cost of being despised by those who labelled themselves virtuous. Could it be that in their frantic search for life they were looking eagerly, if blindly, for the Kingdom of God? Weren't their lives, therefore, embryonically God-filled? And if sex itself couldn't give them the splendour they were desperately looking for – and he would be a conceited fool who imagined he knew for certain how much or how little it did give them, how great or small, frequent or rare, were the spasms of generosity thus engendered – these people, none the less, were desperately aware of their longing and had given up a great deal in their attempt to satisfy it. And could one doubt that in the end God would reveal to them the splendour of His encompassing presence and fill them with His own fullness? Was I from time to time allowed to anticipate this ultimate destiny of theirs? And was that the reason why in their company I was sometimes immediately aware of God's glory?

Perhaps that was a pointer to an answer. But who can tell? God's ways aren't our ways and He tends (as Job discovered) to make havoc of our attempts at explanation.

Among the more unlikely occasions when a fit of awareness came upon me was one which occurred in the Arts Cinema in Cambridge during the Judy Garland film *A Star is Born*. I had gone to the cinema because I felt depressed and defeated. In the story of the film Judy Garland had tried to make her mark three or four times and had failed completely on each occasion. So discouraged was she by this succession of failures that she decided to give up all attempts at a stage career. At this point an oldish, somewhat matriarchal woman gave the defeated Judy Garland a lecture on the necessity of perseverence. The road to success was always strewn with failures, and therefore you had to be tough and believe in yourself so that you would get up and try again however often you failed.

The words of this matriarchal figure came to me as the voice of God. They thrilled me. And in the thrill I was aware of God's presence with me in the cinema giving me new life and inspiring me with fresh courage. I had often read in the works of German Protestant writers how God spoke to people as a living voice when some passage or other of the Bible laid hold of them, and that it was in this sense that the Bible could be called the Word of God. Now I knew what they meant; only for me that afternoon the Word of God came not from the Bible but from a Judy Garland film. I was first aware of the mystery of God's living presence with me, and then, a little later, delightedly amused at the means chosen to make His presence felt. Within me, therefore, praise and laughter were mingled together. The matriarch's utterance undoubtedly verged on the corny. To speak to me deeply and powerfully by means of it seemed to me grotesquely funny. I couldn't deny the reality of the experience, but it was precisely its reality which made the occasion of it so hilarious. There was no knowing where God would explode next. On my way home I looked about me for somebody to slip on a banana skin. But nobody did. God, apparently, had exploded enough for one day.

Another occasion when I was overwhelmingly aware of God's glory occurred in a context which was more accountable.

A pupil of mine was in hospital with terminal cancer. He was a person of very great ability and promise, a devout Christian, with an informed and disciplined passion for social justice. He was a born leader who would certainly have made his mark on the world. He was still an undergraduate when I left Cambridge for Mirfield. On a visit back to Trinity I naturally went to see him in hospital. We exchanged the kind of remarks usual in those circumstances: how long had he been in hospital? How was I finding Mirfield? What was the news at Trinity? What had I come to Cambridge to do? Was he in much pain? Did he find it boring in hospital? How well did I think the Government was doing? But underneath these surface civilities we were both being hammered as if by an iron bar with the inescapable question: Why? Why was he dying, this young man who seemed set to do such great things for mankind? I realized that there was nothing I knew which from his own experience he didn't know much better than I did. It would have been utterly inappropriate and impertinent to preach at him. In any case I wouldn't have had any idea at all what to say. But without words he communicated his own vision to me. He wasn't in bed.

They had allowed him to get up, and we were sitting in a sort of common room. Looking at him I saw him as if covered by the words with which in St John's Gospel Jesus greets the certainty of his own death: "Now is the son of man glorified and God is glorified in him." This young man – his name was Hugh – was dying with Christ. That was the offering and service God had called him to make by means of the destructive evil of his cancer. And because he was dying with Christ he was also caught up in the power of Christ's resurrection, so that his dying was his glorification, as it was also Christ's.

Explained in this way what I am trying to describe must seem no more than a piece of cerebral theology, and, as such, an almost downright callous reaction to Hugh's suffering and death. But in actual fact it was an immediate vision and intuition of God's encompassing and victorious love. In this sick and dying young man, amid the surface banality of our conversation, I had been made aware of God's glory flooding into his world. And I came away from the hospital with the absolute certainty that all shall be well and all manner of things shall be well.

Of the occasions when God's glory broke in on me I must add one more example, since it remains too vivid in my memory to omit.

It was during a performance of the *Nutcracker* at the Festival Hall the first time I saw the ballet. Whoever designed the sets that year had splendidly managed the transformation scene when the drawing-room in which the children's party is taking place becomes the enchanted forest of the little girl's dream. But what hit me wasn't the scene in general but the transformation of the Christmas tree. In the drawing-room it was a common or garden tree hung with the usual tinsel decorations. But in the child's dream it grew visibly upwards and outwards until it became something tall, great and mysterious, no tree in a wood, let alone a drawing-room, but something of mythical proportions which shed abroad from itself what seemed a more than earthly power. It transmitted to me an overwhelming sense of God's immediate presence in all the unutterable majesty of His homeliness, and I was filled to the brim with adoration and praise. The rest of the ballet was for me a doxology of dance proclaiming unceasingly: "Glory to God in the highest; Glory to God in the highest."

When the performance was over and I was leaving the Festival Hall I had once again to try to make sense of my experience. The phallic significance of the tree shooting upwards was obvious, and no doubt some important part of me had been immediately stirred by what it recognized as the sexual imagery with which it was confronted. But, though plainly, it seemed to me, this was the case, yet sex here, it seemed equally plain, was no more than the vehicle and conveyer of what transcended it. For the feelings aroused were not at all sexual, at least in the narrow genital sense. They were made up *de profundis* of worship and a glowing reverence, although, of course, I was aware that in all deep worship of God our sexual instincts play their important and necessary part. What, it seemed to me, was being worshipped on this occasion was the mystery of Godhead encompassing the Christmas tree and the children's party which was its occasion, the mystery which by means of her dream of the enchanted forest the little girl had been allowed to discover.

The vision (if I can call it that) was of God's splendour filling His world and most truly and fully present when His children enjoy themselves and play. For the God who is behind or beyond His world, and continually gives it its derived reality, is also at the same time always within it, so that it is everywhere ablaze with His presence. And that, I concluded, was the truth, alive and resplendent, which I had been permitted in some measure to see that evening at the *Nutcracker*.

I have been to the same ballet several times since then, but the immediacy of the vision has never returned. What the ballet has given me on these subsequent occasions is no more than a memory of the initial rapture.

3

I HAVE NEVER hitherto mentioned what I have called these fits of awareness either in preaching or in anything I've written. That is because I was so extremely uncertain of their spiritual significance and religious value. The spiritual (that is, God) must needs communicate itself by means of the human psyche. But it is difficult to disentangle on the one hand the spiritual present through the psyche and, on the other, what is simply an affair of the psyche alone. And to confuse the two is to become the easy victim of illusions. Most of us have reserve funds of untapped emotion, and these can surface on occasions and invite us to luxuriate in them. So long as these emotions arise within us uninvited and aren't artificially stimulated by drugs or communal hysteria, there is no harm in them. The harm comes when we imagine that the strength of our emotions indicates an advanced spiritual condition.

But there is also the contrary danger of our being tight-arsed old maids incapable of accepting any advance the spiritual makes to us. We must recognize that God does indeed make Himself known to us by means of what we feel, and that our emotions can often be the angels of His presence. Thus, I believe, we must gratefully and joyfully accept the experiences of delight He sends us, but take care that they don't in any way lift us up in boastfulness or make us imagine that we are somehow better and more deeply Christian than those to whom they aren't given.

In my own case I can't any longer doubt that in my fits of awareness God sent me glad tidings of great joy for which I thank Him with all my heart. He showed me Himself alive in His creation and in myself as part of it, so that (to use the words of the psalm) when I lift up mine eyes unto the hills, it is indeed the hills from whence cometh my help because they are alive and glorious with God's own presence – like the rest of the world, only it is easier to see Him in some places than in others, though He is everywhere.

But, it must be stressed, these revelations to me were spasmodic, a matter of fits and starts. Perhaps they could be described as invitations to the waltz. They were certainly not the waltz itself. And if indeed God was calling me to dance with Him, then the dance could hardly be said to have begun.

IT MUST NOT therefore be imagined that life for me during this period consisted of little more than waiting expectantly for the next time when the encompassing mystery of Godhead would break in on me. That was very far indeed from being the case. Most of the time I still felt empty and dispossessed. With great bitterness I cursed the luck which had forced me to live a life of fundamental isolation, and I longed desperately for what could never be. I had a grudge against God for loading the dice against me and I hated the ecclesiastical duty which made it necessary for me to go to chapel and hear the hymns in which His devotees flattered and cajoled Him in the attempt to insinuate themselves into His favour. I found myself whispering an early poem of Frances Cornford:

> "I will not join the hymns men raise
> Like slaves who would avert in vain
> Your blundering and cruel ways."

to which I added my favourite line from A. E. Housman:

> "Whatever brute or blackguard made the world."

Often God seemed to me not to exist, being no more than the projection upon the heavens of infantile fantasies. I found comfort in the idea that we are the products of blind random forces which might as probably destroy us as they had produced us. I remembered with pleasure some words I had read of Bertrand Russell: "The hand which every day feeds the chicken eventually wrings its neck."

I don't think it at all strange or unusual that such thoughts and feelings should exist in somebody to whom God had revealed Himself in the ways I've described. On the intellectual level my fits of awareness could easily be explained away in terms of some psychological theory or other, while on the spiritual level it is notorious that faith and unbelief can – and often do – co-exist and alternate with each other like Box and Cox. Nor in my case (as no doubt in many others) was it always a straightforward contest between the two.

It was partly that. I had been given a pile of components with which to fit together a life, and I thought it horribly unfair that there were missing from the pile several of the components which most other people had been given. Thus I often refused to play. This refusal was a fundamental form of unbelief, but it could be cleverly rationalized into weighty intellectual arguments against belief in God. I am not for one moment suggesting that atheism invariably has this sort of basis. But the mind is more the plaything of our desires than we find it comfortable to admit.

There was, however, for me (as no doubt for many) a complicating factor. For some at least of my unbelief was a paradoxical bid for faith. That was because the god in whom I disbelieved had about him the vestigial remains of the old tyrannical idol whom I imagined I had killed off for good. Dead and buried he might be, but his ghost could still haunt me like a foul fiend and often threw something of his filth upon the face of the true God. After all, a great deal of what is said and sung in church is a tribute to the malevolent tyrant and an attempt to placate him. So it isn't all that difficult to confuse the true God with the idol. And it was, I now believe, against the idol that a large part of my resentment and unbelief were directed.

For it isn't easy to feel angry with a God who suffers with and in His children, a God who in the Christian scheme is represented as a baby born of a peasant woman in a stable who, when grown to manhood, knew agony and bloody sweat and died a painful death upon a cross.

So, I'm reasonably certain, my unbelief was (and is) at least partly a clearing-up operation, making straight a highway for the God who disclosed Himself to me in my fits of awareness.

I used to find particular comfort and encouragement in the first movement of César Franck's Symphony in D minor. For here (I think I'd seen it suggested in some programme notes) there seemed to be a gigantic struggle between faith and unbelief. And when it looked as if unbelief had gained the upper hand, faith won gloriously in the serene and majestic chord with which the movement ends.

I also found courage and hope (as must all who know it) in Beethoven's Ninth Symphony. The slow movement seems to speak of a harmony and love which passes understanding, while the final movement is a supreme act of praise flowing from a faith which was superhumanly heroic considering Beethoven's disabilities, especially, of course, his deafness. "I will seize fate by the throat," he had written to a friend. The symphony showed how he had done it.

It seemed to me odd, yet also typical, that Christians had never thought of making saints of the great creative artists of the world. For if anybody shows forth the glory of God, they do. But they can't be fitted into the ecclesiastical straitjacket labelled goodness, and few, if any, of them cater for the ecclesiastical obsession with virgins. Ecclesiastics prefer to keep God safely in His box as if He were a biscuit.

I used to find pleasure and relief in the songs of Noël Coward which made fun of this oppressively narrow outlook:

> My family has traditions.
> I've heard them a thousand times.
> My relatives were not excessively bright.

They loved to go off on missions
To rather peculiar climes
And lead the wretched heathen to the light.
Some of them got beaten up
In course of these rampages.
My great-aunt Maud got eaten up
While singing Rock of Ages.

Or there is the young couple in love who dream of being:

Far from the preachers
Who always beseech us
To mind our Ps and Qs.

Or, best of all, there is Mrs Wentworth Brewster who, reprimanded for her behaviour in Capri by her conventionally minded children (who begged her):

" 'Leave these men, mama,'
Answered, somewhat bibulously,
'Who d'you think you are?
Nobody can afford to be so lardy bloody dar
In a bar on the Piccola Marina'."

I was once lucky enough to meet Noël Coward at a reception. After chatting for a time we walked together to the supper room. In front of us was a fat ugly woman ridiculously overdressed in a gold costume. He nodded towards her and said to me: "Do you think she'll tarnish before the evening is out?"

I always thought his songs showed him to be a moralist *malgré lui*. What he condemned was self-righteousness, pomposity and every other form of affectation. What he admired was realism and the courage to accept reality, especially about oneself, and to use it to create something positive. I was particularly heartened by his song *Sail Away*:

When your heart feels as dreary as a worn-out glove,
Sail away.

and

> When soon or late
> You recognize your fate
> That will be your great great day.

It said more to me than any sermon in church. That wasn't surprising as church services gave me little except either a feeling of remoteness as if I were only an onlooker, or nausea, jitters and (as I've described) plain panic. They smelt too highly of the destructive idol I had formerly worshipped. The chalice for me was, and often still is, potentially a poisoned chalice. That isn't altogether inappropriate. For the central act of Christian worship commemorates, among other things, the murder by organized religion of tenderness and love and freedom. And organized religion hasn't changed its spots much down the ages.

Out of term I never went near a church. But I was grateful when Chris Courtauld tactfully and unobtrusively replaced the placard I used to have put up announcing that chapel services were discontinued until further notice with one which read that they would be resumed on such a date – the beginning of the following term. It was very characteristic of the way in which the chaplains used to look after their dean without appearing to.

5

THERE WAS ONE CHRISTIAN I knew who was absolutely free from any taint of idol worship. So much so that many zealous Christians, particularly of the more Evangelical persuasion, regarded him as a lost soul, while even more moderate or quite High Churchmen tended sometimes to despise him a little for what they considered his laxity: he sometimes turned up late to take a weekday morning service in chapel and he drank and dispensed gin in almost industrial quantities. His name was Geoffrey Beaumont and he was chaplain of Trinity during my first two years there as a Fellow.

His rooms were always crowded with under-graduates and younger Fellows at a sort of non-stop party which invariably went on until the early hours. Geoffrey used to sit at the piano with a cigarette dangling from his mouth, playing and singing the latest revue songs he had written. He wrote the music for most of Simon Phipps's songs and was a close friend of Ronnie Hamilton, then a housemaster at Winchester, who was himself a revue artist of no mean calibre.

Geoffrey was convinced that God wanted people to enjoy themselves, and in his company they always did. People thawed almost at once when he was there. It wasn't simply that he put them at their ease. He made them feel that life was tremendously worthwhile because it was so immensely entertaining. He somehow got it quickly into their heads and hearts that God and laughter are all but inseparable. This wasn't by anything he said. He wasn't a professional funny man. In fact he was often quite inarticulate. It was by the atmosphere he generated. He was extremely shrewd in his estimate of people, but it was hard to get out of him his genuine opinion of anybody when it was unfavourable. If he didn't want to tell you what he thought he would succumb to a prolonged fit of intense coughing which made him go purple in the face, and you would no longer want to know what you asked him because you were afraid that he would have a stroke.

It was during this time that he composed his *Folk Mass*, which was later published and recorded. In his rooms, crowded as usual, the latest bit composed would be tried out in the atmosphere of a saloon bar. The Sanctus finished, somebody would say: "Geoffrey, let's have another gin before we try the Agnus."

I remember Michael Ramsey (then Regius Professor of Divinity) at one of these sessions, trying, not very successfully, to disguise an instinctive aversion by an attitude of official approval, nodding his head every other minute and murmuring: "Yes, yes, yes." At one point this was mistaken as a vote for gin, and I remember his surprise when a beaker of it was handed to him during the Gloria.

When the Mass was completed it was sung one Sunday morning at St Luke's Church in Cambridge with Geoffrey preaching. His text at first puzzled the congregation – "Render unto Caesar the things which are Caesar's". But it gradually became clear that Caesar in this context meant folk music.

From Cambridge Geoffrey went to be chaplain to the British Embassy church in Madrid. I was lucky enough to stay with him there several times. He attracted so large a congregation that he had to have a repeat service on Sundays – one at ten and one at a quarter past eleven. But his popularity was not confined to English and Americans. Within a radius of about a mile around his flat cries would emerge from every bodega or pub we passed: "Mister Jeffrees, Mister Jeffrees," and we would go in and be given a glass of wine on the house. Geoffrey's Spanish was rudimentary, but he had a way of communicating which was independent of vocabulary and syntax. He only had to splutter and cough, and complete mutual understanding was immediately established. His flat was always crowded with an extraordinary assortment of people: two school-mistresses on holiday from London, a couple of bull-fighters, a policeman (who took about five minutes taking off the revolver and other weapons with which he was loaded), the Englishwoman who looked after the stores in the Embassy, a Spanish racing driver, a blonde from New York, platinum but by no means dumb, a taxi driver who had dropped in for a rest, a pianist in tails soon to set off for his night-club. In the kitchen Geoffrey's maid, Marcella, with Casilda, the maid from the flat next door, could be found reacting to the crowd, sitting with their elbows on the kitchen table rocking themselves to and fro and moaning: "*Madre di Dios, Madre di Dios.*" At this point one of the churchwardens, a humourless man connected with some business or other and a devotee of *Reader's Digest*, called unexpectedly to discuss what strength of electric bulb should be placed at the west end of the church. He saw that his mission was hopeless, nodded towards Geoffrey across the room and said to me sadly: "Nobody would think he was an MBE", and with that left.

We seldom went out to dinner before 1 or 2 a.m., which, even by Spanish standards was late. Once we were invited to lunch some fifteen miles from Madrid and returned at 4 a.m. the following morning.

Geoffrey loved life and he loved people. That was because for him God was the air he breathed always and everywhere. And whether the air was cloudy with incense or tobacco smoke, it made no difference. God was there. Hence in Geoffrey's company people were reassured because they felt they were lovable and counted. He never made anybody feel guilty or sub-standard. In face of so much pseudo-goodness, some of it arrogant, most of it simply depressing, he showed what goodness was really like. Even at an Embassy concert you felt nearer to God when you heard him sing:

> "Carmen, Carmen,
> The toast of all the bar men
> And of old avuncular men."

But he could bring healing with him in very different contexts as well. A great friend of mine was in a London hospital dying of kidney disease. The doctors had given him three months at the most. He told me later that when he was at his very lowest, Geoffrey (on leave from Madrid) went to see him and made him laugh for the first time in months, and that it was from that moment that his recovery began.

After five years in Madrid Geoffrey was given a parish in Camberwell. He was adored in all the pubs where he used to go and play the piano and sing. But the parish was an area from which people were steadily moving out. The church was enormous and hideous and few people went to it. He became disheartened and didn't know what to do next. As happens often to people in depressing circumstances, he began to overdo the bottle a bit. Eventually, to everybody's surprise (he was fifty-eight by then) he decided to test his vocation with the Community of the Resurrection at Mirfield.

He was led there by the understanding and vision of Hugh Bishop (he was subsequently to become Superior of the Community and then to leave it), who, alone among ecclesiastical pundits, perceived the saint temporarily submerged beneath the alcoholic. It was the man in the street, the common or garden sinner, who loved Geoffrey. Ecclesiastical worthies were by this time looking down their noses at him. Hugh Bishop was the exception.

But the decision to move to Mirfield seemed at the time to be little short of preposterous. It was like a fish deciding to live on gravel. I myself thought that one of two things would happen. Either Geoffrey would leave after a bit, his last state being worse than the first, or the Community would slowly kill off the Geoffrey we knew and loved – idiosyncratic, immensely fond of fun, never so at home as in a bar or when concerned with a revue – and replace him by a grey figure of conventional piety. In the event neither of these two things happened. Geoffrey remained permanently in the Community and continued to be entirely his old self.

They kept him at Mirfield for over a year without allowing him to go away anywhere. He then came to Cambridge. As the time for his visit drew nearer I became increasingly apprehensive. What changes would I see in him? Would he have become a reformed character like the Jackdaw of Rheims and hop now about with a gait devout? Would he have joined the innumerable company of holy bores? Would he have exchanged real goodness for the counterfeit article of standard manufacture?

He arrived at my rooms earlier than expected while I was entertaining fifteen or so undergraduates. My apprehension had made me on edge, and my mood communicated itself to my guests. The party was one of the stickiest I remember. The young men stood silent and embarrassed, hating every moment of it and obviously wondering how soon they could leave. Then Geoffrey appeared, somebody they didn't know and indeed had never heard of. Within ten minutes the atmosphere had completely changed. The young men were talking their heads off and enjoying themselves hugely, and so was I. They showed no inclination to leave, and in the end I had to turn them out. "Father Beaumont must be starving," I said. "It is time I took him out to dinner." After they had left we had a good gin session. Geoffrey seemed very much his old self. His effect upon the young men had shown that, but I needed a great deal of reassuring. Over dinner I asked him what the other people at Mirfield were like. "Oh," he said, "they're marvellous people. Wonderful." His answer worried me. It seemed the first small sign of the insincerity, the game of let's pretend, which passes for charity among the pious. I wished that, if he didn't want to answer my question, he had coughed himself purple as in the old days. I put down my knife and fork and looked straight at him. "Geoffrey," I said, "please tell me what they are really like." He was silent for a bit, and then in a reluctant whisper he said: "Absolute hell." And then for good measure he added in a growl: "They're boring, devotional shits." He gulped his wine and, putting down the glass, he said: "They're a lot of good things as well." "I'm sure," I answered. "Tell me about the good things." There followed a bizarre catalogue of virtues which sent us both into fits of laughter. I was now certain that Geoffrey was safe and that the religious enemy would not be able to do him violence. He would remain himself for good.

I saw him several times after that initial visit. He was obviously happy in the Community and fitted in well. Certainly he was much loved by the brethren, and he grew to love them. He was at Mirfield when I visited there in 1968, but he had been posted to South Africa before I myself joined up, so we never overlapped in the same place. He died in Capetown before coming home again. The brethren who saw him there in hospital wrote: "At times he is completely unconscious, at other times he is quite round the bend, and at others lucid and the same old G.B., drinking whisky with his doctors, teaching the nurses to sing or composing comic verse." It was observed that within the space of half an hour two clergymen in succession gave him the last rites. When asked what was going on Geoffrey answered: "Well, it gives them great pleasure and doesn't do me any harm."

His last Christmas in England he sent out a poem as a card. It showed, more than anything, what made him tick:

"For the Son of God (Son of Man)
is just as much there in a broken limb
as in a carol or favourite hymn
a children's party or family meal:
and they need to know that he's there for real
in the starving East
or where every beast
on a farmer's ground
is shot for plague; and where war is around
how can they tell
that he is with them
as much as he was at Bethlehem
and that he is in their hell
with them as in Gethsemane
or often Calvary
(not forgetting the close connection
between that and the resurrection –
between present sorrow
and the life of the world tomorrow)
How can they tell?
  Well –
'Inasmuch (said he)
as you have done what you have done
 to one
of the least of my brothers, you've done it to me.'

Jesus was born
and Jesus grew
may he be born anew
in you
and grow
so
that you may find it great to be alive
and thrive."

Geoffrey Beaumont showed me that it is possible to have an idol-free Christianity, however rare a phenomenon it is. And the fact that the Community at Mirfield was able to assimilate without destroying him gave me the courage to wonder whether it would be altogether out of the question for me to apply to it myself for membership. It couldn't, I thought, be too bad a place.

6

MEANWHILE, for reasons already described, I became more and more convinced that I needed to take some sort of radical initiative if I were not to run completely to seed. I could have remained in my job at Trinity until the retiring age and in my rooms until I died. But I came more and more to feel that for me that would be a cowardly option, a clinging to the security of the home I loved but which I now needed to leave if I were to grow more fully into myself.

I was realistic enough to realize that as a human condition there could be no magic answer to my loneliness and sense of dispossession. On that human level I should have to continue for life belonging to nobody. But a transfer to the right environment might make it seem less important, might even to some extent enable me to accept it and thus let loose its creative possibilities in ways so far unknown. For how can life be found except by the willingness to lose it? And the willingness is all. To recognize your fate, to be willing to lose your life in terms of the necessity laid upon you, is to find your freedom – freedom to be, and hence to bring to fruition whatever potential you may possess.

There was, too, another factor by no means the least important. I had grown weary of theology as so much theory and had become disillusioned by it. I began to feel like a Professor of Egyptology who had never been to Egypt (I was told he existed!) or a Professor of the Fine Arts who had seen only reproductions of the world's masterpieces (Carl Winter, the Director of the Fitzwilliam Museum, in a mood of tomfoolery had once insisted that he preferred reproductions to the originals). In the introduction to *The True Wilderness* I had said of preaching: "What was withheld from me was the ability to transmit second-hand convictions whatever their source. All I could speak of were those things I had proved true in my own experience by living them and thus knowing them at first hand." What was true of preaching was becoming true of teaching and study. I felt increasingly disinclined and then increasingly unable to be concerned with the cerebral exercises which were supposed in some way to be descriptions of the ultimate mysteries of existence. And ladling out these descriptions in simplified form for the benefit of students gave me more and more a sense of futility. I wanted to see for myself and in some way or other to become what I saw, not to compare this speculation with that, Nestorius with Cyril of Alexandria, Loisy's view of the Fourth Gospel with Bultmann's. On my side here, there is no doubt, was the real theological tradition of Christendom. St Augustine, for instance, or St Thomas, or for that matter Karl Barth, spoke only of the things which had become part of what they were. Theology for them was not a mere trafficking in other people's ideas, however much they used them as the servants of their experience. To follow in their footsteps was to be, like each of them, somebody who lived in the territory of which he wrote, investigating it for himself and immersing himself in it. To remain for ever in my study comparing and evaluating other people's attempts at cartography was fast ceasing to be for me a live option. I found encouragement in what I took to be the Eastern Orthodox tradition that theology cannot be dissociated from spirituality, what one studies from what one sees by having immediate contact with it.

But to see for oneself, however infinitesimal be the aspect of Reality revealed, required, as I recognized, the discipline of regular prayer and contemplation, involving considerable expenditure of time and effort. And of this I was totally incapable on my own, not least because I shared Harry Lauder's conviction that it's nice to get up in the morning, but it's better to stay in bed. I could not begin to do it, I knew, without a definite rule I had solemnly promised to keep and, even more important, the company of other people doing the same thing. That was the price, I was convinced, I would have to pay in order to exchange speculation about Reality for a knowledge of it at first hand. It occurred to me that what had to be done was similar (though nothing like so arduous) to the hardships and difficulties willingly undertaken by every explorer for the joy of discovery set before him, and that the psychopathology which is doubtless a powerful factor in making a man an explorer in no way invalidates the authenticity of his quest.

There was also at this time something else simmering inside me. It was related to the desire to explore Reality and equally compelling, though not identical with it.

There is in everybody a potential of generosity which actualizes itself in a thousand different ways. No way, it seems to me, is better or higher than another. It is simply different.

I have described how, in the all but intolerable pain of breakdown, I was on two occasions overwhelmingly aware that suffering need not in fact be the dead-end it seemed. On the deepest level of Reality it could be recognized (to use Christian imagery) as an invitation to share to some small degree in the sufferings of Christ, that is, in the birth-pangs of creation by means of which God's one perpetual creative act accomplishes its perfect and glorious conclusion. In other words, when one had done everything in one's power to rid oneself of one's disabilities, those that remained could be used as a prayer for others and thus be a channel to them of God's life-giving love. In Baynard's Park, it will be remembered, there came to me the vision that I was eating Christ's broken Body and drinking his outpoured Blood – that that was the final reality of what I was going through. And the vision had come to me again while listening on the radio to the carols from King's, this time of Christ leading his children on to the place where he has gone, the place of glory because of total self-giving in costly love. On both occasions the vision had been charged with vehement emotion. I had responded to it by convulsive sobbing. It seemed to me that what I was now being called upon to do was somehow to translate my response into a hard fact of daily life free from the agitation and froth which had initially accompanied it. I could, I thought, earth my vision in this way only if in some quite definite and concrete manner I was to offer myself, warts and all, to God on behalf of others. I knew from my own personal experience how people's ultimate need is subtle and indescribable. The last thing I wanted to do was to convert them to any ideology or creed. The challenge with which all people are confronted is to find their true identity in the encompassing mystery from which their being is derived. And I could, I thought, help a few of them to meet that ultimate challenge by a life to some extent devoted to prayer for them. And it would, I thought, only be an extension of how Ken Carey had told me to regard my analysis: "For their sakes I consecrate myself."

I used to speak a little about all this to Ralph Leigh, the editor of Rousseau's letters. (He had been elected a Fellow of Trinity a year after I had. We are somewhat alike in appearance, and he complained that I had for several years ruined his reputation in Cambridge by going to a party in King's and speaking the most appalling French, the company being under the impression that it was him.) He had the advantage of not being a churchman or in any way schooled in conventional piety. But his intimate knowledge of French writers – Bérulle, for instance, and Bossuet – enabled him to some extent to understand the gist of what I was trying to say. He was once in my room when the waiter brought in a tray with afternoon tea and cucumber sandwiches. "Christ, how I *hate* that," I said, looking at the tray after the waiter had left. "Why?" asked Ralph. "Because," I answered, "it symbolizes everything which keeps me in this place." He understood.

I was to be fifty in a year's time, and the magic of numbers asserted itself. At fifty, I thought, I must make a definite decision: either to remain where I was or to effect some sort of radical change. It was then or never. I should be too old, too completely dug in, if I put off the decision further. Would I have the nerve to make it? It occurred to me that during the whole of my life I had never taken any fundamental initiative. I had merely accepted what had been offered to me on a plate – the curacies in London, the chaplaincy at Westcott House, the Fellowship at Trinity. I had not pulled even the smallest string to get any of these jobs. Wasn't I now a bit old to begin making a future for myself and perhaps actually applying somewhere for a place or a job? It had never dawned on me before how protected my life had been. Hitherto I had, without realizing it, assumed that things just came one's way. I had, it is true, lived my adult life in the early postwar period when there was no unemployment to speak of. But people, none the less, did choose to do this rather than that and took steps accordingly. I never had. The possible prospect of it alarmed me not a little.

7

THE SPRING VACATION (it was 1968) promised me some temporary relief from the choice hanging over me. I flew to Shetland for a fortnight's holiday with two of the

Ramblers – Elizabeth Cavendish and John Betjeman. We based ourselves at Lerwick. The morning after our arrival we woke up to find thick snow on the ground which immobilized us for two days. We had to remain in the hotel and read, with occasional sessions in front of the television. Among other things we saw Tony Snowdon's film *Don't Count the Candles*, about growing old, or, more accurately, about growing old in comfortable affluence. The film reminded me savagely (a sign, no doubt, of how good it in fact was) of the choice I had to make. In what context was I to live the rest of my life? I thought it a filthy trick of fate to confront me almost immediately on my arrival in Shetland with the problem from which I had gone there to escape for a week or two. I cursed the snow which had kept us in, and tried to find some relief by repeating several times to Elizabeth and John that Tony Snowdon had made an appallingly bad film. They were surprised at my vehemence and clearly wondered what lay behind it.

Luckily at that point the fishing fleet arrived back in Lerwick, and the fishermen had several weeks' pay to spend. They packed all the pubs, and were not only friendly but embarrassingly hospitable. To remain tolerably sober in their company was no small achievement, but Trinity had kept me in excellent training. As well as drinking in the pubs, they each carried a half-bottle of whisky in the back hip-pocket of their trousers. One of them – he must have been round about twenty-five – slipped in the snow, cut himself slightly and bled a little. Feeling the moisture, he put his fingers to the wound and then sucked them. "Thank fuck," he said, "it's only blood." Altogether it was a diverting evening and I slept marvellously afterwards.

The next day the snow had all but disappeared. The sun was shining and the sky and water were blue. We hired a car and for several days explored what is known locally as the mainland. The bracing air and rugged sea-washed land, looking in the sun like the enchanted and slightly forbidding abode of some sea god who happened for the time being to be in a good temper, left me no space to think about myself. All you saw of land and sea was bathed in an intense and unearthly light which completely monopolized the attention by its power to delight and threaten – a sure sign that it was the home of a god – while the red and purple sea-urchins along the shore looked as if they belonged to his casket of treasures. Inland we saw two or three blue hares – a species I hadn't encountered before.

Walking next day round Lerwick itself I came across the Roman Catholic church and went in. There was displayed there a large poster advertising a call from Pope Pius XII to pray for the conversion of Africa to the ideal of virginity. It seemed to me rather a waste of intercessory effort.

We had a launch at our disposal and, in still brilliant weather, went to Yell and Unst, where we spent a couple of nights, as well as to several of the smaller islands. On Fetlar we were lucky enough to see the snowy owl which was nesting there, and we were most generously given lunch at the home of a kirk elder. He asked me what I did. I told him I was at Trinity, Cambridge. He looked puzzled for a moment and then his face lit up. "Oh," he said, "isn't that the place which Lord Butler runs?" It was an unusual but at the time not altogether inaccurate description of the college. On Vaila we visited a largish house whose furnishings and decoration, all in spotless condition, hadn't been changed since 1880. It was a bit eerie as the old lady who owned the house was bedridden upstairs and her fairly constant geriatric cries and moans made the house feel as if it were haunted. I think we were wrong to visit it. She didn't know we were there and we were intruders. I had agreed to accept her housekeeper's invitation to see the place, and it was certainly a curiosity finding ourselves in a house which looked exactly as it had almost ninety years before. But I felt now that we had been discourteous, to say the least. It was a relief when we left.

On the mainland we were kindly invited to lunch by Sir Basil Neven-Spence, who had formerly been MP for

Orkney and Shetland and was now the Lord Lieutenant. He was medically qualified and had had an interesting career as an army doctor in various parts of the world. Being a widower he did his own cooking and gave us the most marvellous meal. The interior of his house looked as if it had left Harrods only the day before. He had had it refurbished for a recent visit of the Queen. He was much loved in the islands. They told us at Lerwick how his wife had been taken suddenly and fatally ill when staying at the hotel there waiting to board the ship for Aberdeen. I thought him a most movingly gallant person. I shan't quickly forget the victory over misfortune and loss which radiated from him. The only frightening thing was his car. By arrangement he met us at a garage a few miles from his house in order to guide us there. He told us that the garage had warned him that his brakes were almost entirely non-operative. The handbrake worked slightly, that was all. We begged him to leave his car at the garage and get into ours. This he refused to do. As he led us up and down hills and along cliff roads on one side of which was the sea several hundred feet below, I expected him to disappear at any moment and be seen no more. But he didn't. On leaving, we absolutely refused his kind offer to lead us back to the garage. We could, we said, find our own way perfectly well and in any case we wanted to stop quite frequently and admire the view. So he said goodbye to us at the gate of his house.

I have given these details of our stay in Shetland to show how fully occupied we were. Once, on our third morning, the snow had gone there was no time to sit about and brood. By the evenings we were healthily tired and our conversation was naturally chiefly concerned with what we had seen that day and planned to see on the next. All three of us made close friends with Dolly, the barmaid at our Lerwick hotel, a woman of around fifty, who knew a great deal about the lore and customs of the place. We were (somewhat provincially, I suppose) amused by the way the islanders spoke of Aberdeen as if it were a foreign city in the far south, much as we might speak of Milan. John was particularly intrigued by the fact that the nearest railway station was at Bergen. It would be fun, he said, to have it stamped upon one's writing paper.

Easter Sunday came, and I thought I had better go to church, partly out of a sense of duty and partly not to upset John, for whom at that time (he is no longer like that) attendance at the Holy Communion on Sunday was a bit of a neurotic compulsion; all the more so, therefore, on Easter Sunday. So the three of us went to the small episcopal church in Lerwick. There were about twelve other people in the congregation at this eight o'clock service, and the priest was a youngish man attended by the usual adolescent server in his middle teens. We didn't discover to whom the church was dedicated, but for me personally it was quite definitely Trinity church, for it was there that I met my doom. The priest read the usual Prayer Book epistle for Easter Sunday, and a sentence of it burnt itself into me like fire: "Ye died, and your life is hid with Christ in God." The words overpowered me. It was like being struck fiercely in the face. Yet it wasn't like that either. For if the impact of the words was merciless, it was the impact of a merciless mercy. What pounced upon me was not so much a divine imperative as a divine invitation, though I suppose it could be said that these are different ways of saying much the same thing. Yet not always or necessarily. For what strikes somebody as a divine imperative may be a projection upon the heavens of his own pathological guilt-feelings. But an invitation, however compelling, is never compulsive. It has about it a supreme graciousness which frightens only because it attracts so mightily. From that moment I knew beyond a peradventure that I was being invited to die somehow to an old life in order to find a truer identity in the encompassing mystery of which I had been so long aware. In practical terms this meant leaving Cambridge and writing to Geoffrey Beaumont about the possibility of the Mirfield Community's being willing to give me a try.

At the time I said nothing to Elizabeth and John

about what had happened to me in church. I knew them both intimately, but the experience was at the moment incommunicable. In any case, if I tried to speak of it I was sure I would break down, and I remembered that it was their holiday as well as mine. As there would be no change in my attitudes and behaviour, the easiest thing seemed to say nothing. But unperceptive is the last thing Elizabeth ever is. She saw something was up, but with her usual sensitivity she asked no questions. All she did that morning was unaccustomedly early to say: "Let's go and see Dolly and have a drink," to which I agreed with alacrity. The bar was closed. But Dolly was about and brought us large glasses of Glen Morangie.

✤❧8❧✤

I REMEMBER a retreat conductor at Westcott House concluding a fervent address on the necessity of venturing all for God with what he intended to be a climax which would stun us all, "So, brothers," he said (he was the occupant of a snug cathedral deanery), "let us therefore burn our boats and launch out into the deep."

Returning from Shetland I did neither. I was far too cautious and self-regarding. I said nothing to anybody in Cambridge of what was in my mind and merely wrote to Geoffrey Beaumont at Mirfield to make tentative enquiries. Geoffrey's answer was exactly what I should have expected of him. He said it would be marvellous if it eventually turned out to be God's will that I should join the Community. But he refrained from any real enthusiasm or encouragement. He was wise and holy enough to understand that any pushing or pulling, let alone any gush, would be quite out of place. I should, he said, write to the Superior, Hugh Bishop. This I did, and the Superior suggested that I should visit the place for a few days when I was next free, the visit entailing no obligation on either side. In practical terms this meant going in July. Meanwhile I could continue reassuringly as usual.

It must be obvious that in threshing the matter out in my own mind I was aware that I was up against a serious contradiction. What I believed to be the invitation which had come to me so powerfully in the church at Lerwick was not at all an invitation to churchiness or any sort of conventional piety. To lose my current manner of life in order to find a truer identity in God might well for me at this point involve taking vows of poverty, chastity and obedience. For that I was prepared. However difficult the living out of those vows might turn out to be, I felt that at this stage of my life they would, so to speak, be on my side. They wouldn't hinder the search for Reality or the life of prayer for others to which I believed myself called, but might well, on the contrary, help them forward. At worst they wouldn't be a denial of what I was, and in fact would probably be an affirmation of it.

But churchiness was a different cup of tea altogether. I saw no reason to believe that I should cease as if by magic to fear and hate churchiness, nor that the church services, constantly repeated, would no longer bring on those fits of terror to which for so long they had made me liable. And psychopathology apart, it was still my rational conviction that organized religion was often a negation of God, reducing the ultimate encompassing mystery into manipulable counters doled out by hierophants, with all the resultant claims to exclusive possession of the truth (as though salvation could be patented), and all the evil masquerading as goodness (cruelty, for instance, as alleged loyalty to Christ's standards) which inevitably followed. I still thought that there was a serious element of truth in Bertrand Russell's claim, absurdly overstated though it was: "I say quite deliberately that the Christian religion as organized in its churches is the principal enemy of moral progress in the world." For if today freedom is suppressed by totalitarian states, wasn't its suppression anticipated by a totalitarian church?

It was only after they had been deprived of their political coercive power that the churches began to speak so much about freedom:

> "Christians have burnt each other, quite persuaded
> that all the Apostles would have done as they did."

I knew that there were five or six lay brothers at Mirfield,
but that most members of the Community were clergymen. Even worse, they were Anglo-Catholics. Only a few
years before they had regarded themselves as the spearhead
of the Anglo-Catholic movement in the Church of
England, leading, for instance, the opposition to the
proposed Church of South India with hysterical outbursts
about the apostolic succession. But here, I had learnt, the
crisis (as doctors used to describe it) of the malignant fever
had been passed, and the Community was now in a quieter
and more chastened mood.

All the same, was it wise, I continued to ask myself,
to contemplate living in such an ecclesiastical and High
Church atmosphere? Wouldn't the result of churchiness, let
alone of incense with everything, at best be nausea? Yet
how else, except by putting up with churchiness in some
form or other could I live the life to which it seemed I was
called? The alternatives to Mirfield looked even worse, and
they hadn't, as far as I knew, been put through the test of
assimilating a Geoffrey Beaumont without destroying him.
It must, I concluded, be Mirfield or nowhere. In any case
how could I tell about a place without visiting it? That
would be to let prejudice rule.

9

THE SUMMER TERM in Cambridge ended and what Geoffrey
used to call Balls Week began. I went only occasionally to
the Trinity May Ball, and didn't go that year. But at seven
o'clock the following morning the assistant head porter
came into my bedroom and told me that a pupil of mine
had been involved in an extremely serious accident while
driving to Ely for breakfast with his girlfriend after the ball.

The fact that the assistant head porter came himself to tell me the news instead of telephoning it from the porters' lodge indicated how grave he had been led to believe the accident was. I telephoned the hospital at Ely and they told me that the couple were on the danger list. I then telephoned my pupil's parents in Hampshire, asking them to telephone the girl's parents, as I didn't know who she was. I then went immediately to Ely. On the road I passed the wreckage of my pupil's car (it had collided with a lorry, whose occupant was unhurt). It looked no more than a tangled screwed-up bit of metal. It seemed to me incredible that anybody could have come out of it alive. It was an RAF hospital to which my pupil (his name was David) and his girlfriend had been taken. By each of their beds there was a nurse whose sole charge each of them was. Both sets of parents arrived by the afternoon. The girl was unconscious for a number of days and her father and mother used to take it in turns to sit by her bed. Her father later told me of the first sign of her recovery. He had been out to get some lunch (a salad) while his wife kept watch. On his return to the hospital he took his wife's place. After about an hour his daughter, aware of his presence for the first time, looked at him and said: "You smell of garlic." It was a declaration that she would survive.

David remained for much longer on the danger list. It was decided that he needed the kind of equipment the RAF hospital at Ely didn't possess. So he was rushed in an ambulance with police outriders to Addenbrooke's in Cambridge and put on a life-support machine. His parents camped out at the hospital while for what seemed an endless number of days he hovered between life and death. The situation was made all the more poignant by the fact that his father had died some years earlier (his mother had married again), and he was the only child of that first marriage. He was therefore the only successor to his father's name and family. His mother and stepfather were heroic beyond belief – calm, perfectly self-controlled, enduring their agony of waiting as though it were all a matter of course. With an entire lack of self-consciousness they radiated a profound and simple faith so that in their company you knew you were on holy ground.

My last memory of David before his accident was when he had come to take his final terminal exeat – he had finished his three years in Cambridge and was going down. I saw him put something on the floor his side of the table opposite me. As he got up to go he lifted whatever it was from the floor and looking rather embarrassed gave it to me. It was a bottle of Tio Pepe.

I have spoken of him at some length because of the part his accident played in the decision I had to make. God had invited me to dedicate myself to Him in prayer for others. And here were three people (I hadn't then met David's half-brothers and sisters) who desperately needed every ounce of prayer available. And I suppose that in a way I asked the Lord for a sign. I didn't bargain with Him in the sense of saying: "If David recovers I will go to Mirfield." That, it seemed to me, would have been superstitious and crude. But I did say that his recovery would make it easier for me to decide to go. Perhaps the difference was no more than a face-saving rationalization. For religious thought and feeling are susceptible of distinctions every bit as fine and subtle, and maybe as ludicrous, as the class structure in England! Anyhow, David did recover, and some years later I had the privilege of taking his wedding.

❧ 10 ❧

I WENT IN JULY to Mirfield for a week. I had been twice already some twenty-five years before (on both occasions to attend a retreat), so I knew what the place looked like and its general layout. But now I had somehow to assess its atmosphere, and its Superior had to assess me.

I didn't as it happened learn a great deal. When I chatted with members of the Community I found that my social instincts came into play so that I automatically spoke of things which I thought would be congenial to them, which meant chiefly the Anglo-Catholic priests, pundits and places of worship with which I was familiar. "You must have known Father Humphrey Whitby," I said. "Oh yes indeed," came the answer. "I remember twenty years ago how he dealt with some Protestants who complained that St Mary's didn't seem an Anglican church at all." I connived at the fun described, more as a matter of courtesy than anything else. I was used to joining in conversation with strangers as a matter of good manners without being at all involved in it.

An old Father sitting on a garden seat called me to join him. "I want to tell you about something wonderful," he said. Clearly this time I must be prepared to listen properly and learn. But the wonderful thing (I found it very reassuring) turned out to be Marie Lloyd. The old man when young had been a student at the theological college in the grounds and, against the rules, had secretly broken out one evening to see Marie Lloyd in Leeds. Here, I thought, was a sign of spiritual health.

Geoffrey Beaumont was in residence. But we knew each other well already and there was little point in our getting together, especially as on a fairly recent visit to Cambridge he had told me how apprehensive he was about his imminent posting to South Africa, and I didn't want to cut into the short time he had left at Mirfield.

On Sunday morning (I was the only person in church who wasn't a member of the Community) one of the younger Fathers in a long intense sermon lashed out at the Community, condemning it for the blatant social unrighteousness of a recent business transaction in which he alleged it had been involved. At breakfast afterwards it transpired that he had got his facts all wrong and that the Community had never even remotely done what he accused it of. It was nice to know that more than one form of lunacy existed in the place. A great deal of indignant breath may have been wasted, but at least it wasn't about the apostolic succession.

Indeed there was a certain atmosphere of reform about the place. Only the older men said private Masses. Most people communicated at the communal celebration. A Father, fairly advanced in years (he was a retired bishop), tried to drag me into the controversy which reform always brings by encouraging me to insist on saying my own Mass every morning. But this, for obvious reasons, had no attraction for me whatsoever. One morning I could hardly believe my eyes and thought I must be dreaming. I was sitting in the church by myself when around half past ten the Superior came in with five or six of the other brethren. In complete silence – it was rather like a nightmare in an Ingmar Bergman film; all the actors were dressed in black – the Superior and his companions began stripping the High Altar of everything, crucifix, candles, frontal, fine white linen cloth, leaving it completely naked with its dull pink bricks looking insolently unashamed.

But I didn't enquire much into these things. In fact I took in extremely little of the place. I realized later that I didn't want to.

Fundamentally important decisions are seldom if ever made by putting two and two together and seeing what they add up to. Fundamentally important decisions are invariably made at a far deeper level of the personality than the conscious mind, and all one does is to discover the decision one has already made. I see now that I had already decided to go to Mirfield if they would take me. And I felt like the brother officer of a friend of mine in the Italian campaign during the war. Relieving this officer of guard duty my friend asked him what was going on in the enemy positions opposite and received the answer: "I haven't dared look." On this visit I took in very little about Mirfield because, I am sure, like the officer, I didn't dare look.

The Superior had a long talk with me and explained the mechanics of entry into the Community.

If he accepted you, you became before arrival an aspirant. On arrival you became a postulant, which meant

that you lived in the place and kept the Community Rule
(it is printed and I was given a copy to study) but still had
access to your own money. After three months or so, if the
Superior thought fit, he admitted you as a novice. From
this point you ceased to have access to your own money
and were under the direction of an official called the
Novice-Guardian, who acted as the equivalent of a sort of
old-fashioned nanny and gave regular reports about you to
the Community. After two years of this the members of the
Community would discuss you and a secret ballot be taken.
If elected you would be admitted as a full-blown member
of the Community, solemnly declaring your intention of
remaining in the Community for life but vowing to do so
only for the next three years. After that there would be
another discussion and ballot and, if all went well, you
would vow to remain in the Community for life. Poverty
meant having no money of your own and, if you earned
anything, paying it into the common purse while the
Community undertook to look after your essential needs.
Chastity meant not marrying or entering into a relationship
which in ordinary circumstances would naturally lead to
marriage (in plainer speech it meant no sex or petting).
Obedience was not to the Superior but to the printed Rule.

The Superior said that I should need two or three
references and would have to have a medical check-up (he
knew of my analysis) and that if these were satisfactory, as
he anticipated, he would accept me as a postulant.

Clutching at a straw (for we are all a mass of
contradictions) I told him that I was due the following
academic year for a sabbatical. Could I try myself out at
Mirfield during that period before resigning from Trinity?
He laughed and said that that would be quite out of the
question. I should have to resign from Trinity before
arriving as a postulant or indeed before joining the list of
aspirants.

Having described the mechanics of entry the
Superior spoke of more personal matters. Did I think I was
being driven to Mirfield by guilt? Here I could confidently

say No. Fourteen years of psychoanalysis had destroyed my capacity for irrational guilt. In any case I was now certain that the game people played was nothing like so important as the game which was being played on them. When everything, every wheel within a wheel, was taken into account it seemed to me that most people were much more sinned against (by life, that is) than sinning. The evil people suffered was generally far greater than the evil they did. I had long noticed, for instance, that if people were nasty it was because they were unhappy.

The Superior then said to me: "If you come here, you mustn't regard it as in any way a denial of your past. Your past is what you have ɔ contribute to the life of the Community." I thought of my hatred of churchiness (the Superior obviously shared it to some extent) and was glad that even that might perhaps – though it seemed unlikely – be able to give something to the place. And, although I was ready now to give up sex as I would be required to do, I was glad that that too, all the past tenderness of receiving and giving and the intimate personal knowledge of others thereby made possible, would not now have to be denied or rejected as evil, but brought with me thankfully to my new life in the form of whatever degree of love and sensitivity and understanding I was capable of.

One final question the Superior put to me: "What are you going to do if you come here? Being a Religious (monk) isn't a job, at least nothing like a full-time job." I dithered a bit at this because of my disillusion with the academic study of theology. But eventually I said: "There is a very good library here, isn't there? Perhaps I could study and write." The Superior looked a bit sceptical at this. I was later to discover why. Quite a number of brethren had declared their intention of writing about this, that and the other (a biography of A. N. Whitehead, for instance, of all things!). But of these only two of late had actually produced anything.

The interview ended by my agreeing to write to the Superior about my decision a week or so after my return to

Cambridge. I was still trying to kid myself that the decision hadn't been made.

Altogether I got the impression that the Superior, Hugh Bishop, was a man of great personal authority from whom I should be able to learn an enormous amount as he obviously had a very great deal to give. In the event he never gave it. But that belongs to a later stage of the story.

I still have a cherished memento of that visit to Mirfield which I carry about with me everywhere in a small plastic box containing odds and ends. It must have been very nearly the last of its kind to be bought or sold in England. A crucial button from the top of my cassock, holding one side to the other, came off the second afternoon of my stay. I was no doubt tugging at the cassock in nervous agitation. I didn't know that there was a needlewoman in the place who would have sewn it on. So I walked down to the small town where, in a delightfully amateur sort of shop run by a Yorkshire lass of no mean age or proportions, I bought a small card of black safety-pins. They have all long since disappeared, except one. And that I hope to keep with me till I die.

11

A FEW DAYS after returning to Cambridge I wrote to the Superior and asked to become an aspirant, adding that I would keep to the arrangement which had been proposed of arriving at Mirfield as a postulant in a year's time. When the Superior had written to accept my application I wrote to Rab Butler as Master of Trinity resigning my Fellowship from the end of the academic year 1968–69 and explaining the reasons. I had now burnt my boats even if I hadn't yet launched out into the deep.

It might be supposed that having once definitely and irrevocably made the decision to try myself out and be tried out at Mirfield some sort of relief would follow. But it didn't. I was able for much of the time to push the decision to the back of my mind. I was extremely reluctant to talk about it and hated other people doing so. It was as if they were jabbing their fingers into a sore place.

In private there were times now and then when I couldn't stop myself realizing what I had done. And around those sporadic occasions there gathered a sort of manic-depressive condition, using the phrase in the loose conversational sense and not with any clinical precision.

There were times when I would be immensely excited by the prospect before me. "The Holy Ghost shall come upon thee and the power of the Highest shall overshadow thee." When I was in a manic mood I was thrilled to think that those words were and would be true of myself. It was as if I were standing in a place resplendent with spiritual glory and I used to weep at the goodness of God in bringing me there. A favourite gramophone record of mine was of Sandy Wilson's *Valmouth*. One of the songs was sung by a nun who was enjoying her one talking day a year and describing how she was going to make the most of it. Tomorrow, she said, she would have to be silent and sad and glum again. This amused me because I thought how wrong she was. To be enfolded in God's love was the richest, most joyfully satisfying, thing that anybody could be given. Then I used to play Noël Coward singing a number from *Bitter Sweet*:

> I'll see you again
> Whenever spring breaks through again.
> Time has lain heavy between
> But what has been
> Can leave me never.

Hadn't spring broken through again for me so that now I saw again the face of God's dear Son, so long obscured? And if from time to time I had seen it before in those occasional fits of awareness which I've described earlier on, I was now seeing it in a new and better way because I had now committed myself totally to it by my decision to go to Mirfield.

For some years the only prayer I could say *ex animo* (I've mentioned it before) had been: "O my God I hope in Thee for grace and for glory." Now it felt as if the prayer was being answered. The splendour of God had broken upon me and I was caught up in the radiance of His love.

I was by no means altogether taken in by this manic mood. There was about it, I knew, a great deal of sheer egotistical self-dramatization. I was aware that in practice God's love was sternly matter-of-fact, revealing itself much more in the giving of a cup of cold water (or gin) to a person in need than in high-flown visions of delight. Its coming upon me when I allowed myself to think of going to Mirfield was, I knew, little more than a sign of acute spiritual indigestion, and not by any means only spiritual either. I was preening myself in the centre of my own stage, singing some sort of equivalent to the song from *West Side Story*:

> I'm so pretty, O so pretty,
> I'm pretty and witty and bright . . .

I was more taken in by the occasional depressive moods. When these occurred it was generally at night. I then had dreams of utter gloom, finding myself lost in endless wastelands wandering about in despair. In one dream there was a man in the wasteland lying on the ground. I went up to him and found he was dying. "But," I said to him, "they told me there was a Hilton Hotel here." He just had strength enough to shake his head before he died. When in this depressed state, I used sometimes to wake up in a cold sweat as though some dreadful catastrophe had just occurred. Regaining consciousness it slowly dawned on me that the catastrophe was my going to Mirfield. There were occasions when I didn't go to sleep at all, but just lay in bed quaking with fear at the decision I had made. After a more than usually severe bout of fear I did one night eventually drop off to sleep. And then I dreamt that I was confronted by Keats's Belle Dame sans Merci. And with mounting horror I slowly realized that she was Hugh Bishop.

I kept these manic–depressive fits entirely to myself and said nothing about them to anybody, except, of course, to Christopher Scott, my analyst. He wasn't very perturbed about them. He thought that in the circumstances both the mania and the depression (in the loose sense in which I am using the words) were more or less inevitable and would pass to the degree in which in course of time I had assimilated the decision I had made.

He turned out to be right, but not before I had made a final protest, this time of a psychosomatic kind. Just before leaving for Mirfield I came out in spots, which itched terribly. I went to my Cambridge doctor (my GP). I had no temperature and didn't feel ill. The doctor said that the spots indicated nothing infectious or contagious. All I needed was some soothing ointment. During my first three months at Mirfield the spots grew in number and itching virulence. But they never appeared on any part of my body that was visible. I didn't tell anybody about them or go to the Mirfield doctor as I thought that my having them would be taken as a sign of nervous disability showing that I was unsuitable for my new life. So I used to go to a chemist in a neighbouring town and buy ointment for them, which I put on at night. My legs, feet, trunk and the tops of my arms were covered with them. But there was no sign of them below my shirtsleeves or above my collar. I used to scratch them in my sleep as well as when awake and there was often blood on my pyjamas and sheets. But I folded the sheets in a way which hid the bloodstains when I put them in the laundry basket, and nobody saw my pyjamas (we do our own washing except for sheets and towels). In time the spots cleared up and have never appeared again. What interested me was the control which saw to it that no spot ever occurred on any part of my body I had to display in public.

12

ABSTRACTING THESE FITS of mania and depression in order to describe them has made them look far more important than they were. They occurred only spasmodically. For the most part I was able to keep the future at arm's length, pushing it out of sight as much as I could. This showed itself outwardly not only by reluctance to talk about it or have other people mention it to me, but once by an act of rudeness at a party in London. On arrival I saw that at the other end of the room there stood a Mirfield Father – Augustine Hoey. I deliberately avoided him. I hadn't joined up yet. It was with that plea that I excused my rudeness, but the plea didn't impress me very much.

In spite of my having a sabbatical I had a great deal to occupy me. At the end of July I went with a Rambler, Graham Storey, to Athens for a fortnight and then on to a three weeks' tour of Iran, escorted by a member of the British Council there who had been a pupil of Graham's at Trinity Hall. I then went to the USA for a lecture tour and made enough money to fly back first class by day on the Yankee Clipper, its comfort, food and drink being a spiritual experience of no mean order. My medical checkup showed that I was about to have a rupture in two places, so I went into hospital and had these dealt with. Then I went to Malta, Cornwall, Naples, the Sorrento peninsula and Rome, followed by a visit to Ireland. And between trips I had the debris of eighteen years to sort out and dispose of. There was little time for what Byron called "that blight of life, the demon, thought".

13

FOR ALL MY RELUCTANCE to talk about going to Mirfield, I had to tell people about it. And this had to be done as opportunity offered. I couldn't put a notice in *The Times*: "Harry Williams is grateful to the Community of the Resurrection at Mirfield for undertaking from July next

year to see if he would be the slightest good as a monk."
But informing people piecemeal in this way brought the
unintended advantage of my being able to observe their
reaction more carefully than I could otherwise have done. I
noticed that in a number of people it obviously stirred
latent unconscious forces which manifested themselves in
various ways.

The first person to know was Rab Butler because of
my letter of resignation. He gave me the impression of
being slightly hurt as though, through lack of confidence in
him, I had resigned from a government ministry of which
he was chief. This showed, among other things, in his
obvious delight in having hooked a bishop (John
Robinson) as my successor. He was, as always, consistently
kind and friendly, but I detected in him a subtle instinctive
resentment as though he felt, against all reason and
proportion, that I had somehow betrayed him. I could see
also that he thought me a fool (though he was far too nice
ever to say so). But in that more than half of me entirely
agreed with him.

Mollie was her own marvellously sympathetic and
supportive self. Her eyes told me that she thought I might
be making a big mistake, but she did everything in her
power to boost my morale and make me feel it was a
worthwhile if foolhardy risk I was taking. She understood,
I think, better than anybody the turmoil I was going
through. But then, of course, she was used to explorers.
Her first husband had been one. I am sure she hasn't the
slightest idea how much easier she made things for me
during that final year at Trinity before my departure.

I would like at this point to say that I am not at all in
a position to classify people's reaction to my decision into
right, wrong, fair, and so on. I was (and am) myself such a
bundle of contradictions that everybody was right and
everybody wrong. Nor am I yet, even after an interval
of some thirteen years, in any position to assess the various
verdicts given.

One of my closest and dearest friends, Elizabeth

Cavendish, was totally opposed to what I had done. Her views had enormous weight with me, not only because of our friendship, but also because she had no personal axe whatever to grind and (as I've said before) she is a person of very penetrating perception. And transparently she was concerned in this matter entirely and only for my welfare.

In the spring of 1969 I stayed with her and John Betjeman in Cornwall. I arrived very het-up because of an incident at the end of the Lent term which had wounded my *amour-propre*. It was silly of me to get angry about it. It was only a matter of a speech. Its upsetting me so much showed what a volatile condition I was in. The atmosphere at Trebetherick with the company of Elizabeth and John soon put me once again on an even keel. After a week, when I was fully stabilized, I felt at dinner that something was in the air. I was right. It fell upon me like an avalanche while after dinner we were sitting round the fire. Elizabeth told me straight out that she thought I was making the most catastrophic mistake in going to Mirfield and said she was going to spend the evening telling me why.

I remembered how her mother one evening at dinner in Derbyshire had said that Elizabeth had a rough tongue but a kind heart. The two of them on occasions used to have the most passionate quarrels, not in the least on any personal or family matter, but about Cyprus, or Africa or the welfare state, Moucher (Elizabeth's mother) defending views similar to those of her brother, Bobbety Salisbury, while Elizabeth would condemn them as politically inept, out of touch with reality and inhuman. By the end the two would often be shouting at each other things like "If that's what you mean, then for God's sake say so," and so on. But the quarrel left no trace of any kind whatever after it was over. Half an hour later you would never have guessed it had happened.

Sitting that evening at Trebetherick I remembered those occasions, fastened my seat-belt, and prepared for the worst. John's face, meanwhile, was a mixture of concern, anxiety, amusement and reassurance. He remained silent

most of the time, but every now and then he interjected a
sort of miniature scherzo which sounded irresistibly funny.

"First of all," said Elizabeth, "you enjoy conviviality. You get a great deal of pleasure out of parties and
dinners. There's nothing wrong in that, and it's just silly to
cut yourself away from it. It's a much more important side
of your life than you imagine and you'll feel the loss of it
desperately."

At this point John interjected the first of his
scherzos. Sounding like the Walrus in *Alice in Wonderland*
he said gravely: "I suppose you reach a state where a *petit
beurre* tastes delicious."

"And then," Elizabeth went on, "what about your
holiday travels? You've often said they're the best part of
your life. Certainly they liven you up. Won't you be more
than half-dead without them?"

"Oh, those ceramic tiles at Caltagirone. I shall never
forget them," said John.

I had no secrets from Elizabeth. She knew all about
me, and she continued: "And young people, the undergraduates and those you've been able to make permanent
friends of like Simon and James and William and that
young man – what's he called? – who works at Rota's, and
those amusing young Fellows, what's the name of the one
who's such a good mimic, you know, the one who's a
scientist? And that lovely old man who kissed me when I
came to the Ladies' Night, the Russian, Susie, no, Bessy,
something – won't you be cutting yourself off from your
life-blood if you can't see them?"

"I thought that young man in front of us in church
on Sunday was very handsome. Do you think he noticed
us?" said John.

"What I'm getting at is this," said Elizabeth. "What
you say and write is of enormous help to hundreds of
people. I know because I've met a lot of them. It's not
conventional parson's stuff. You go to the heart of things.
But this depends upon your imagination. And imagination
needs to be fed. It's parties and travel and young men,

however much it sometimes hurts, and interesting people, which feed your imagination. It'll dry up without that sort of stimulus. And we shall all be the losers. And for what? I'm going to have my say. For a fit, for what is probably no more than a passing fit, a fit of – yes, I'm going to say it – a fit of conceit. Yes, I don't care what you think, of conceit, spiritual conceit. I don't know the technical name for it, but I'm sure it exists. Is it 'accident' or something like that? And it won't work because you're simply not like that. You're not the stuff from which stained-glass windows are made."

"Kempe's windows in Wakefield Cathedral are rather good," said John.

"I'm sorry," said Elizabeth, "but I've got to say what I think. I think you're being madly silly, utterly insane, criminally stupid."

She paused and I said, "But I've done it now. I've resigned from Trinity."

"Yes, I know," she said. "But there are dozens of other things you could do which would keep you in circulation. One thing you must promise me – if when you go to Mirfield it doesn't work, you must be humble enough to admit it frankly and leave. I mean this with all my heart – you mustn't be wasted. People need terribly what you have to give them."

"I would like a glass of port," said John.

The attack was over. It worried me, of course, because I thought she might well be right, and I still wonder how far she was. But it didn't upset me fundamentally because it was so obviously the sincerest expression of affection. And her attack was open and above board. What gets under the skin is unconscious or semi-conscious aggression, the sneaking onslaught which hasn't the courage of its own intentions. "The words of his mouth were softer than butter, having war in his heart: his words were smoother than oil, and yet they be very swords." Of that there was no trace whatever in what Elizabeth had said. Perhaps a rough tongue is always the kindest. And among my friends it was Elizabeth and John who came to

Mirfield for the ceremony by which I was made a full member of the Community, Elizabeth giving me a gold pencil with my initials on it and the date – 1 January, 1972.

The only other person who took this uncompromising line, though much more light-heartedly and half in joke (but only half), was a charming man in Rome to whom Monsignor Gilbey had given me a letter of introduction. He was the representative of the English Benedictines to the Holy See and (as I proposed to do) had become a monk later in life, joining Downside or Ampleforth (I can't remember which), having first been a professional soldier in a Guards regiment and for some time ADC to the Governor of Malta. He said he knew nothing about the Anglican Community of the Resurrection, but was talking in a general way from his own experience. "Don't do it," he said, when I told him of my being an aspirant, "don't do it. You'll hate it. They'll take years to forgive you for having had a successful career before joining the Order. They'll think it's God's will that they should keep you continually in your place and treat you like the lowest of His creatures. You'll be utterly miserable. I was, for years. You've still got your freedom. Keep it." He was able to combine looking serious with the very slightest suggestion of a twinkle in his eye. I left him feeling that he had meant me to read either between the lines or along them, whichever I chose. I stopped at a nearby café and had a Campari soda with gin, known locally as a Cardinale, and thought things over.

An exactly opposite view to the two preceding was taken by Ann Tusa, the wife of John Tusa the journalist and television commentator. I had known them both fairly well when they were at Cambridge some eight or nine years before and had taken their wedding in Trinity chapel. Ann, I suppose, would describe herself as an agnostic, though, having read the History Tripos she knew a fair amount about Christianity. Around this time she came up to me at a party in London. I felt embarrassed as I knew she had heard the news about me. Seeing me look a bit shy she said: "I don't think what you're doing is at all odd. Quite the reverse. I know you, but I don't know you well. I mean I don't know all about your dreams and struggles. I'm judging the thing not in terms of what you're like but in terms of Christian principles and claims. What you're doing seems to me the logical outcome of what Christianity is about. It's Christianity taken to its ultimate conclusion, if, that is, it has anything to do with Jesus as represented in the gospels." This detached and somewhat academic verdict was refreshing. It was followed by her opening her bag, taking from it a paperback edition in English of the Rule of St Benedict, and giving it to me. She made me feel very grateful to her and I kissed her.

I gave the news to my old friend Simon Stuart (as yet unmarried) during a weekend house party at his place in Sussex. On the evening of our arrival we found ourselves sitting alone together on the terrace before dinner while the rest were changing. I said – it must have been somewhat portentously (we had driven down from London alone together) – "Simon, I've got something I want to tell you about myself." He turned white and looked very frightened. When I told him what it was a look of enormous relief came over him. He knew I'd been to the doctor lately for a checkup and thought I was about to tell him an incurable disease had been diagnosed which would kill me in six months. He was so pleased that I wasn't ill after all, that my going to Mirfield seemed to him for the moment a cause for celebration and he gave us all a very jovial weekend.

His London housekeeper in those days was a woman of great character called Nusha. She was a Yugoslav of farming stock who filled the flat by her presence and had decided views on most things, even if a view could change to its opposite within the course of a single conversation. Once, after I had been at Mirfield a year or two, I arrived at the flat on a Friday evening – I was, I think, preaching at Westminster Abbey on the Sunday morning. Nusha, opening the front door, welcomed me with an earnest piece of advice. In her broken English she said to me: "Mr Williams, why don't you stop preaching and get married?" Her peasant's intuition had in a short sentence gone directly to the heart of the matter.

James and Janice Mitchell were apprehensive but extremely comforting in all ways possible. Like many shrewd and successful businessmen James is an easy weeper. (The death of Puccini's Mimi always sends him into floods.) So he wept as we spoke about my move, while Janice looked very sad. But James did more than weep. With his business partner, John Beazley (to die tragically young of cancer a few years later), he volunteered to guarantee me a job in his publishing house if Mirfield didn't work. He said it would be a safety net which would tide me over at least temporarily until I decided what I wanted to do. That is the sort of thoughtful generosity one never forgets.

James's father, Bill, had the same generous nature. When I stayed with them once in Gloucestershire the other guests were an army man and his wife, desperately worried by their inability to meet their children's school fees. The next day they looked happy and relieved, and the man told me that Bill had undertaken to meet whatever financial liabilities they themselves were unable to meet. It was Sunday and Bill's birthday. He and I went to church together and sat in the front pew. Immediately after the sermon while there was still complete silence in the church Bill said to me in a loud stage whisper: "You stay on here. I'm going to put some champagne on ice. I've invited the vicar and his wife." To which in a loud, stern voice the vicar replied, as though determined not to be side-tracked: "Hymn number 345."

There was one reaction to my going to Mirfield which still makes me laugh. It came from people who thought – I don't know why – that they ought to be appreciative and were afraid I might think them too Philistine to be so. Their efforts to dispel this imagined impression resulted in statements like the following:

"While I'm lying in bed at nine o'clock in the

morning it'll be a wonderful help to me to know that you'll
have got up at half-past five."

"When I'm at Covent Garden to hear Callas sing
Tosca it will refresh my jaded soul no end to think of you
in church at Mirfield."

"As with the usual gang of friends we eat our dinner
of grouse and Château Lafite it will be a real spiritual
inspiration to know you're having a meal of bread and
water." These remarks were made with all the passion
which only simulated sentiments can arouse. I adored them.
They seemed to me the very quintessence of comedy. And
as in all comedy they made the speakers rather lovable. A
certain genuine humility is needed for people to be vacant
enough to make themselves look completely ridiculous.

A more honest but unintended reaction came from
a college employee who was the head of his department. I
went to see him at his office about something and he
showed me a letter he had received that morning from a
former undergraduate who had gone down the year before.
It was to cancel a perfectly ordinary and honest arrangement he had made and could have been done in a couple of
lines, especially as it was for three months ahead, so that the
cancellation caused no inconvenience to anybody. But as
the totally irrelevant reason for his change of plan the
young man had written pages and pages about his having
given his heart to the Lord Jesus and living now only to
witness for him. After I had spent about eight minutes
ploughing through the letter, the college employee said to
me: "People like that generally end up in a monastery."
Then he went red in the face and corrected himself – "I
meant a mental hospital." He then went redder still. I
wanted to laugh, but something told me it would be more
tactful to suggest that young people did get aberrations of
that kind, but that as a general rule they were only
temporary.

The Fellows maintained a sensitive and compassionate silence about my decision, saying only that they
were sorry I was going. The welcome they have given me

on my return visits encourages me to believe that they meant it. One Fellow, Bob Robson, wrote the words of a farewell song which was subsequently set to music and sung in my room by the chapel choir. It can be found only in a strictly private collection of Bob Robson's domestic poems. To publish it here would not only be an abuse of his kindness but might lead to more than one misunderstanding. I was, of course, delighted as anybody would be and, when it was sung, rather weepy if also a trifle embarrassed.

14

ANOTHER SONG had already been sung about me at the end of the Lent term. At that time each year the undergraduates get up a revue which among other things generally contains a number of topical allusions and songs. (Kitson Clark's name used often to be brought in to the annoyance of Simpson, who once said to me: "He doesn't realize it's only because his name is easy to rhyme.") That year, 1969, to the tune of "Lily the Pink", they sang:

> "Let's get drunk, get drunk, get drunk,
> For Harry the monk, the monk, the monk."

It was all very good-natured and hilarious, and was so funny that I didn't feel even slightly embarrassed.

Prince Charles was in the cast. As is now well known, he is a marvellous comedian. But his presence meant that the song was published the following morning in the *Telegraph* and other national dailies.

Except to say how profoundly grateful I am for the privilege of Prince Charles's friendship, I don't want to abuse it by writing small talk about him. But his being at Trinity at this time meant that the Press were eager for any tit-bits of news and gossip they could scrape up. A man becoming a monk has in itself for English people – heaven knows why – a certain minor publicity value (as, did also, eleven years later, the Fellow, a Professor of Mathematics and an FRS, who became an Anglican clergyman), but the royal presence in the college enlarged it out of all proportion and I began to feature in gossip columns and so on. It was all very harmless stuff and no more than a minor irritation.

What really annoyed me was when a clergyman I knew vaguely, who had himself been at an Anglican community for a number of years and then left, wrote reproving me severely for the publicity and saying that that was no way to become a monk. If I had left a religious community I don't think I should have written to reprove somebody I scarcely knew who was about to join one. But that apart, my correspondent should have known what is obvious to anybody with a grain of sense, that the fierce light which beats upon the Royals casts some of its glare on those who for the time-being are their associates. The publicity is thrust upon you willy-nilly, not sought after.

Another clergyman I knew who had seen in *The Times* that I was to "retire and go to Mirfield" wrote me a snarl of a letter to say how lucky I was to be able to retire at fifty in a blaze of footlights.

The consecrated claw, I'm afraid, can often be irresponsible in the victims it chooses to scratch, and seems quite unaware (at least one hopes so) of the impulses which animate it. These letters would have been unpleasant to receive at any time. But in the unsettled condition I was then in (and the clergymen should have known that it would be a difficult period for anybody) they were very nasty indeed.

To counterbalance them I had a most encouraging letter from Michael Ramsey (at that time, still being Archbishop, he was the Mirfield Community's Visitor). It is no surprise that he understood that I was no more than standing at the gate, certain only of my weakness and muddle, and desperately needing the kind of support and heartening which he gave.

What sustained me a great deal during this time were the novels of Graham Greene I had read over the years. For he so clearly and deeply understood that God's grace is given not only to virtuous and worthy people but also to mixed-up sinners like myself whom life had broken into a number of pieces which wouldn't fit together, and who had to be content to live like a jigsaw puzzle too difficult to remain anything else but a heap of bits. One phrase I remembered in particular – I think it was from *The Heart of the Matter*: "When the moment of grace comes our prayers will rise like a flock of birds." And I hoped that included our unuttered prayers, those buried wishes which rise to the surface every now and again and quickly disappear once more below ground. I hoped that when their time came those buried wishes as well as my articulate prayers, so few and far between, would rise to assault Mercy itself and bring me – well, I didn't know what, except perhaps, vaguely, deliverance from the pride which prompted me in effect to thank God I was not like a good sound churchman, as though the publican in the parable were to thank God he was not even as this pharisee.

But more often than not at this time such edifying thoughts were crowded out by festivities of one sort or another. In May I had my fiftieth birthday and James and Janice Mitchell gave me a dinner at the Savoy, ordering a birthday cake which arrived with my name and age on it in no more than twenty minutes! Then Mollie and Rab Butler generously said they would give me a farewell dinner. I could choose any twelve people I liked and Mollie would not only write to invite them but offer to put them up in the Master's Lodge if they needed accommodation. It was (as always in the Lodge) a very happy and enjoyable evening, but for me at a deeper level it also seemed inevitably something of a funeral wake. When the party broke up soon after midnight I went to my room and sported my oak. I heard some people banging on it and calling my name. But I wasn't in the mood to continue the revels, so I didn't open up and they went away.

Then on the first day of July there was Prince Charles's Investiture at Caernarvon Castle. It was a glorious occasion, and the dedication of which it spoke did a great deal to invigorate my own faltering resolves. In the train on the way back I was lucky enough to share a compartment alone with George Thomas, then Secretary of State for Wales. He told me a charming story about his appointment to that office which I'm sure he won't mind my repeating. Harold Wilson, he said, after offering him the post added: "I think I ought to be honest with you, George, and tell you that you were not the first person on my list for the job." "I think I should know who was," George Thomas replied. Harold Wilson smiled for a moment and then said: "It was your old mum." At this point Jim Callaghan came into the compartment to congratulate George Thomas on the outstanding success of the day. For George Thomas he ordered some kind of soft drink and gave me a large gin and tonic. It almost persuaded me to vote Labour at the next election, but didn't quite.

My last party was a barbecue given by the Cobbolds on the banks of the lake at Knebworth. There were a lot of former Trinity undergraduates there whom it was fun to meet. But I've mentioned the event for another reason as well: it was the occasion on my part of a ritualistic act. The evening was coolish and everybody was dressed in sweaters and jeans and so on. But I decided to wear my clerical evening clothes and to look as smart in them as I could. For this would be their positively final appearance and I wanted to say goodbye to them in style. I didn't, of course, tell anybody what I was doing, and when the party had livened up I noticed some of the guests looking at me with a certain surprised curiosity. But from a clergyman anything is expected and everything forgiven. So nobody actually said anything to me about it. The suit then went to the Mitchells' house in Hampstead to be stored in a cupboard. When on a visit there some years later a wave of nostalgia prompted me to examine it, I found it still had some pieces of grass on it. It's odd how life solidifies itself in things. The barbecue was more immediately present to me in that suit with the grass on it than when it was actually taking place.

15

LIFE, HOWEVER, DURING THESE LAST DAYS wasn't all beer and skittles. I had a great deal of clearing up to do.

My official college papers and correspondence were neatly sorted out by my secretary and locked away in the appropriate files. It was my own personal junk I had to deal with.

For eighteen years I had kept all my letters, bundles of newspapers, journals, photographs, menu-cards with the customary signature of friends on them, programmes for every sort of occasion – the usual rubbish one accumulates when one hasn't the heart (or more likely the strength of will) to throw away ephemera. It made an enormous pile which reached almost half-way to the ceiling. I decided to tear everything up and burn it. It was two-thirds a commonsense decision (I knew there would be precious little room at Mirfield for anything but essentials) and one-third another ritualistic gesture signifying a break with the past.

There were dozens of bread-and-butter letters. Glancing through them I noticed with amusement that they all followed more or less the same pattern. They said that the food was very good, but (in case the writer should seem too concerned with his belly) the conversation was even better. In fact the exact opposite was almost uniformly true.

Then I came across a letter from an undergraduate who had gone home to attend the funeral of a rich bachelor uncle from whom the family obviously had expectations. With the innocence of youth he commented on the uncle's death: "Everybody seems to have taken it very well." The sentence conjured up a scene rich in comic possibilities.

Next I examined a number of those long heartfelt letters from the close friends of undergraduate miscreants who pleaded that the misdemeanour should not be treated too severely as there were extenuating circumstances of this and the other kind. Young people always stand by their friends and do everything they can for them in a way calculated to revive any flagging faith in human nature.

I then picked out a letter from an undergraduate the College Council had had no option but to send down. It thanked me for my concern and was signed "Yours affectionately". Anybody capable of that sort of generosity was, I thought, bound to make good. This young man certainly did.

Then I found postcards from honeymoon couples I had married – coloured pictures of Taormina, Amalfi, the Scottish Highlands, and, best of all, Southend, with happily facetious greetings at the back like: "You should try marriage. It's bliss," or "You seem to have done your work at the wedding splendidly." One bride had been thoughtful enough to write: "I have an awful feeling you didn't get any wedding-cake."

The letters from colleagues were fewer. There were a number from Lord Adrian when he was Master of Trinity about this and that, one of them announcing that at a forthcoming memorial service he intended to wear only a gown. I hadn't suggested what he should wear, but I remembered answering on a card that I hoped he wouldn't find it too cold, and then feeling frightfully scared that he wouldn't be amused. Luckily he was. When he laughed and his eyes twinkled at you he was quite irresistible. I would have died for him.

Both Kitson Clark and Patrick Duff, my old tutor, had always been very good to me. I was amused, therefore, to find a letter from Kitson telling me that an event I had mentioned in a sermon as occurring in 1863 had in fact occurred in 1862 and giving me the appropriate reference. I remembered that when I had looked it up I found that it had occurred in December 1862, so that I was not all that wide of the mark. Patrick's letter belonged to four years previously and read: "Dear Harry, As your old tutor I feel I ought to tell you that it is time you learnt not to spell 'all right' 'alright'. Yours ever, Patrick."

From Simpson there was a fairly large bundle of letters. Would I stop the organist from playing too loudly?

Would I stop the leader of the choir from beating time? Would I stop the chaplains at Sunday Evensong from praying for things like Vietnam? Could we not sometimes at weekday services have the prayer of St Chrysostom, as the phrase "when two or three are gathered together in Thy name" was on those occasions so entirely appropriate? Some of his letters were appreciative. He liked my preaching, which I found flattering, as he wasn't easy to please in the pulpit. And once when circumstances had given me an extra amount of very taxing work he had written to remind me that God strengthened the back of the mule according to the weight of the burden it had to carry. He always wrote in his own hand, but signed the letter with a rubber stamp as though the final effort of writing his name would be too much for him.

There were letters in abundance from Mollie Butler – many of them invitations, but some of them written on occasions when she intuitively recognized that I was under strain or sad. She always knew, for instance, when a sermon had been particularly difficult to deliver and wrote at once to thank me for it. And there were also a number of pure fun letters; she had once disguised her handwriting as I had told her jokingly that the porters would be raising an eyebrow at the volume of our correspondence.

There were also, of course, letters which had no connection with the college.

Before the Wolfenden Committee was appointed I tried to organize a letter in *The Times* signed by a number of eminent people asking for the setting up of a Royal Commission or something similar to consider the law concerning sexual offences, particularly what were then homosexual offences. I found in the jumble a letter from Geoffrey Fisher, then Archbishop of Canterbury, saying he was entirely in favour of the setting up of such a commission and would certainly give the idea his public support and blessing, but that it was his practice never to sign letters to *The Times* in conjunction with others except for Roman Catholic and Free Church leaders on strictly church matters. I also found a letter from Bertrand Russell saying he would certainly sign. I hadn't pursued the matter further because I then went to Madrid for the whole of the long vacation as temporary chaplain to the British Embassy church there, the former chaplain having left and a new one (it was to be Geoffrey Beaumont) having not yet been chosen. During my time in Madrid I saw in the English Press that the Wolfenden Committee had been appointed, so there was no more to do.

Radio and television broadcasts had brought stacks of letters. Radio brought me more than television. Perhaps my voice is nicer than my face, but it was also because old retired people in those days used the radio more than the television, and they were the people who had time to write. A few of the letters were abusive, quite a number complimentary, and some from puzzled listeners. An anonymous person sent me a postcard every time I gave tongue on radio or television. I found a bundle of them. They all had a background of crayoned purple and red against which was always inscribed in large green capital letters the announcement: "The kingdom of heaven shall consist of four hundred and forty thousand bachelors." I didn't know whether it was supposed to be good news or bad.

Among this collection of letters I found one even more peculiar. It was from a person well known in religious circles in this country and greatly respected and valued. He had written to tell me that as a result of watching my television broadcast on Easter Sunday about Christ's resurrection a friend of his had shot himself. I had thought this over very anxiously for some days and then come to the conclusion that if anybody shot himself as a result of seeing any television programme he must have been pretty dotty in the first place. About fifteen years later (I was at Mirfield by then) I was gossiping with the head of an Oxford college about this and that, and he said: "I did a television broadcast about six months ago. A few days later so-and-so (my correspondent) wrote and told me that somebody had shot himself as the result of seeing it. I'm pretty certain, you know, that he had made it up." "You're perfectly right," I said and described the letter sent to me.

Among the rest of the rubbish only one thing brought back really vivid memories. It was a theatre programme of the production at the New Theatre (as it was then called) of *Romeo and Juliet* with John Gielgud as Romeo, Laurence Olivier as Mercutio (they exchanged parts), Peggy Ashcroft as Juliet, and Edith Evans as Juliet's nurse. Alec Guinness, I think, had a very small part as the Chorus. The programme contained photographs of the four leading characters and they transported me back to that miraculous afternoon – I went to a matinée. I was fifteen and had saved up enough money for the fare to London and the ticket. Although I had already, when staying with my Aunt Nellie, seen Gielgud as Hamlet with Jessica Tandy as Ophelia, it had had nothing like the same impact on me as this production of *Romeo and Juliet*. I was totally enthralled and forgot entirely that I was sitting in a London theatre. I was part of the action on the stage, and not only was I in Verona but each of the characters seemed to be myself. It was I who stood both below the balcony and on it. It was I who was Romeo suffering the pangs of love. It was I who was Mercutio making fun of him for them. It was I who was Juliet's nurse making her shrewd, down-to-earth comments. Inconsistently it was all I could do not to shout at Romeo that Juliet was only drugged not dead. And when he drank the poison and Juliet, waking to find him dead, killed herself, I felt that life had ceased for me as well. The finer points of the play and dialogue escaped me, of course, completely. But I had never before entered with such complete abandon into the reality of life and love and death. It was in fact too much for me. When the performance was over and I stood outside the theatre in St Martin's Lane I discovered that I had a severe migraine. It was chiefly the play. But it was also partly, I'm sure, the punishment I unconsciously gave myself for my wickedness in going to the theatre at all. So impotent, when it comes to it, are the rational convictions and judgements on which we pride ourselves. But it was worth the price every time and in every way.

Finding the old programme reminded me of that great afternoon, bringing back its past reality into the present. I now saw that it had been the first step along a road which was to lead me through great torments to freedom and the inalienable inheritance of my humanity. The last step of that journey was still in the far distant future and might never be taken in this life. But that first step, I thought as I examined the programme, belonged to the past. And to clutch at the past nostalgically only falsifies the present. So I tore the programme up, having first kissed the four photographs it contained.

There is a sense in which the best things in life have to be surrendered as well as the worst, the good as well as the bad. For it isn't only good food which grows stale and rotten if kept too long.

PART FIVE

Mirfield Father

AS THE DAY of my departure for Mirfield drew nearer I began to feel like a soldier on leave from the front who, knowing that his leave will soon be up and he will have to quit his family for the front once again, mesmerizes himself into feeling that he has still an eternity of time at home.

There were still two full weeks before I left for Mirfield. Then there was one whole week. Then there were forty-eight solid hours.

I was spared the ordeal of having dinner in Hall my last evening as the Butlers invited me to dine with them privately at the Lodge. In the event Mollie was ill in London with a throat infection, so I had dinner with Rab alone. Nobody could have gone out of his way more than he did to be paternal and comforting. My sincere gratitude was mixed with a certain sympathy for the poor man for being loaded with this chore. It was a relief that one could ask him questions about public and political affairs. He told me, for instance, who he thought would certainly not be the next Archbishop of Canterbury if Edward Heath happened to be Prime Minister when the vacancy occurred. It was somebody regarded in church circles as much the most likely candidate. As it happened the favourite died prematurely and, in any case, it was Harold Wilson who appointed.

I had hired a car and driver to take me to Mirfield. The car was waiting for me outside the Great Gate at eleven o'clock the next morning. Luckily I got through Great Court without meeting anybody. Then just outside I saw approaching a former pupil of mine who was by then a Fellow. I shall always be grateful to him for what he did, or rather, for what he didn't do. For he didn't come up to say goodbye, but merely smiled at me and passed on.

Our journey started, and after what seemed to me a short time we stopped at a garage. But we didn't buy any petrol. I looked at my watch and saw it was half-past one. My driver (he had driven me a number of times before and we knew each other fairly well) got out and obviously expected me to as well. He led me to a roadside café attached to the garage and pointed out what was on offer for lunch. It was the most dismal meal I have ever eaten. But it was soon over and we were *en route* again.

It was a dull day with black clouds and intermittent rain. I noticed that the farther north we got the more dismally disapproving my driver's face became. With every mile passed his face disseminated a bit more gloom. Then, towards the end of our journey it suddenly lit up. The reason was our approach to a signpost pointing in a direction it described as Royston (a village near Barnsley). With the insane hope born of utter despair my driver said to me brightly: "That isn't our Royston, is it, Sir?" I wished devoutly that it were.

Eventually we arrived at the House of the Resurrection at Mirfield. I sent the car away and rang the bell. Nobody answered. After ringing three times with no result I pushed open the front door and went in. The place looked like the *Marie Celeste*. It had all the signs of being inhabited but not a soul was about. Eventually a cassocked figure appeared. "Excuse me," I said, "but I've arrived here according to arrangements made. My name is Williams. I'm the new postulant. Could you tell me what I should do or who I should see?" "I haven't the slightest idea," the cassock answered and scuttled away. After what seemed an interminable interval another cassocked figure appeared and I asked him the same question. He looked entirely blank. But, recovering, he said he would go and see whether the Superior was in. He wasn't. (He was in fact away.) But his secretary, a very capable woman, came to my rescue. She asked somebody to discover where my room was and to lead me there.

I knew the room would be small (it was ten feet by

seven), but I didn't expect it would have only one chair – an upright at a table. I unpacked the few belongings I had brought and sat at the table. It had on it a Bible, with the Apocrypha included, in the Revised Standard Version. I began reading the Everyman edition of *Little Dorrit* I had brought with me.

About an hour later somebody appeared whom I recognized from my visit the previous year as the Novice-Guardian. He took me on a quick tour of the main buildings, introducing me to one or two Brethren we happened to meet on the way. They were all in a great hurry. Leaving me back in my room the Novice-Guardian said: "Evensong is at seven. If you arrive in the church five minutes early I'll show you where to go." I sat at my table again and read *Little Dorrit*, feeling like one of those unwanted children sometimes called an accident or a mistake. And my spots itched horribly.

After Evensong the Prior (the second in command), Donald Patey, gave me a friendly welcome and said that, although it couldn't be repeated, since this was my first evening I could as a special privilege sit next to him at supper. By the end of the meal I felt almost cheerful. Somebody gave me a postcard which had already arrived for me that morning. It was from a clergyman friend in Malta – a reproduction of a painting in the Roman Catholic cathedral in Valetta of the Beheading of St John the Baptist. On the other side the message was brief: "I expect you feel you've lost yours too." On reflection I discovered that I didn't.

❧‖2‖❧

MIRFIELD is in what used to be called the West Riding of Yorkshire, ten miles from Leeds on one side and five miles from Huddersfield on the other. It is a smallish town with its main shopping centre about a mile from the Community house.

The nucleus of the house (known as the House of

the Resurrection) is a mansion built by a wool spinner who had made his pile by selling cloth to both sides in the Franco-Prussian war. The house was bought by the Community in 1898 and over the years a number of wings (including a guest-house with thirty-five rooms) were added with other extensions of various kinds, most notably a large church designed by Walter Tapper. From the outside the church looks ugly, but inside the proportions are extremely good, and the building combines great simplicity with great dignity. The ambulatory, with its succession of small arches, seems to me particularly fine, especially at night when it is lit up. Of the building as a whole you never grow tired, thanks, I think, to its complete lack of fussiness.

The wool spinner had obviously employed a very competent landscape gardener to lay out the grounds. They are on different levels and contain lawns, flower-beds, a small wood, a large field (known as the cricket field, though I've only seen teams from the neighbourhood play there, and that only about once a year), an orchard and a vegetable garden where we grow a great deal, but by no means all, of our fruit and vegetables. From the lowest level of the grounds you can see the land sloping down to the River Calder (reputed to be the most polluted river in England). On the other side of the river the land goes upwards in green fields. What luck, I wondered, had preserved them from being built over?

In the Community grounds there is a theological college, that is, a postgraduate college where for two years men are trained to be Anglican clergymen. It generally has a complement of about forty students, and four out of the six members of the staff belong to the Community. The college is self-sufficient in the sense that it has its own buildings, including a library, dining hall and chapel, though the students (only of course during term) attend sung Evensong from Monday to Friday in the Community church and also the sung Communion with sermon on Sunday mornings, some of them standing decoratively about the chancel as extras.

The Community was founded in 1892 by Charles Gore, later Bishop of Oxford and a noted Anglican theologian. And the Community's Rule (more or less in the form now printed) was written in the course of time by Walter Frere, an immensely learned man who later became Bishop of Truro. The Rule has been only slightly modified here and there since Frere's time to meet new conditions. By constitution the Community is a democracy. Important decisions can be taken only by the Brethren voting in General Chapter (a sort of Parliament) on the principle of one man one vote. The Superior is in charge of personnel and is generally responsible for the welfare both of the Community as a whole and also of its individual members. He decides where a Brother is to be posted or what job or jobs he is to do. He is chairman of General Chapter, where he can exercise influence but not power. He is elected by a two-thirds majority of the votes in General Chapter (those abroad voting by post), nominally for a period of three years, though in practice he generally stays in office for nine or twelve years, no other candidate being proposed at the triennial elections. I imagine that one of the more trying facets of a Superior's job is the necessity to deal patiently yet firmly with people of limited wisdom who are very much in earnest. I suspect that a number of such people are found in most, if not all, Religious Communities.

The Community has houses in South Africa and Zimbabwe, one in London, and a contemplative house (whose only work is prayer) in Sunderland. Until recently it also had a hostel in Leeds for university students, but the fabric was costing too much to keep up and we sold the building to the university. Mirfield is the headquarters or the Mother House and contains around forty Brethren. The whole Community has between seventy and eighty members, the numbers fluctuating as people die and join.

The Community is financed by investments. (A London committee of stockbrokers generously gives us the benefit of its advice.) A Brother can leave his capital to whoever he likes, but I suspect that in the early years of the

Community, when people still had money, quite a number of Brethren left it to the Community. We also continue to receive legacies. Anything earned by a Brother goes, of course, into the common purse. And we have charitable status as far as tax goes.

The printed Rule starts off on its title page with a contradiction: "The Community of the Resurrection shall consist of celibate priests and laymen who combine together at the call of God to reproduce the life of the first Christians." But most of the first Christians were married, and if they reproduced anything, it was themselves by the ordinary biological processes. The New Testament, however, is a screen on which all sorts of different things can be projected. Within certain limits you pays your money and takes your choice. I don't think Walter Frere realized this at all, and he also lived before the days when English theological scholars properly understood how radically different from each other successive cultures are. As A. J. P. Taylor wrote once in a review: "That the past is not the present is hard doctrine." Frere imagined that a condition alleged to have existed in first-century Palestine could be transported bodily, like a sort of Holy House of Loreto, to twentieth-century Yorkshire. And in his day scholars had not yet understood what a highly idealized portrait of the first Christians is given us by the author of the Acts of the Apostles, the truth, seeping out from the Pauline Epistles, being very different and far less edifying.

The beginning of the Preface in its amended form is far more informative:

"The Community shall be occupied in pastoral, evangelistic, literary, educational and such other works as are compatible with its common life and worship, and are in accordance with the special gifts which God has given to its members, provided always that it be kept in view that the immediate worship and service of God must take first place in the lives of those who would truly after Christ's pattern minister to men."

An ordinary day begins with Matins at 6.45, followed by the Holy Communion. Breakfast is at 8 o'clock. There are generally various chores to be done until about 9.30. You then answer letters and get on with your own work until 12.45, when there is a service of about fifteen to twenty minutes. After lunch (it is the main meal of the day and is called dinner) you garden or go for a walk until tea at 4. Tea must end at 4.30, and you get on again with your own work until 7, when Evensong is sung, followed by supper. After supper you can have half an hour off, and then get back to your work. The last service of the day, called Compline, is at 9.45 and is generally over soon after 10, when, if you wish, you can go to bed. Silence is kept from Compline until 9 o'clock the following morning.

In addition to these services you undertake as a minimum to spend three hours a week in meditation or contemplation, and half an hour in praying for the Community and its members. But most Brethren do much more than that.

At any one time a number of Brethren may be away from the Community House on work – taking retreats, giving lectures, preaching, looking after nuns (since all communities of nuns have what is called a warden, who is always a priest and who goes and stays with them from time to time to give advice and so forth). There may, therefore, on any one day be considerably fewer than forty Brethren in the House. But there will also be guests, on an average five or six at a time, except when there is a retreat or conference, when there can be as many as thirty to thirty-five.

❧❧ 3 ❧❧

AFTER TWO or three months at Mirfield my chief feeling was one of relief. The place wasn't anything like as bad as I thought it would be. I was like a bather on some English coast who is afraid that the sea will be very cold, but who, when eventually he plunges into it, finds it is exhilarating instead. I didn't remember that if he stays in the water long the cold will begin to bite. For at the moment I was happier than I had been for some considerable time.

My happiness was the result of a number of things.

The most important, I think, was to do with prayer. Nothing is easier than to speak glibly about prayer and nothing prevents people more than such glibness from apprehending what prayer really is. I hope in a later chapter to struggle to see whether I can say anything about it of the slightest value. Here all I want to do is to say how enormously (when there was no stale Anglo-Catholic posturing going on) the atmosphere of the Community church helped me to pray, both on my own privately and also communally with the rest of the Community in the recitation of what are called the Offices, that is Matins, the Midday Service, Evensong and Compline. I was aware in church of being supported by the prayers of the other members of the Community, past as well as present. And I knew that in that place the words of St John's Gospel were true of myself: "Others have laboured, and you have entered into their labour." And that, inevitably, brought richness to my life.

And then there was ample opportunity for reading. At Cambridge a lot of my time had been taken up with administration, and the books I read were mainly concerned with what I had to teach – dreary things like the latest book about the authorship of the Pastoral Epistles or (admittedly much more interesting) the relation between the persecution of the early Christians and Roman Law. Now I could read widely as I chose and my choice had no longer to be determined by the nonsense that the latest piece of scribbling is necessarily the best. I read all Nicolas Berdyaev's books and all John Oman's, three volumes of Karl Barth's *Church Dogmatic*, several of W. R. Inge's books, including his Gifford lectures on Plotinus, all the novels of Dostoevsky, and some old ground new to myself like Gabriel Marcel's *Being and Having* and Karl Jasper's *Philosophical Faith and Revelation*, not to mention the varied offerings of Harvey Cox and the more consistent ones of Alan Watts. My mind was in a ferment of pleasurable excitement.

When in the 1890s a steam yacht was chartered to take some English schoolmasters on what, I suppose, was the first Hellenic Cruise, Owen Seaman wrote of them:

> "'Twill be among their purest joys
> To work it off upon the boys."

Well, I worked it off in a sermon of sadistic length in Westminster Abbey at the consecration of Robert Runcie as Bishop of St Albans. (The sermon was subsequently published in the May 1970 number of *Theology*.) Robert was awfully nice about it and so were Michael Ramsey and Eric Abbott. Eric Abbott obviously found the occasion irresistibly amusing, for on the too few occasions when we meet he always reminds me of it and laughs for sheer delight – "I saw the Archbishop touch his mitre and look more and more desperate." The other bishops present, including my old headmaster, were absolutely livid as it made them very late for luncheon appointments with their wives or boyfriends in their various clubs. My headmaster subsequently wrote me a letter of reproof (it was the length not the content of the sermon which enraged everyone), telling me that it was all too horribly obvious that I was only a novice.

But all that is by the way. I was happy because in large part I was being fed (or over-fed) by my reading.

With regard to chores I was afraid that as I came from Cambridge I should be put to work in the library. That would have bored me and I should have done it most inefficiently. I have always sympathized with Benjamin Jowett, of whom an Oxford colleague said: "How he hates learning."

However, no doubt with the laudable intention of breaking me in properly, I was put to work for an hour each morning in the kitchen. The powers that be didn't realize how pleased I always am to be close to food, and how deeply I shared Algernon Moncrieff's conviction: "I hate people who are not serious about meals. It is so shallow of them."

The kitchen was a friendly and welcoming place. Three Yorkshire lasses from the town worked there. Like all Yorkshire people they were extremely kind and warm-hearted, and full, too, of humour, some of it very shrewd. On one occasion there was an ecumenical get-together at the House, which doubled the number of residents. About this, one of the Yorkshire lasses – a widow lady with a grown-up son – said to me: "I don't see the point of it, Father. After all, we all go to the same place in the end, don't we?" I couldn't have agreed with her more. I've always thought that ecumenism is the last refuge of the religious bore, making a great song and dance about what is represented as a technical operation when all that is really important is mutual good will, kindly feeling and a sense of proportion.

In charge of the kitchen and catering was a youngish lay brother called Alan. I discovered that we had a great deal in common. For not by the very longest stretch of the imagination could his interests possibly be described as ecclesiastical. It meant that he had time for ordinary people like myself who wasn't ill with heart trouble, or worried by doubts about the Real Presence, or in difficulties with my marriage. His friendship was entirely unprofessional and quite untainted by notions of doing good. He was an expert on the theory and practice of yoga. Maybe some people looked down their ecclesiastical noses at him for his apparent lack of piety or real lack of conventional piety. But it was the old story of the last being first. For whatever the crisis in the kitchen (and on occasions when there are fifty or sixty people to feed there can be severe crises) he was never in the slightest degree het-up or showed the slightest sign of being in a flap. If a Brother failed to do what he was supposed to do – lay the tables for instance – Alan always took it with the utmost philosophic calm. One morning I was angry with him for something he'd said. I refused to answer when he spoke to me and just ignored him, scowling. About an hour after I had left the kitchen, he came to my room with some magazines saying: "You said you would like to look at these. Well, here they are." We were friends again at once.

The kitchen was by far the snuggest berth I could have been given, not to mention the entrée it procured for me to pantries and fridges where I could help myself if hunger threatened.

Gardening was difficult. I hated it. One afternoon I got out of it by the simple expedient of listening to a Brother who was supposed to be gardening with me, but instead gave me an hour's exhortation on what he called the grace-bearing properties of the work. Eventually I got out of it altogether, since, by a stroke of luck, the Novice-Guardian himself hated gardening and kindly exempted me from it.

When I arrived at Mirfield there was no other postulant or novice as the stream had dried up altogether some time before. As a new boy I wasn't allowed into the Community common room and had to sit in solitary splendour in what was called the Novice Parlour – a potentially pleasant room, but at the time dreary in the extreme. It looked as if it hadn't been decorated for about thirty years and the apology for a carpet was no more than a piece of rag. There were no pictures on the wall, only a gaunt crucifix. In one corner there was a bookcase containing the most depressingly dingy collection of Tractarian theology, all published well before the First World War. And the room had that terrible smell which seems to be peculiar to institutions of piety. But there was a fairly new electric stove of large proportions which gave out a splendid heat, so that, *faute de mieux*, you could at least bake yourself in front of it.

After six weeks or so a second postulant arrived. He called himself Stephen and I was pleased to discover that he was even older then I was. I was fifty; he was sixty-three.

Of Anglo-Irish stock, he had spent most of his working life as a missionary in Central Africa and had had close connections with the Community, since in his youth he had been a student at our college, where he was a contemporary and intimate friend of Gilbert Harding, the television personality, who decided in the end not to become a clergyman.

Like all members of the Church of Ireland I've been lucky enough to meet, Stephen was a charming and perfectly delightful person. But he was much more than that. His maturity was a great source of strength to my rawness, and his knowledge of the Community was also most valuable. He used sometimes – not very often – to indulge himself by telling me that the great days of the Community were in the past and that it was now running downhill without any idea of where it was going. At the time I thought that what he said was simply old man's talk, but in fact a great deal of his diagnosis turned out for that particular period to be correct. He had a tremendous sense of duty, being as faithful in that which is least as in that which is much. This led sometimes to amusing results. The Novice-Guardian used to give us periods of instruction about the Religious Life in general and the life and customs of the Community of the Resurrection in particular. Stephen realized that in this matter we were disciples and he thought it was the duty of disciples to ask questions. He thought up a good many. He was able to because he already knew the answers. One day after a period of instruction, he was a bit stumped for a question. But he wasn't the man to give up easily, and asked: "When in church should one hold one's hymn-book with one hand or with two?" It was a more fruitful question than first appeared, as the discussion it engendered lasted for seven minutes at least. Like most Irish people he had some odd ideas. He once said to me quite seriously, and indeed with concern, about an officer of the Community: "He lies every evening in a bath for half an hour. That can't be normal, can it?" I answered that we couldn't all go native as he had. In those days (it has now been altered) the Rule compelled one to get up, even on holiday, not later than seven thirty. Stephen always woke up early and would like to have got up before six. But he told me that on his first holiday from Mirfield, out of a kind of loyalty to the Rule, he used, rather against his will, to stay in bed listening to his radio until 7.29 and then get up.

Alas, he was posted to Rhodesia (as it was then) soon after becoming a full member of the Community, and I see him now only on short visits when he is on furlough.

The Novice-Guardian was Eric Simmons. He has since become the Superior and, by his wisdom and singlemindedness, saved the Community from shipwreck and restored to it once again its sense of purpose.

In my early days at Mirfield, however, all that was in the future. Eric was thirty-nine when Stephen and I arrived at the Community and it must have been an awful bore – not to say strain – for him as Novice-Guardian to have to be in charge of two old men. On my own side I discovered that an old man of fifty is by no means exempt from hangups about authority. I found myself beginning to feel about the Novice-Guardian the sort of things I had recognized many of my pupils used to feel about me. I was now on the other side of the desk in the pupil's shoes. The result was that we were incapable of communicating with each other on any important level. When he used to give me a routine interview we were like two people looking at each other through unopenable windows in parallel stationary trains. David Loveday, my old headmaster, showed me what I was missing. Retired from his bishopric, he came to stay at Mirfield for a week. One day at dinner he said to me: "Who is that sitting at the end of the next table? He has the most beautiful and deeply sensitive face." I looked with some curiosity to see who it was, since David Loveday's comments about people were seldom altogether kind, if always very amusing. It was Eric Simmons.

There were two other contributory causes to my sense of relief after a few months at Mirfield.

At Cambridge I had drunk quite a lot and I wondered how I would react to the absence of alcohol. Here I was lucky. I discovered that I had the sort of biochemistry which doesn't miss alcohol at all. As nobody had it, I never thought about it. (The Community is not teetotal by conviction, but there is no money to buy booze.) It is only honest to add that I feel no better at all for not drinking, nor has it done anything whatever to diminish my weight.

The other thing was getting up early. I find I can say my prayers best first thing in the morning, so I try to be in church at a quarter past six (I don't always succeed). This involves getting up at a quarter to six. But I discovered it was no harder to get up at a quarter to six than at nine o'clock. What is hard is getting up earlier than usual. Of course we go to bed early – soon after ten or thereabouts.

I began to wonder what coming to Mirfield was going to cost me. I had to wait a bit before in course of time I discovered, as everybody else does, what the snags were. Some of them were fairly minor, others fairly major. But they were things I had more or less and by and large anticipated, in theory at least. But the greatest and most costly sacrifice I was called upon to make was something I had never thought of. It had never entered my imagination. And if it had, I should have been certain that Mirfield was the very last place where it could have been demanded. God seems awfully fond of surprises.

❧4❧

THERE WERE TWO SNAGS, one minor, the other major, which, since they, unlike the others, were only temporary, are perhaps best dealt with straightaway so that each may be disposed of and placed for good on the shelf.

When I first arrived at the Community many of the Brethren were friendly enough, but I found that quite a number of them were definitely on the defensive. They showed signs of being threatened somehow by my presence and reacted accordingly. It amounted to only a minor strand in my new life, but it caused me some very unpleasant moments. To give examples of what I mean: one evening just after supper a small group of Brethren were discussing a play which two of them were to see on the following evening. In an attempt to be social I asked by whom the play was being performed. "Oh, by a repertory company in Dewsbury," I was told, and my informant added: "You see, we're not like you. We can't afford to go to expensive theatres in London and to Covent Garden. We're just unimportant people." Between old friends, and said in a friendly ragging voice, such a remark could have been a joke. But I wasn't an old friend and the voice was distinctly unpleasant and hostile, what Blake would have called sneaking. Realizing on arrival at Mirfield that every word and action of a new boy is always everywhere charged with significance, I had been particularly careful about what I said and did. I had never once mentioned the theatre, let alone Covent Garden. The Brother's remark was a projection on to me of something in his own mind.

On another evening (I was still a postulant with access to my own money) I took out a packet of a quite ordinary standard brand of cigarettes. A non-smoker, for the benefit of the bystanders, said to me: "Oh, of course, you have the most expensive luxury cigarettes. That was to be expected," and he went on like that for several minutes. I always think it particularly nasty when a person selects a victim for the purposes of playing to the gallery. I ignored his remarks, but they had begun to make me feel like Coriolanus: "You common cry of curs."

On the first day when the students returned to the college for the autumn term the Novice-Guardian told me that I was not on any account in any circumstances to hear their confessions. Such an idea had never entered my head. I was far too occupied with the Brethren in the Community to think at all of the students at the college. As far as I was concerned they didn't exist, and my views on sacramental confession I have already described earlier on. In any case I shouldn't have been up to the standard of the Brother, Peter Hewitt of blessed memory, who said to a student in the confessional (or so at least the young man reported afterwards): "Now, my dear, there is no need to go into details as God knows all about it and I have an extremely shrewd idea."

One day when we were clearing dinner the oldest of the lay Brethren (we got to know each other well later on and, like everybody else, I grew extremely fond of him) said to me: "I can't understand why you're so marvellous. What on earth is it which makes you so special? I can't see it. You look very ordinary to me." There was an openness, a sort of cleanness, about this attack which made it much less offensive than it might otherwise have been. I answered that, although I was a fool, I wasn't quite such a fool as to think myself marvellous or special.

I thought this attitude of defensiveness must be due to the gossip column publicity to which I'd been exposed. It was reasonable for people to be narked about it when they had had no experience themselves of how it was forced upon you willy-nilly. But there was also another factor of which at the time I was unaware and which I pieced together only later from what was told me by various people here and there. Somebody important in the Community (it certainly wasn't Geoffrey Beaumont or Eric Simmons) had gone round telling fishermen's stories about me in which I was the fish. Such stories must have been extremely irritating, to say the least.

Yet there was a certain element of fact and truth in the attitudes which these Brethren largely projected on to me. Although on arrival at Mirfield I kept a low profile and was very careful not to say anything which might cause offence or alarm, in my own secret heart things were not quite the same, and no doubt something of my inner self was somehow intuitively perceived.

I thought that the Community's *raison d'être*, its whole value, lay in its religious and spiritual nature. It was, I thought, a band of people who, in the words of the Rule, had "combined together at the call of God". In earthly, this-worldly terms I didn't think that the Community had much or any prestige, compared at least to the place from which I'd come. In a purely mundane scale of values I didn't think Mirfield ranked very highly. Its value lay, I thought, in its being a place of prayer and worship and the works, spiritually extremely important but in terms of this-worldly calculations unprestigious, which followed from them. It never occurred to my blindness that some at least of the Brethren regarded their membership of the Community as a sign of professional and indeed of social success. (I had forgotten what the English Benedictine in Rome had told me.) Yet this view of theirs was understandable and reasonable. Some of the lay Brethren had had to wait for membership of the Community before becoming personages, while as for some of the clerics, at university they had stayed in the Community's hostel at Leeds; they had then gone to our own theological college and after a brief time in a parish which doubtless had close connections with the Community, they had returned to Mirfield as postulants. It was quite natural and right that they should take a good down-to-earth pride in the place and consider it, if not the heart of the English Church when true to its Catholic inheritance, then at least an important centre of affairs in which, if lucky, they could carve out a career for themselves in terms of being Priors and Superiors. (Reassuringly the careerists never get the jobs they want; they live at too close quarters to the electorate.) It was I who in my inner feelings was being insensitive.

Mercifully my own muddles and general incompetence became in time obvious to everybody. And the troubles I have described faded completely away.

❧ 5 ❧

THE OTHER and major snag which was also only temporary, none the less dragged on for quite a time. It centred on Hugh Bishop, who was then Superior of the Community.

He was, as I've said, a man of great personal authority who had given an enormous amount to all sorts of people (you still meet them everywhere) and it looked as if the Community as a whole and its members as individuals could receive a very great deal from him. His interests and contacts were wide and he was quite free from any of the narrow parochialism to which from time to time the rest of us might succumb. I was certain that he could teach me many of the things I badly needed to know. He was a man of stature.

It became slowly clear to me, however, that his heart was no longer in the Community, but elsewhere. I'm not suggesting that that in itself was in the slightest degree blameworthy. God plays all sorts of tricks on us by means of our heart, and the result is generally to make us greater and deeper people. But I do think that Hugh Bishop should have realized that what was now his permanent state of mind and absorbing interest rendered him unfit to be any longer the Community's Superior, and should therefore have resigned. If he had, he could still have remained a member of the Community, or, if he wanted to leave it altogether, there was at hand in the printed book constitutional machinery to enable him to do so without attaching to himself any kind of blame or stigma.

But he went on being Superior long after he had ceased to believe in the Community life he was supposed to lead. Indeed he often apologized for it, speaking of this or that feature of it with a kind of despairing disdain. He seemed to have little use for the spiritual values it existed to embody, appearing to regard them as a nuisance. Again I'm not suggesting that there was anything wrong in this in itself. It is perfectly possible to outgrow something which in the past has given a great deal. People often need to move on from one form of life to another, and the need can be a sign of growth, of God's educating of us. But nobody can properly run a system in which he himself has ceased to have any confidence. However much he goes through the motions of outward observance, his fundamental disillusion is bound to manifest itself and infect the body politic.

There were growing signs of this in the Community. Four or five Brethren left it and of the novices who arrived a year or eighteen months after Stephen and myself (there were several of them) only one finished the course. That, it is true, might have happened anyhow, but in the minds of many of the Brethren it was inevitably connected with Hugh's being still in charge. I remember one of them saying (he was filling a hot-water bottle at the time): "I much prefer this place when the Superior is away." It was a stronger statement than it will seem to outsiders, since once a Superior is elected he becomes very much a sacred cow it is impious to complain about.

Concessions were made to individual Brethren which shouldn't have been made. If a Brother demanded that something brand-new should be bought for him when what he already had was only two or three years old and would have been perfectly serviceable for another eight or nine at least, the demand was complied with. Demands of this sort were sure signs in themselves that the Community's morale had sunk to a low ebb. They were hardly in the spirit of poverty.

And within the House there was a growing amount of indiscipline which it isn't necessary to describe, except to say that it brought adverse comment from outside.

Around this time I had been a full member of the Community for just over a year. I knew I was indebted to Hugh Bishop for being elected, since there was, I was told (not by him), a fair amount of opposition to my election. In view of this opposition and the fact that I was very much a new boy I didn't think I could go to Hugh as a representative of the Community and tell him what I thought. I felt that it would be presumptuous, and in any case I was fairly certain it would do no good. That was doubtless in part a rationalization of my cowardice, but there was at least a certain objective validity to it. Could I go over the heads of the major officers of the Community who had been here for years? I did speak to these major officers, but they said that everything was all right. The Community wasn't falling apart. I hadn't, they said, experience enough of the place to understand it.

The *dénouement*, when it finally occurred, was swift.

During a General Chapter (parliament) in January 1974 the Prior (the second in command) received one afternoon out of the blue a telephone call from the Archbishop of Canterbury, Michael Ramsey, saying that as the Community's Visitor he could no longer put his confidence in Hugh Bishop as Superior. The Prior telephoned back to Lambeth to confirm the message. And Hugh Bishop left the House the same day and has never entered it since.

I wouldn't have mentioned the telephone call but for the fact that Hugh Bishop himself made as public as possible the manner of his leaving the Community, first in a printed letter he sent to a lot of people, including the Religious Director of the BBC, and then in a television programme on BBC1 which was seen by almost everybody I know. But neither in the printed letter nor in the television broadcast was the crucial telephone call from Lambeth mentioned.

If, as Hugh Bishop did, you are going to make the facts of a situation public before millions of people, it should, I think, be the full facts. And in this case it should include a fact of central significance which in the stress of the moment Hugh Bishop had doubtless forgotten.

The whole thing was a tragedy in the proper sense of the word. For it was Hugh's great and good qualities – his personal authority, his breadth of outlook, the humility which made him ready to grow and change, the courage which enabled him to refuse to deny his God-given humanity – things which could have given so much increase of strength to the Community; it was precisely these things which went awry.

And as in all tragedy proper it left questions it is impossible to answer. How far was the Community itself responsible for what happened? I'm not referring to what its major officers did or didn't do, nor to the provisions of its printed Rule and Constitution, but to deep-grained attitudes – the fundamental feelings and outlook of a man, the largely unconscious condition of his heart and mind, the unknown things which make him tick. How far in these deep unconscious areas was Hugh the victim of what the Community had subtly made him? Was he therefore unable to break out of the Community without waving a bloody flag and banner of defiance? Had life in the Community inculcated in him a degree of pathological guilt from which he couldn't free himself without making a great deal of noise? And if so, was it right for people to live in the sort of context the Community provides? Even with the provision of constitutional machinery to release a Brother from a life-vow, was it right for him to vow solemnly to stay in the Community for life in the Name of the Father and of the Son and of the Holy Spirit Amen? To claim to have the answer to such questions would be indeed to rush in where angels fear to tread.

Many of the Brethren, especially the older ones, were deeply wounded by the television programme. They had given Hugh a great deal of loyalty and affection and service only to hear him tell the world that the Community meant nothing to him at all. No wonder that from that point its morale reached an all-time low.

But death was in due course (why did we ever doubt it?) followed by resurrection. It was of this Easter story that the Archbishop reminded us when he came to install the new Superior: "And they were saying to one another, 'Who will roll away the stone for us from the door of the tomb?' And looking up, they saw that the stone was rolled back; for it was very heavy."

PERHAPS this is a convenient point to describe the place of vows in the life of the Community.

When Charles Gore founded it in 1892 the Brethren

didn't take life-vows. Gore wasn't an Anglo-Catholic in the sense that he didn't think it necessary to imitate Roman Catholic structures. Quite the opposite – so much so that a very Anglo-Catholic Superior in the 1940s, Raymond Raynes, ordered a whole trunk full of Gore's papers to be burnt because he thought them heretical (i.e. the views they expressed were not Roman Catholic) – an act of vandalism which will pass beyond the belief of anybody who has had no personal experience of the destructive potential of religious zeal.

It was during this Anglo-Catholic period of the Community's existence, beginning in the late 1930s, that life-vows were introduced, and the structure of vows remains the same today as it became then.

When a man passes from the novitiate to become a full member of the Community he publicly declares his intention of staying in the Community for life, but vows to do so only for the three years next following. After that period, if the Community thinks fit, he solemnly vows to stay in for life.

After witnessing the tragedy of Hugh Bishop and the terrible distress of those four or five Brethren who left the Community soon before or after Hugh, I asked the Community whether I need take life-vows when I was due to in January 1975. I also asked that the whole question of vows, their nature and *raison d'être*, the way in which they functioned, and the effects they produced, should be thoroughly examined and recommendations made accordingly. The Community agreed that in January 1975, instead of taking life-vows, I should be allowed once again to declare my intention of remaining in the Community for life and vow to do so once again for the next three years. A committee was also set up to investigate the nature and functioning of vows.

The committee had no option but to suggest that the procedure with regard to vows should continue as it had become in the 1930s, since the replies to a questionnaire made it clear that that was what all the Brethren wanted. I myself had hoped that we might return to a modified form of the original state of affairs whereby people who wanted to take life-vows because they found in them a source of strength and stability should be allowed to do so, but others, who found them a difficulty or scandal, while declaring every time publicly their intention of remaining in the Community for life, should be allowed to vow only for the next three years or so.

My difficulty with regard to life-vows wasn't only what I had witnessed in Hugh Bishop and the others, but that, however certain a man might be in the present that it was God's will that he should remain in the Community for life, that present certainty did not qualify him to dictate to God what the divine will must be for the rest of the man's life. That seemed to me to make absolute (God's will for always) what was in fact only relative (a man's conviction in the present of God's will for him). And the making of the relative absolute is generally considered the essence of idolatry. I was quite ready publicly and solemnly to declare my intention of remaining in the Community for life, because that, in being less binding, left a space for the admission of human fallibility. And in any case it was, and always had been, my intention to do so.

When, at the end of the extended period of three years, I told the Community that I wasn't yet ready to take life-vows, they allowed me once again to declare my intention of remaining in the Community for life but to vow again only for the next three years. However, they added a very firmly worded declaration that this must be their last concession, and that after this further period of three years was over, I must either conform or get out. I must take life-vows or leave the Community.

This put me into a double-bind. To state it bluntly: I thought it was God's will that I should remain in the Community (I had never had any other intention); and I thought it was against God's will that I should take life-vows. What, then, was I to do? It was a choice of evils. I was reasonably certain that if I left the Community I should spiritually go completely to pieces. To leave, I was sure, would be spiritual and perhaps even moral suicide. But to take life-vows was against my conscience.

In the end I decided that the lesser of the two evils was to conform and remain. I was helped here by remembering something my analyst, Christopher Scott (he had since died), had said to me in Cambridge: "You'll be all right at Mirfield so long as you don't take it over-seriously." I therefore arrived at the view that if to remain in the house of the Lord I had to bow myself in the house of Rimmon, that couldn't be helped. I certainly did feel that being forced to take life-vows was a violation of my intrinsic tenderness, but from my early days as a child I had been accustomed to that tenderness being trampled upon by the hobnail boots of other people's intense religious convictions. So it was no new experience. The only difference was that now the boots need not hurt, at least anything like so much, because it was with a shrug of the shoulder and a large pinch of salt that I could go through the motions of taking life-vows. So I took them in January 1981. Perhaps I had better repeat that it had always been, and was still, my intention to remain in the Community for life.

The occasion reminded me of a passage from D. H. Lawrence I had read years before: "It was the mania of cities and societies and hosts, to lay a compulsion upon a man, upon all men. For men and women alike were mad with the egoistic fear of their own nothingness." The sacred canopy held over the occasion was unable to disguise what was really going on, and in the event I was unable to find the salt and was pushed to the verge of breakdown.

❧❧ 7 ❧❧

BEFORE I GO ON to describe what life in the Community is fundamentally about, this is a convenient place to give some sort of picture of its less important aspects. I say "less important", but that is probably misleading since the less important things are often the vehicles or expressions of what is basic and central. They are like the small rock pools which the ocean fills.

One of the Community's great Superiors, Keble (Ted) Talbot, is recorded as saying: "The Religious (monastic) Life would be all right if it were not for the Brethren." Brethren aren't necessarily friends. Friends are chosen because they are congenial or you have common interests or share a certain outlook or find the same things funny. Brethren, on the other hand, are like relatives. And it is tempting to quote Algernon Moncrieff once again: "Relatives are simply a tedious pack of people who haven't the remotest knowledge of how to live nor the smallest instinct about when to die." In Community you have to live at close quarters with people some at least of whom you will find temperamentally incompatible. That is an essential part of the discipline of Community life. You must be prepared to associate constantly with at least a few people who get on your nerves. This, however, is ameliorated to some extent by the protection given to Brethren from each other by the provisions of the Rule, especially the regulations enjoining silence. The rules of silence safeguard for each of us an important degree of solitude. So, for instance, a Brother can't visit another Brother after Compline and talk about his soul until the early hours. The Greater Silence from after Compline until 9 a.m. next day forbids it.

But protection is something negative. The positive challenge of those you find temperamentally incompatible is that of discovering the real and lovable person hidden behind the temperament. I'm aware that many Brethren have done this in my own case, refusing again and again to be put off by the superficial and objectionable aspects of what I am, and penetrating to the person behind the enveloping façade. And I have sometimes been able to do the same with regard to others. The result is that you often begin to have a real affection for the people you initially found offensive. They still sometimes jar on you as, no doubt, you do on them. But the jarring is more and more confined to isolated occasions and seems less important as affection grows. One of the most remarkable things about the Community is the combination, on the one hand, of realism in our estimate of each other and in the honest recognition (and verbalization) of our hostile feelings and, on the other hand, of our realization that what we find objectionable in anybody is only a tiny fraction of the full truth about him, as we hope it is also about ourselves.

The overall result is an atmosphere of acceptance. It has nothing sentimental or romantic about it as it is an acceptance very much aware of warts and all. But it does give you a sense of being supported. You begin to realize that you are not on your own because all the time you have behind you the prayers and good will of the Community as a whole. And that supplies some (but not all) of your need to belong.

Not all, because in the nature of the case there can be between us no intimate or tender feelings. It isn't that they are frowned upon or forbidden but that they just don't arise. There is a sense in which Brethren both care and don't care about each other. They care officially as a Christian duty, but don't care personally. Thus a death in the Community is greeted with perfect equanimity (unlike the death of a Fellow at Trinity). This may be partly due to a firm belief in the resurrection of the dead. It is due much more to the fact that the departed leaves no sense of personal loss. This in large measure is because there is no opportunity for Brethren to get to know each other as colleagues at Cambridge do. That sort of knowing depends on evenings spent together in an atmosphere of conviviality. And in a Religious Community there is no time or place for social intimacies of that kind. That is why, in spite of everything Mirfield has given me, I still regard Trinity as my home. Mirfield is school: a school which evokes gratitude and loyalty because it gives me what I most need. But still school, situated within at least walking distance of the waters of Babylon. We are, many of us, I think, not mature or robust enough to leave school. But that doesn't in any way invalidate our vocation to the Religious Life. God, said St Paul, has chosen the weak things of this world. It does, however, sometimes cause irritation: when I am doing a chore there are occasions when I feel that if I were a man instead of a mouse I shouldn't, for instance, be cleaning out the refectory or be standing at the kitchen sink washing up dinner for forty to fifty people. But that, I'm pretty sure, is only the old farce of self-dramatization put on for my own benefit. The poseur within me dies hard, even though rationally I know that chores of this kind are a form of prayer.

Of course I have found a number of Brethren immediately congenial on the ordinary natural level. I have already spoken of Alan, who was in charge of the catering. There is also, for instance, the Brother who, when twelve or thirteen years ago we began using one of the revised services of Holy Communion in which we had to give each other the greeting of peace, took my hands in his and, instead of saying "Peace be with you," said to me soulfully: "We can't go on meeting like this." His humour is a constant delight. Or there is the Brother who cares enormously but unostentatiously about people and who, after we had once had to listen to a piece of high-flown spirituality, said calmly and quite unemphatically: "It's all bogus, you know." His unshowy piety and level-headedness are always immensely reassuring.

Here I can say that I have found that fervent religious zeal is almost always in inverse proportion to that sensitivity by means of which alone we can love our neighbour. In that sense zeal is a substitute for love. Those least capable of the empathy by which contact is made with others are invariably those most ardent for religious exercises. It is a contrast Dostoevsky drew in the *Brothers Karamazov* between Father Zossima, the saintly elder who brought help and healing to the multitudes who came to him for succour, and Father Ferapont, who saw nobody but was "a great ascetic who prayed day and night (he even dropped asleep on his knees)" and who condemned Father Zossima: "He was seduced by sweetmeats, ladies brought them to him in their pockets, he sipped tea, he worshipped his belly, filling it with sweet things and his mind with haughty thoughts."

Those two types are still recognizable today in Religious Communities, if not in the exaggeratedly dramatic form in which Dostoevsky presents them to us. The essence of the Father Feraponts is that they use intense devotionalism as a defence against self-knowledge, without, of course, realizing that they are doing so.

I believe that the signs of genuine nearness to God are the relaxation and laughter which give out an atmosphere of human warmth. So (to take a trivial example) when a service in church goes wrong and mistakes are made, those near to God are amused, not upset.

Two or three years ago a group of Brethren, after much serious discussion and consultation, drew up a new form of ritual for the weekday celebrations of the Holy Communion in which seven or eight Brethren trailed up to the altar in long white robes. On seeing this for the first time a Brother from another house in the Community said to me: "I so much enjoyed the new ritual. It is exactly like the old film of Eddie Cantor in *Roman Scandals*."

❧❧ 8 ❧❧

THERE IS, I believe, an important bond between Brethren which is discussed without affectation and with considerable humour by some Brethren and never mentioned by others. It follows from the fact that clergymen in the Anglican Communion are allowed to marry.

In my experience if men are emotionally capable of marrying, they do. Anglican Religious Communities tend therefore to be composed very largely of people whose emotional hangups have in some way or other prevented them from doing so. It may be because by orientation they are homosexual or the woman they passionately loved was for some reason or other unattainable or, although attracted to women, they hadn't the psychic courage to stake their claim for one. But, whatever the cause, they are people who in some way or other have been wounded in their sexuality. Some find it easier to speak about it, generally in a light-hearted sort of way. Others find it easier to remain silent. Their reticence always deserves respect. The common bond is no less binding for being unspoken. In some cases the wound heals in a Brother, and he is then confronted with the agonizing problem of how to remain most true to himself and his God-given nature: should he remain in the Community in spite of the healing which has come to him? Or should he apply for release from his life-vows, leave the Community, and get married? It is very far indeed from being an easy or obvious choice. What does the Community the greatest credit is the way in which it respects and honours a Brother's decision to leave and gives him a warm welcome should he return on a visit.

The real danger in these matters is self-delusion: imagining that for God's sake one has voluntarily renounced the happiness of having a wife and children when in realistic terms there has been nothing voluntary about it at all. That, of course, is not to deny that there are Brethren who have made that renunciation in full freedom and whose decision to adopt the celibate life has been entirely voluntary. But I believe they are very much in the minority.

❦❦9❦❦

ANOTHER OF THE FACTS OF LIFE we have to live with as Religious is that collectively we are a focus of people's projections like, say, TV personalities or the royal family.

These projections are by and large of two kinds.

People who are only vaguely, if at all, religious regard us with a combination of incredulity, benign amusement, and a sort of puzzled respect. They imagine that life in a monastery is one long cartoon from *Punch* or the *New Yorker*, an unending series from morning to night of cracks in the cloister. They think our main characteristic is being jovial people who enjoy our food. Quite often they imagine that we produce it all as if we spent the whole day fishing and were equipped with our own slaughter-house. "Do you produce all your own food?" is invariably the first question which strangers ask, though admittedly they ask it more with the calm of courtesy than the eagerness of interest, and doubtless my own figure does something to prompt the question as I don't look exactly underfed. I was a little less pleased when somebody asked whether we were allowed to use deodorants, but, on reflection, I was certain that there was nothing personal about the question. Once when arriving somewhere for lunch dressed unaccustom-edly in a suit instead of a cassock my hostess (I knew her quite well) asked me what had happened to my skirt and said she would knit me one, though she hasn't so far.

I find it fun being the object of good-natured laughter. How else can one repay people for their kindness? Monks as jokes is a pleasant projection and not all that wide of the mark. There is a sense in which we are rather like the clowns of God, though we don't try to be or think of ourselves in those terms, and certainly we can't levitate like Nijinsky, the self-styled clown of God.

The other kind of projection can also be amusing if you are in the right mood, but, since you seldom are, it is more often irritating and, if taken seriously, it can be dangerous.

Simply in virtue of our calling we tend to collect around us a crowd whose dominant religious characteristic is *sancta simplicitas*, and it makes them imagine that we are the next best thing in this world to saints. It never seems to occur to them that we are ordinary people like themselves who often lose our temper, say nasty things about people behind their backs, have a sharp eye for our own comfort, grumble about the chores we have to do, positively hate Brother Aloysius for blowing his own trumpet when we want desperately to blow our own but are too spiritually proud to do it, and who cast longing glances at the attractive girl or boy who has turned up for dinner.

No; for these pious people we are figures of holiness, virtue, benevolence, unselfishness, generosity, devotion, with a wideness to our good-heartedness like the wideness of the sea, and who, by comparison, would make Sir Galahad himself look like a rake.

It is on the second Saturday in July that we become most aware of what people thus make of us. For then we have an open day when three to four thousand people parade round our grounds and greet us with the admiration and reverence they think we deserve while we walk about looking too good and kind to be true. Fortunately our visitors aren't allowed into the house so that we can ourselves go in and put our feet up when the effort of looking virtuous and friendly becomes too exhausting.

The danger of the projection upon us of sanctity is that it may tempt us to imagine that we really do have the best spiritual answers to the problems of life. I think that that is an attitude into which some of us sometimes fall, imagining ourselves experts in goodness and religious truth who have exactly the sort of food the hungry sheep most need.

I think it would help people much more if they saw us as we really are: ordinary Christian folk like themselves who in spite of our many imperfections and severely limited wisdom do none the less try to love and serve God as best we can. Being considered a spiritual élite falsifies our relation with people from the start if only because it leads them to confuse earnestness with insight, fervour with understanding and zeal with love.

What saves us here is the way in which we criticize and laugh at each other. The Community is the last place where a person can get away with any spiritual pretensions. He is seen through at once and becomes a figure of fun. That abrasive atmosphere is one of our chief health-giving properties. It is when we are away from the Community that we may be tempted to think that we are – well, rather spiritual, however hard we imagine we are trying to disguise it from others. On our return we are soon put in our place once again.

But spiritual pretensions can be communal as well as individual. And here the corrective isn't so easily available. I remember Rab Butler once saying to me in a grudging voice (it was a characteristic piece of his humour): "The letters C.R. after your name look like a decoration." I think that as a Community we sometimes imagine that the letters are some sort of spiritual decoration. But that is less the case now than it was forty years ago. It does, however, remain the besetting temptation of many Religious to feel that they have continually to justify their existence to themselves by means of increased religiosity and the multiplication of pious practices. So long as this is a voluntary and private matter all one need do is to mind one's own business. But the self-justifying urge pushes itself into a Community's public statutory services by embroidering them with extensive devotional embellishment so that their length can be doubled. This may seem like an assertion of what Jesus denied – that God does indeed hear us for our much speaking. But it is far more an attempt to increase our spiritual capital, making us feel a little more justified in the pursuit of our calling while we forget that it is precisely the rich who are sent empty away. One other favourite means of self-justification is "asceticism". I have put the word in inverted commas since it never connotes anything of real hardship but only such things as are calculated to irritate by making life slightly more uncomfortable than it need be. It is as though the road of martyrdom and endurance had been reduced to the painted canvas of a stage set so as to give us at least the illusion of walking where the palm branches grow and leafy honours can be gathered and worn, not least by those responsible for painting and setting up the scenery.

❦❙10❙❦

AS I SETTLED in at Mirfield I discovered that the inability ever to give anything to anybody was more of a privation than I had anticipated. I'm not referring to generosity on a large scale (I was never financially capable of that) but to small things like Christmas presents or taking people out to dinner or the theatre or tipping a godchild – those tokens of friendship which are one of the pleasures of life.

And as far as seeing friends was concerned, any initiative I now made about meeting them had to take the form of my proposing myself as their guest. That is all right when I know people well and can take it for granted that their open invitation is a genuine sign that they want to see me. But even here I have a horror of imposing myself on people – I know from Cambridge days what it is like to be imposed upon when one is busy. And there are also a number of people I should like to see from time to time and who, in normal circumstances, I should invite to a meal or a party, but don't know well enough to thrust my company on them at their expense.

Friends, including a number of old pupils, have been immensely generous in their hospitality and that has meant a great deal to me. But I should like sometimes to be able to ask them back. We can, of course, have guests here, but unless they are madly religious there is nothing for them to do, and one has to leave them by themselves for large parts of the day, while the fare, though invariably good and appetizing, is hardly abundant.

I am particularly grateful to John Betjeman, who has given me a key to his house in Chelsea so that I can always stay there when I have to be in or am passing through London, and to Elizabeth Cavendish for always keeping open house as far as I am concerned, so that I can drop in for dinner any day. It is difficult to exaggerate how much their friendship and generosity mean to me. They make me feel not that I am being entertained but that I am a member of the family who has come home for a day or two. And I rely very much on their advice, which is always informed and wise. It is they, I think, who have kept me sane.

One of the professional hazards of being a Religious is the ease with which one can develop the mentality of a scrounger. One has constantly to be on one's guard against becoming pauperized. The Community pays for all things necessary – shelter, heat, food, clothes, books, postage, dentist, oculist, medical prescription charges – and gives you eight pounds a month pocket money and ninety pounds a year for holidays (1981 reckoning). It is easy enough to expect one's friends to supply luxuries. Two of them, Simon and Deborah Stuart, have been extremely generous in taking me abroad with them. But I have constantly to remind myself that this is a spontaneous and undeserved kindness. It isn't one of my rights to have a holiday in the sun, and the uncertainty of it sometimes makes me feel gloomy.

There is, too, the contrary danger of feeling, however well you are treated, like a poor relation to whom it belongs to keep in the background and not to say that you would like very much to do so and so and drive to such and such a place. It is a mean and most ungracious response to people's friendship and goodness to feel within yourself like a governess in one of Charlotte Brontë's novels. Such guilt and awkwardness in receiving is a sign of pride, the clinging to a false identity which you feel you must always prop up. It is, I suppose, useful as a reminder that reality hasn't kept up with your spiritual aspirations. Luckily I've never found it a very strong feeling, but I'm aware of it on the periphery, waiting for an opportunity to come to the centre.

11

ONE FEATURE OF LIFE in the Community which has to be negotiated with some care is the difficulty of finding diversions when you need to relax. There are plenty of things to read: we take in daily and Sunday newspapers and three or four of the standard weeklies; and the library contains an excellent section where you can find novels and forms of light literature. We also have a television – an old black and white – but our timetable enables us to see it only between 8.30 and 9.30 in the evening, and that period always includes the news at nine on BBC 1. We have also a music room with a piano and a hi-fi with a large collection of records. But here again time is the enemy. There is generally on Sunday evenings about an hour when we can play records, but not much opportunity otherwise.

If you don't belong to the area (some Brethren do) there are no friends around whom you can visit. So you never go out, unless you enjoy spending a day with little money in Leeds or Bradford.

And yours is a seven-day week. Sundays are the same as other days except that the services are at a slightly different time and the Holy Communion in the morning is sung with a sermon.

Most Brethren cope with the situation by going away on work fairly frequently: taking retreats, hearing confessions (in spite of the availability of local clergy), preaching, lecturing, giving talks, looking after nuns. Such expeditions are a welcome break from the monotony of life here, and they have the added advantage of relieving the other members of the Community of your company for a few days.

I am myself very uncertain of what strategy to adopt in this matter. On the one hand I feel very strongly that the main point of belonging to a Religious Community is to be there. I feel that the monotony is part of the unavoidable discipline of the life of prayer. There should be a way not only of tolerating it but also of transforming it into something positive, and using it. On the other hand I am aware that if I stay put here for four or five months on end I go a bit potty and begin taking it out of the others by being bad-tempered and morose. Then I think that all I am doing is trying to live beyond my spiritual income, which is the quintessence of pride. So I begin once again to accept the invitations that come to me to do this and that, tired though I often become of having to sing for my supper. But the invitations are generally to places in the south, which means I can see friends in London *en route*.

Technically it is the Superior or his representative who decides when and where you should go on work. But in practice (rightly in my view) you are treated as an adult who must accept the responsibility of making his own decisions.

In an important way I am luckier than most Brethren since I am allowed a generous amount of time for writing. I have never had any *folies de grandeur* about myself as a writer. I know that what I write is, most of it, pretty mediocre stuff. But writing is the quickest way out of Mirfield. I don't write easily. It all has to be ground out slowly with immense labour. And therefore it is exhausting and by the end of the day I long for the kind of relaxing diversion which isn't available. Yet it is precisely the life of the Community and its atmosphere of prayer which provide me with the wherewithal to write at all. So I am greatly in its debt, not only for the time it allows me but also – and more important – for giving me a context which evokes whatever little I have to say.

In any case it is sheer childishness to expect to have all your vitamins in the same pill. Life always involves choosing this rather than that, and each will have both its advantages and disadvantages. I am reasonably certain – most of the time, that is – that the life I've chosen is the right one for me. And on the deepest level I don't in fact feel at all separated from my friends and the people I love. On that deepest and most real level I know beyond a peradventure that in the presence of God they are always with me. But that statement requires to be expanded and explained if it isn't to look like wishful thinking or escapist piety. It requires an attempt to describe the life of prayer. I shall have to approach this from a certain distance.

❧§‖12‖§❧

I HAVE NEVER KEPT a commonplace book, but sentences (generally short ones) which seemed to have some significance for me have remained at the back of my mind and have come to the front of it when called forth by some occasion or other. When first read and remembered these sentences didn't reveal to me anything with much real bite, but I felt them to be important in a vague sort of way and, if called upon, no doubt could have made a good theoretical case for them. But their power as yet was only potential. They were not for immediate consumption but for storing. According to ancient Chinese wisdom it is only when the pupil is ready that the teacher comes. So these sentences had to wait in the back of my mind until I was ready to receive them. And when their time did come I was lucky in remembering not only the book in which I had found them, but that they came near the book's beginning, middle or end, so that I could find them again without too much difficulty. On looking them up I discovered that my memory of their gist was generally correct, but that storage for a number of years in an inferior mind had often made them go soggy and robbed them of their crispness of expression. But since their original form was easily discoverable, that didn't matter much.

During my last two terms at school, after getting a scholarship to Trinity, I had read (it seems to me now a very strange choice) Carlyle's *Sartor Resartus*. I had forgotten its content entirely except something Carlyle had said about man's misery being bound up with his importance, since both had something to do with eternity. After I had been at Mirfield about three years I remembered this passage and looked it up. It read: "The misfortune of man has its source in his greatness; for there is something infinite in him, and he cannot succeed in burying himself completely in the finite." That sentence seemed now to sum up the attraction Mirfield had for me.

I wasn't much attracted by the sort of life lived there

in terms of its external structures. The services (five of them
every day) often had meaning for me and were helpful, but
sometimes they seemed like a relentless treadmill –
something positively malignant which frightened and
sickened me. This was especially true of the fussy Anglo-
Catholic ritual of High Mass and Solemn Evensong. These
can be fun now and again. But having to endure them
every single Sunday and major Saint's Day I found
nauseating.

Nor, at first sight at least, were most members of
the Community the sort of people I should naturally have
chosen as friends. Their predominantly ecclesiastical interests and High Church jokes were what, in the normal
course of events, I should have run miles away from.

But these disadvantages were totally outweighed, as
far as I was concerned, by the opportunity the place
provided of finding the something infinite in myself of
which Carlyle had spoken. I knew (as I've said) that
without the discipline provided by a Religious Community
I should try to bury myself completely in the finite. And I
also knew that the attempt was bound to be tragically
unsuccessful and that its result would be an ever-increasing
degree of sterility, isolation and unhappiness. And it would
also be to deny and shut myself away from, not something
vague and distant of which I was hardly aware, but
something which had come upon me from time to time
with superlatively attractive power.

In this most important of all areas of my life,
Mirfield, I had found to my relief, was giving me what I
had gone there to obtain. Putting up with the other things
was a price infinitely (for once the adverb can be used in its
literal sense) worth paying. I had no doubt about it, at least
for most of the time. I was aware of a richness. But it wasn't
of an obvious or superficial kind. It didn't consist of strong
feelings which could be whistled up on demand as you can
whistle a cab from a rank. It was a richness deep down
which often seemed no more than a dim sort of joy in the
background; so dim, in fact, that it was frequently overlaid

by more superficial feelings, like those, for instance, of irritation, anger, loneliness, despondency or a longing for the bright lights and convivial chatter of former days. But I came to see that the depth of a feeling is much more important than its strength. The richness was there, deeply, if not as a rule strongly. And under God I had Mirfield to thank for it. So far, then, all was well.

Yet there were times when I wasn't so certain. From one point of view that was inevitable. For complete and permanent certainty belongs only to the insane. But in particular what worried me during these phases of uncertainty was integrally connected with the challenge with which life in any Religious Community must confront its members: the necessity of relating the something infinite within them to all that is finite. For the relation of finite to infinite isn't only a problem in metaphysics. It has also to be figured out in the ordinary practical business of daily life.

The difficulty is that the infinite and the finite aren't two different quantities which you can mix in suitable proportions as you can mix twelve ounces of coffee with four ounces of chicory. Indeed to imagine that the infinite is a quantity different from and opposed to the finite is paradoxically to treat it as though it were another alternative finite, thus making it into a false infinity.

Religion as a specialized activity can very easily become the worship of an alternative finite, of a false infinity. Instead of worshipping the true infinity, the ultimate mystery which, for all its homeliness, dwells none the less in thick darkness or in the light which no man can approach unto, people can worship the Catholic God, or the Protestant God, or the God of the healthy-minded, or the God who is the psychiatrist's assistant – in all cases an entity neatly packaged and easily describable. The idol to which I was once enslaved was a bogus God of this kind, though for some people he can be cosy and comfy, a perfect darling, instead of the sadistic monster he was for me.

It is to false infinities of this kind that people of

religious zeal invariably dedicate themselves. And their idolatry makes them either too good to be true – the sort of people to whom you long to tell a dirty story – or religiously feverish and hectic types who do whatever is the contemporary equivalent of crying out loud and cutting themselves with knives. It was, incidentally, this unnaturally placid or unnaturally hectic fixation on a false infinity which Freud identified as religion. No wonder, then, that he described it as a universal obsessional neurosis.

When people demand more of the infinite and less of the finite (it could be a demand for more time in church, more time for devotion, and less for reading or going for a walk or enjoying other people's company) they are like people demanding that the mixture should contain more coffee and less chicory. They don't see that their demand might well be a denial of true infinity altogether.

For true infinity – and this is the absolute crux of the whole matter – doesn't lie outside the finite (that would make it another alternative finite) but includes the finite in its own infinity. The glory of man, for instance, isn't an alternative to the glory of God. In the glory of man God's glory is embodied and shown forth. That is what, in the Christian scheme, Jesus stands for.

But if this is so – that the infinite includes the finite in its own infinity – then how can anybody still try to bury himself completely in the finite? Or, in terms of my own history, why did I leave Cambridge for Mirfield?

❧§‖I3‖§❧

THE ANSWER is that people can be totally blind to the infinite which the finite contains and expresses. And when this happens they are like people who can't see the picture for the paint. As a parable we can imagine somebody looking at a Turner and seeing in it no more than so much pigment which could be scraped off and weighed. And where, he then asks in desperation, can he find the beauty and attraction in a pile of pigment?

Here I had better say that I am myself fully convinced that people can discover the something infinite within and around them and express it in their finite lives without necessarily being at all aware of what they are doing. They are like the sheep in Jesus' parable of the sheep and the goats. I agree therefore with Paul Tillich (however unfashionable it may be now) that people who have found depth in their lives have found God. Indeed there is a certain sense in which the agnostic or atheist can find the true infinity better than the religious person, because the so-called unbeliever has no temptation to treat the infinite as though it were another finite. He isn't susceptible to the lure of a false infinity. The point can be made clearer by a prospectus of a public school I saw some years ago. Each page illustrated what the school had to offer – learning, sport, art, music and (on the last page with a photograph of the chapel) religion. God had here become a commodity along with geography and golf. Conversely, a publisher of religious books told me that he once approached the late Barbara Pym and asked her if she would write a spiritual book. Clearly she understood the true infinity, since she answered that she must refuse his request as her spirituality was in her novels.

Many people find the something infinite within them without thinking of it in those terms: in a deep loving personal relationship, for instance, in the homeliness (if it is homely) of home, in their response to some other person's need, or to the glories of the natural world (seeing eternity in a grain of sand but not putting it like that), or of art (like my friend, the Director of the Fitzwilliam Museum, who used to sit silently in front of a picture or sculpture) or (since I've lived most of my life among academics) in the excitements and aridities of their research. The examples could be multiplied indefinitely.

But for me none of that was possible. The finite for me remained no more than frustratingly finite. I couldn't maintain a deep personal relationship since I was unable to evoke a corresponding response. I had no home. I enjoyed the beauties of nature, but it was little more than the enjoyment of a tourist. I also enjoyed art and music, but it was, if anything, slightly less than the enjoyment of the average educated person. I could talk about art and music all right, but they didn't engage me to any real depth. And with my work, with the theology of the schools, I had become, as I've explained, disillusioned. It seemed to me no more than a collection of clever ideas, or of pious ideas dressed up to look clever, a continual shaking of the kaleidoscope to make new and temporary patterns.

To find that something infinite within me I had, therefore, to live in an atmosphere where I was continually being reminded of it, and in the company of people who were themselves continually looking for it. I had to live a life to which there was no point of any kind whatever unless you were fundamentally concerned about it. That was the price I had to pay to escape hell, not the hell of ecclesiastical convention, but a hell of ultimate frustration as I tried hopelessly to bury myself completely in the finite. And life at Mirfield provided me with what I desperately needed.

Or did it? For there were times, I said, when I was uncertain. The uncertainty, I came to see, was the recognition of a real danger. For the pursuit of the infinite as a full-time calling can become all too easily the pursuit of a false infinity. You can begin to think of it as one calling among others. You can begin to imagine that you have chosen the pursuit of the infinite as others choose the stockmarket or the law. And you can thus begin to make of the infinite a finite possibility. So, for instance, in a prayer which is sometimes said in the Community church we compare ourselves to the apostles Peter, James and John, who are represented in the gospels as the specially intimate friends of Jesus. By becoming Religious (monks) we have, the prayer announces, joined this circle of three so that we are now ourselves among the specially intimate friends of Jesus. The prayer thus reduces the search for the infinite to membership of an exclusive club. The prayer, however, isn't an official pronouncement of the Community. The Rule, of course, is. And in the Rule, chastity (which here means celibacy) is enjoined so that we may "follow the Lamb with an undivided heart". If anything expresses a false infinity, that does. For it can only mean that a man who has taken upon himself the finite cares of wife and children can follow the Lamb only with a divided heart, almost turning a wife and Lamb into sexual rivals. That St Paul took this view in one of his earlier epistles doesn't alter its character.

Turning the infinite into a false infinity, that is into something finite, is in my view an attempt to compensate ourselves for all those finite things which have failed to come our way. Other men may have a wife and children, but we have something much better: an undivided heart which makes us an élite – God's own cronies.

I believe that the Religious (monastic) Life can be lived fruitfully only if those who enter it are constantly aware that they have done so, not because they are more spiritual than others, but because they are less. Unable to perceive, or (still more important) to take to themselves, the infinity which beckons in the rich variety of finite things, they have had to pursue the infinite by means of a life specifically concerned with it. To use the roughest of parables, they are like children who, because they are unable to manage their pocket-money, have to be kept in to do sums in simple arithmetic. It must not, however, be forgotten that by means of doing the sums the children may in time be able to manage their pocket money properly, some of them perhaps better than the average child. So the Religious (monks or nuns), in so far as they pursue the true infinity, may be able in time to see it gloriously present in the finite world, a few of them, perhaps, more clearly than many outside the cloister. From what I've witnessed I know that that does happen. And in any case it is there for everybody to see in the works of Thomas Merton. When a Religious is shown to have that sort of vision, it answers one's uncertainties about the Religious Life and vindicates its validity. To put it succinctly: the degree in which a monk or nun is able to see God's glory everywhere is the degree in which they have truly seen that glory in their own distinctive way of life.

❧❦ 14 ❧❦

INFINITY IS A BLEAK WORD. It probably conjures up the image of an empty immensity. But when we speak of something infinite within and around us it isn't of emptiness that we speak but of fullness – the absolute fullness of the ultimate mystery in which we live and have our being. To obtain some impressions of that fullness we have to use emotive words. I have already spoken of a richness deep down and of joy – if only of a dim sort of joy in the background. Some people have spoken of deep love; some of beauty ever old and ever new; some of peace which passes all understanding; some even of the loud conviviality of a banquet – "the shout of them that feast". Such expressions are valid signposts to the fullness of infinity. But none of them – not even deep love or joy – are anywhere near adequate or literal descriptions of it. For the fullness pointed to is too full and too real for the human mind to grasp except by means of hints and pictures. And the hints and pictures can only suggest to us what the fullness is like. They are unable to describe directly what it is. Yet we can certainly experience it at first hand, even if we can't express it in words and therefore in thought. For in experience we can know what passes knowledge.

It is, as we say, within ourselves that we can experience the fullness we call God, or at least something of it, and it is thus that we know what passes knowledge. It is a daunting and at first sight ridiculous task to try to speak about what by definition is unspeakable because unthinkable. Yet we can nevertheless set out to discover how far along that road we can travel. And it is a journey we can certainly begin, for it is ourselves we can take as the starting-point, and we can talk about ourselves.

WHAT, THEN, we can ask, is me? Me consists of a number of me's and I can make the mistake of identifying myself entirely with only one of them. There is, first of all, the me I put on for the benefit of other people. Then there is the me I put on for my own benefit. Then there is the me I have locked away out of sight (my own sight) in a dark cupboard because it is too painful to look at, since it is a me damaged and made ugly by the adverse chances of life. But this me, locked out of sight though he may be, can still exercise a malign influence on the me's I put on for my own benefit and that of others.

When I try to bury myself completely in the finite it is with these three me's that I identify myself without remainder. I am, I think, only them.

But there is also another me – the me in which there is something infinite, the me where God and fullness dwell, and dwell not as a stranger or a visitor or a permanent guest but as far more fully myself than the other me's. For the sake of convenience we can call this me, where as my own fullest self God dwells, the final me.

The rest of what I am can often be completely out of touch with the final me. It can go on living as if the final me didn't exist. When this happens and I am aware of no more than the superficial me's, then I am the slave of whims and fancies and fortune, pushed around by illusory fears and destructive passions lest I become what I imagine the world of circumstance and other people are trying to make me. What shadows we are, said Blake, and what shadows we pursue. As a general rule this out-of-touchness with the final me isn't complete. It's a matter of degree, and the degrees differ from day to day, from hour to hour.

The superficial me's are often attracted by the final me. They recognize intuitively, if often only dimly, that the final me alone can bring them the fulfilment for which they crave. But they are also very frightened of the final me because they feel he is a threat, as indeed he is. For the final me loves the other me's and wants to give them the freedom of being part of his own infinite self. But this will entail a change in the other me's, a transformation of them so radical that it will be a veritable death and resurrection. In order to become organically part of the final me, the other me's will have to die to what they have been in order to be raised up as living and active expressions of the final me. And only so can these other me's become solidly and satisfyingly themselves instead of the shadows they are.

❦❘16❘❦

PRAYER is the means by which we become aware of the final me. Prayer is going down deep into myself to the place where I can find the final me. Prayer is anything which puts me in touch with the final me. It may be in the guise of what prayer is conventionally supposed to look like, or it may be in a totally different guise, unrecognized by anybody except myself. What counts here isn't the trappings, but the getting in touch with the final me, however the contact is made. Where there is that contact, there there is prayer.

But in prayer I not only discover and get in touch with the final me, I also increase the influence of the final me over the other me's. In prayer the final me gradually permeates the rest of what I am so that I'm ready, after all, for it to die and be born again. This doesn't happen all at once and it has very little, if anything, to do with overwhelming emotions. It is like the seed growing secretly in the earth. The influence of the final me over the other me's is as silent as the holy night of the Christmas carol. It is generally unperceived, and to try to measure it is almost certainly to get it wrong. The earth beareth fruit of itself. So also does prayer. If our concern is to be in touch with the final me, the rest will be added to us in due time. There is no need for anxiety and fuss. We can leave the transformation of the other me's, their death and rebirth, to look after themselves. That doesn't mean that it won't be painful. Death and birth always are. But it does mean that however perturbed we may be, and however much we may be hurt, there is no ultimate cause for worry. The final me is indestructible, and it kills the other me's (whatever the pain involved) only to give them life – full life for half or quarter life.

17

WHAT I'VE TRIED to say here isn't the result of theorizing. It was beaten out on the anvil of my own experience.

By means of what is conventionally called a breakdown I was driven to discover the final me as my one and only security. The other me's were, for the time being, completely broken up so that (as I've described) I was unable even to walk out into the street. The discovery of the final me was a gradual process or, perhaps better, a matter of fits and starts, and it certainly had no sudden magical abracadabra effect. I often lost sight of it and then, of course, I wasn't able to rely on it at all. And that still happens quite often and in varying degrees. There are times when I'm less in touch with the final me than I am at other times. But on occasions I have known, none the less, what it is to be truly in touch with the final me and the blessing of the life he gives to the rest of what I am, so that on those occasions I've been able to rely on the something infinite within me.

And it is in this connection that life in the Community at Mirfield has been of the greatest assistance. It has provided me with a context which has constantly reminded me of the final me and has thus enabled me constantly to resort to him. That doesn't mean at all that the other me's don't often decide to go off on a trip of their own and thumb-nose the final me, nor that I'm now entirely free from neurotic fears and phobias. Far from it. But life at Mirfield has radically undermined my estimate of the importance of these excursions when the other me's go off on a tangent. I can sense their hollowness even when for the time being I am in their power. They can no longer permanently obscure from me what I most truly am. They can hurt, sometimes like hell. But it is as if the poison in their sting has been removed.

What in fact Mirfield has most deeply done for me is to enable me to assimilate by means of prayer what first came to me by means of breakdown and the fourteen years of therapy that followed. I've said already that Christopher Scott, as well as being a skilled and experienced analyst, was also in his ultimate outlook a mystic. And in fourteen years a little of that couldn't fail to rub off on me. So in this most important respect my analysis turned out eventually to be a preparation for the life of prayer. I see now that at the conclusion of the analysis it was all but inevitable that I should feel drawn to join a Religious Community. The relation between the two – analysis and Community – was hidden from me when I applied to join up at Mirfield. The final me was at work without my being aware of what he was doing.

❧❧ 18 ❧❧

BUT THE READER, particularly if he is religious, will by this time be puzzled if not exasperated by my continual reference to the final me. What, he will want to ask, is the theological status of this final me? Or, in plainer language, what has this final me to do with God? Indeed the reader may say that it sounds as if I'm making myself God, though, if he is charitable, he will add that surely that can't be the case. After all I am a Mirfield Father, as Robin Hood was a gentleman.

The answer to that question is very proper material for this autobiography, for one of my main tasks at Mirfield (if not my main occupation) has been to work out in thought how the final me can be related to my religious beliefs. In prayer I've been immediately aware of the relation between God and the final me. But that doesn't absolve me from the task of figuring out the relation in terms of intellectual description. How can it be described rationally by the discursive understanding?

19

IT IS A COMMONPLACE of theology that God can't be directly described. He can be thought and talked about only by means of images and pictures which point to Him – some of them homely images like our Father, some of them metaphysical like causality. What is less often perceived is that whatever pictures or images we use they all have to be put into a frame which is itself a kind of image or picture. The frame into which all the images and pictures have to be fitted is the image of objectivity.

Objectivity is an ambiguous word. It can mean a lot of things. So when you use it you should always describe what you mean by it. Here I am using the word to mean not something's independence of myself and my perception of it (the tree is there whether I'm looking at it or not, whether I die or was never born) but the way in which I look at it, the way I think about it and describe it. I am using the word "objectivity" to signify the mental apparatus by means of which alone I can perceive something or think and talk about it. In order to inspect anything or think about it I have to turn it into an object so that there is a mental distance between myself and the thing I'm inspecting or thinking about. I am one thing (the person looking or thinking) and what I'm inspecting or thinking about is another thing (the object of my attention). Without thus putting a mental distance between myself and the object of my attention I can't think about it at all. Suppose, therefore, that I apply the word "objectivity" to the Alps. It could mean that the Alps are there in total independence of myself or anything I am. That is true, but it isn't the sense in which I'm here using the word. What I mean is that to see or consider the Alps I have to put a mental distance between them and myself so that they become the object of my sight or thought.

I must thus objectify a thing in order to think of it at all. I have to put it over against me in order to consider it. So objectification is the necessary mental apparatus of all rational knowledge. Yet here I'm caught up in an inescapable contradiction. For although I have to objectify something in order to know it, yet objectifying it also separates me from it. I don't see or know the thing as it is in itself. I know it only as the object of my sight and knowledge. To put it simply: I can see the thing only in the light of my own eyes so that what I see is only partly the thing itself because it is also partly the light in which I see it. The knowledge, therefore, which unites me to the thing observed also partly puts me at a distance from it. Knowledge joins me to its object and also separates me from it.

In order to think or speak about God I have to objectify Him in this way, since I have no other mental apparatus at my disposal. I may think or speak about Him in images or pictures, but these images and pictures have to be made into objects, they have to be fitted into the frame of objectification, for me to be able to consider them at all. In terms of my mental apparatus, of my thinking, God must therefore necessarily be an object, something over against me like the Alps. I am in this place looking at Him, and He is in that place being looked at. There is a distance between us – the unavoidable distance which stands between perceiving subject and the object perceived.

This distance or separation, however, is a limitation only of thought. I have to *think* of God as there over against me, but what about the knowing which passes knowledge? If that phrase (and it is in the New Testament) means anything, it means that God's relation to me isn't confined by the limitations of thought. In His relation with me God breaks through those limitations so that the distance between subject and object is overcome. However much I may still have to *think* of God there and me here, in terms of the ultimate truth about our relation that distance or separation doesn't obtain. We could say, therefore (and we speak still only in pictures), that God is in what I am and I am in what He is. It is true that, like the Alps, God's reality is totally independent of my own. In that sense He is infinitely other than myself. But since the distance between subject and object is a necessity only of thought and isn't the ultimate truth, it is also true that God is what I am and I am what He is. That is why it is by going down deep into myself that I find Him. Indeed many of the saints have testified that God was more truly themselves than they were. We need only think of St Catherine of Genoa saying: "My me is God, nor do I find my selfhood save in Him."

It is at this point that we can return to what, for convenience, I've described as the final me.

God isn't the me I put up for the benefit of other people; nor is He the me I put up for my own benefit: nor is He the me I've locked away in the dark cupboard out of sight. For these me's, in so far as they are out of contact with the final me, are illusory me's or shadows, however powerfully destructive such illusions can be. God isn't these illusory me's. But He is the me which, using the unavoidable spatial metaphor, we can say lies beneath these more superficial me's. God is the final me, and is present and at work in the other me's when they have become organically part of the final me, even though we must also think of Him as infinitely transcending the final me. For haven't we seen that infinity includes the finite and takes the finite to itself?

In my experience of God I thus find what for thought is a contradiction – He is both me and infinitely other than me. If in prayer God remains always a Thou (to use the favourite phrase) He is also at the same time what I myself ultimately am.

Such statements often startle Christians, especially if they are unaware that the distance between subject and object is a limitation only of thought. But the statements go no further than St Paul: "It is no longer I who live, but Christ who lives in me" (Galatians 2:20). If anything does, that describes an experience of God as at one and the same time greater than the self and identical with it – "great enough to be God, intimate enough to be me". And it doesn't in any way involve an absorption or annihilation of individual personal identity. On the contrary, individual personal identity is thus confirmed in its fullness. The saints have shown us that a man is never so fully himself as when it is not he who lives but God who lives in him. For then all the me's I am express and articulate the final me, the "my me" which, as St Catherine said, is God, the God in whom alone I can find my selfhood.

❦‖20‖❦

THERE IS A RESEMBLANCE between the relation of the superficial me's and the final me and the relation between the perceiving subject and the object perceived. As a general rule the superficial me's are half in touch with the final me and half out of touch with him, while the perceiving subject by his act of knowledge is both united to the object known and separated from it. On further investigation it looks as if what we have here is more than a matter of mere resemblance. For the relation of the perceiving subject to the object perceived depends upon the relation of the superficial me's to the final me. To the extent to which the superficial me's are in touch with the final me, to that extent the relation of the perceiving subject to the object perceived will not be confined within the limits of the laws of thought. The relation, in other words, won't be one of externality – one outside inspecting another – but of union reaching the point of identification.

Two examples of what I mean can be taken from what I've already recounted of my own history.

When on that afternoon in Regent's Park I saw the beauty of the winter scene and felt desolated because I knew myself totally excluded from it, my exclusion sprang from my being totally out of touch with the final me. I hadn't found my selfhood in God and therefore the beauty of the park was something I could only inspect from the outside as a hungry man inspects a shop window of food. It remained external to myself because for me God also remained external to myself. However consciously sincere my worship and service of Him may have been, He remained, as far as I was concerned, an object over against me. In my knowledge of Him I was confined within the constrictions of the laws of thought, though at the time I wasn't at all aware of it. A year or two ago I came across a saying of the Indian poet and saint Kabir (he died in 1518) which sums up what I've been describing: "If thy soul is a stranger to thee, the whole world becomes unfriendly."

When, on the other hand, at Lacona I was radiantly aware of myself belonging to the sea in which I swam and the coast which I saw as though they were somehow part of me, that was because I had begun to be in contact with the final me, and the initial effect was intoxicating. I had begun to find my selfhood in God and therefore my relation to what we call the external world was no longer a relation of mere externality because I was able from time to time to transcend the confines of the laws of thought so that I lived in what I saw and it lived in me.

It was inevitable that the experience of knowledge as union to the point of identification should, when it first came to me, arouse in me the strongest emotions so that I felt it thrilling me through. It frothed up like champagne when the cork bursts from the bottle. But a part of me realized that much of it was indeed only froth and that the experience would have to sober up and calm down before it could be consistently appropriated. That was also true of all the similar experiences which came to me and which I've somewhat clumsily called fits of awareness.

21

AFTER TWO OR THREE years at Mirfield there were no more excitements of that kind. That, I knew, was a good sign. It showed that the initial froth had subsided, that the largely projected raptures of the honeymoon were over, that the invitation to the dance had been replaced by the dance itself, and that I had begun to get down to the sober everyday task of allowing the final me to assimilate the rest of what I am. There was nothing dramatic about this process of assimilation. There were occasionally days when it felt rewarding, leaving a warm glow in the heart. There were other days when the temperature dropped considerably, falling sometimes to below zero, and I began asking myself: "Who is able to abide His frost?" My selfhood in God then seemed about as attractive as an iceberg. The chill ascended from feet to knees and everything I was. There were again other days when I was just plain bored. The search for my selfhood in God seemed utterly pointless, a chasing after fantasies which eluded me, so that "I struck the board, and cry'd, No more". But I went on none the less, because somewhere within me I knew that in spite of appearances I was on the road to fulfilment and joy, and in any case I had taken to heart the warning that strait is the gate and narrow is the way that leadeth unto life.

There is no need to enlarge on these various types of experience. They are the staple diet of all who dedicate themselves to the life of prayer, and an endless number of books has been written about them.

22

IT IS, I THINK, much more important to examine what I initially apprehended at Lacona and on subsequent similar occasions: that the final me, the selfhood I found in God, included the whole world. It wasn't only the world around me in a literal or physical sense, but the places and people I knew and could therefore imagine. As far as the places were concerned I could no more than feel at one with them either with gratitude if the place was, say, the Bay of Naples or with concern and discomfort if it was the Neapolitan slums. The people, on the other hand, were all, like myself, final me's with whom I knew myself identified, distinct from myself though, of course, they also were.

When therefore in prayer I found the final me, my selfhood in God, I found other people there. I recognized them as included in what I was because I was no longer separated from them by the limitations of the laws of thought. It is true that I had first to think about them, considering what at the time I deemed to be their particular happiness or need. In that sense I had to put between them and me the mental distance that thought requires. But that was only a preliminary. For I knew with first-hand immediacy that in a most important sense I was what they were as they were what I was. So no prayer of any kind could possibly be a flight of the alone to the Alone. Finding God in myself necessarily involved finding company. No doubt the company was in fact the whole world of people living and departed. But in prayer the human imagination still remains human, which means that it still remains limited. So for practical purposes the company I found in the final me (St Catherine's "my me is God") was the company of those people I had got to know by the chance encounters of life. And again, for practical purposes, there was the necessity of being selective even about these people. I couldn't think of everybody I had ever met. So the company within me consisted, as far as my awareness was concerned, of my relatives, those people I had come to know well, and those at any particular time in special need.

Because of the company of people contained in the final me, that final me is by nature an intercessor. The final me can't live or die to itself. It must by its nature live and die for the whole company within.

Hence the most important work we do at Mirfield is the work of intercession, that prayerful concern for other people who are always present within us as we lift up our hearts to God.

Such intercession isn't a condescending activity as though we were superior persons helping those inferior or weaker than ourselves. For we are aware that what we receive from them is as important as what they receive from us. In the final me separability is transcended so that the whole company both gives and receives from each other.

If there is nothing of *de haut en bas* about intercession, neither is it the power game it is sometimes represented as being: I can't influence you by anything I say or do, so I'll bring to bear on you the secret influence of praying God to give you somehow a kick in the backside so that you'll be what I think you ought to be and do what I think you ought to do. Intercession isn't giving God instructions about how He ought to deal with people. I can't myself pray that so-and-so may become religious or be converted to Christianity, since religion (including the Christian religion) can all too easily be used as a bulwark against the final me, a flight into a false infinity in order to escape the true.

Intercession is realizing my identification with the company within, so that, whatever form my prayer takes, it is their prayer as well. To be properly aware of this coincidence does, I believe, require me to think regularly of each member of the company within, and to consider their circumstances, their happiness, their needs and problems, and maybe their sufferings, not in order to tell God what to do about it, but just to lift each one up in His presence and hold him there for a short time. It is like putting myself at their disposal before God. A man puts himself at his own disposal when he summons up his intelligence to solve a problem or his skill as a mountaineer to climb the Matterhorn. In intercession I don't try to solve other people's problems for them, but I do offer to God my own resources so that He may use them according to His wisdom to help the person I'm praying for.

Doing this can be very hard work. It can require the spending, not only of time, but of energy — spiritual, mental, and physical — sometimes of a very great deal of energy. But it is only by being willing to give ourselves in this way that we can become properly aware that we are part and parcel of the company within as they are of us. It is only in the exercise of mutual giving and receiving that we can come to the knowledge of our common identity.

BUT THERE IS MORE still to intercession. The true infinite (as we saw earlier on) includes the finite in its own infinity. Otherwise it would be only another and alternative finite. But our finitude makes us vulnerable to the thousand natural shocks that flesh is heir to. It involves us in suffering and ugliness and death. So when the infinite includes the finite in its own infinity, it includes these horrible and destructive things. What the cost of that inclusion is we can scarcely even guess. In the Christian scheme that cost is represented by the figure of a man dying in agony upon a cross. But when, at a cost we may not know and cannot tell, the infinite includes within its infinity all in the finite which is tormenting and hideous and death-dealing, then those evil things suffer a sea-change. They become something rich and strange. They are transformed into what is glorious and beautiful and life-giving. I have discovered only recently how this truth was expressed by Jakob Boehme (he was a German mystic who died in 1624). He said that the dark principle in nature is as it were the fuel which eternally feeds the eternal love and joy which constitute the life of God. Love and joy are, as we saw, two possible ways of indicating the absolute fullness of the infinite. Boehme has put with a simplicity beyond my reach the experience I've been trying to describe.

This transformation isn't something we can objectify, setting it at a mental distance from ourselves so that we can inspect and consider it. For it passes beyond the capacities of the necessary laws of thought. But we can know it by the knowing which passes knowledge. We can experience it within ourselves in so far as we are in contact with the final me. In that innermost sanctuary where "my me is God" and we know our selfhood only in Him we can apprehend, however dimly, that suffering and glory are the obverse and reverse of the same thing. In so far as we are in contact with the final me, to that degree we know with immediacy that the infinite takes the finite into its own infinity. And with that knowledge we can perceive with the same immediacy that what in terms of finitude alone is suffering is in fact much more than suffering since it is also (if we may so put it) the raw material from which the infinite weaves a garment of glory.

That was the truth which came upon me overwhelmingly when I was unable to sit any longer at my parents' dinner table and went for a walk in Baynards Park, and also on that Christmas Eve when I listened on the radio to the carols from King's. Only at that time it remained a truth I couldn't yet appropriate to any significant degree. It came certainly in its full force as though God were battering my heart. But then (to mix metaphors) it slipped off me like water from a duck's back.

The apprehension of suffering as glory doesn't mean that suffering ceases to hurt. It goes on hurting, but we can see beyond the hurt to its sea-change into something rich – the richness which can't be objectified and therefore described because we can't put it at a mental distance from ourselves. We can only be it.

When in intercession we realize our identification with the company within, we shall find ourselves identified with a fair degree of suffering, adding to what may be our own sufferings the sufferings of those others who are also ourselves. To intercede for people is to be willing, in some measure at least, to share their hurt so that it is felt to lie on our own shoulders as well as theirs. Intercession can, therefore, demand from us not only an expenditure of energy, but also a willingness to accept pain – the pain of others which we recognize as our own. Intercession can sometimes demand from us that we share the bloody sweat of Gethsemane. It is certainly to rejoice with those who do rejoice, and that is a marvellous and heartening thing. But it is also to weep with those who weep.

For if in terms of the final me we are them and they

are us, we can't avoid bearing their griefs and carrying their sorrows as they do ours. But in experiencing the hurt, the final me also experiences the transformation of the hurt into the richness and glory which passes knowledge. And he experiences it not only for himself (for he experiences nothing for himself alone). He experiences it on behalf of those for whom he intercedes, since his awareness of the glory is his contribution to the awareness of the whole company within. It is his personal addition to the common stock. St Paul once said: "So death worketh in us but life in you." To use Christian terminology, intercession can often be the sharing of other people's Good Fridays in order that they may see, in however distant or obscure a way, their Good Fridays irradiated with Easter glory. And that vision is always life-giving in the sense that it makes us all willing to die in order to live.

Intercession can exhaust and it can also hurt. But by its nature it can't fail to put us and keep us in touch with the final me where God is. It leaves us both poorer and richer: poorer in our reserves of energy and often in our sense of well-being, but richer in our awareness that "my me is God", and that that is true also of all those for whom we have prayed, however much or little (if at all) they realize it. Indeed it may be our task and privilege to realize it for them.

🌿24🌿

ONE OF THE RESULTS of joining in the life of prayer at Mirfield was that the events in the gospels became less and less important to me as historical happenings and more and more important as the externalized poetic or narrative representations of realities which occurred or were found in the depths of what I was – in what I've called the final me.

So, for instance, the Annunciation spoke to me profoundly of God's intimately personal invitation to union with Himself. Whether or not anything approaching what is described in St Luke's gospel ever happened to Mary seemed to me more and more a matter of indifference. Or again, the Ascension of Christ into Heaven was centred now for me upon the fact that we can ourselves "in heart and mind thither ascend", and not upon an historical event which may or may not have happened on a hill near Jerusalem. The gospel seemed more and more to be about realities which were present and inward, not about alleged incidents which were past and external. I could no longer understand the claim so often made by Christians that externality was somehow a guarantee of validity. The fact that such-and-such a thing happened as a matter of objective history seemed to me irrelevant. What counted was that I could see and experience it happening now in myself and in the world. That was a conclusion to which I was driven apart altogether from the considerable difficulties of establishing what in fact did happen on any particular occasion. But obviously the conclusion had for me the incidental advantage that my union with God was independent of the caprices of New Testament criticism. Some New Testament scholars allowed more in the gospels to be historical, others less. But for me the Annunciation, the Christmas story of Bethlehem, the Baptism of Jesus and his temptations in the wilderness, his healing power, his passion, death, resurrection and ascension were, all of them, living contemporary realities whose saving truth were quite independent of the latest bulletin issued by New Testament scholarship. And I have the impression (though, of course, I can't be certain about it) that this was in the last resort true also of those who worshipped with me in the Community church. Certainly they *thought* that on the feast of the Annunciation or of Christmas, Easter or Ascension Day they were celebrating an historical event and they would be horrified if it were suggested that they weren't. So much so that, for all practical purposes, they left even the most conservative kind of New Testament criticism at the church door as they came in, even if they had allowed it to impinge upon them seriously anywhere at all. But the real power and splendour of these celebrations lay in their contemporary significance within and among us. It was to us now that the Angel Gabriel appeared announcing the birth within us of God's son. It was within us now that God at Christmas was born. It was we now who had to die and be raised from the dead so that it was we ourselves who could now in heart and mind ascend into heaven and there continually dwell.

If these present realities seemed totally dependent upon the alleged historical events in which they were represented, the reason seemed to me not difficult to find. The stories of these alleged past events were charged (as Jung so clearly saw) with psychological power. The inward realities needed the outward representations to spark them off, keep them alive, and increase our awareness of them. We felt that the truth for us now was more real as we celebrated the stories in which it was portrayed. But in actual fact, so it seemed to me, their present truth for us didn't in the least depend upon the historical accuracy of the story being celebrated.

This was the more borne in on me when as an Anglican in Europe I went (as I often did) to a Roman Catholic church on 15 August when the corporeal assumption of our Lady into heaven (declared and dignified as a dogma by Pius XII) was being celebrated. Nobody could fail to be aware of the power exercised over the large congregations by what was being commemorated. It obviously had the deepest and strongest meaning for them. The alleged historical event of the Assumption put them in contact with potent psychic and spiritual forces within themselves. It made them aware of an immensely important aspect of their personal identity. Yet there isn't a single shred of historical evidence for the corporeal assumption of our Lady. It is a pure invention of the pious imagination (Charles Gore used to speak of it as "that Roman doctrine so rightly called the assumption"). The assumption, in short, never happened. But its power to move and enlighten those who celebrate it isn't thereby in the slightest degree diminished. For what in the last resort is being celebrated has nothing to do with a historical figure called Mary. It is a spiritual reality, always contemporary, within the hearts of the worshippers.

That is an inference which an Anglican can legitimately draw. But if he does, he can't escape the consequences. And the consequences will lead him far outside the reserve of even Anglican orthodoxy. For if what is beyond question a non-event as far as history is concerned can still stir the hearts and minds of worshippers and make them aware of realities within, what about those supposed historical events which can certainly be found in the four gospels, but for which the historical evidence, when critically examined, turns out to be slight, obscure, muddled, or sometimes non-existent?

It seems to me a waste of powder and shot to try to show with immense labour that this or the other detail in the gospel narrative may after all be historical when a generation of scholars has concluded that it isn't. The real and important truth remains whatever the status as history of the story in which it is represented. If we have God truly present with us now, and if He can be truly incarnated in what we are today, and if we can know at first hand what it is to die and be raised again from the dead, what importance still survives in historical events alleged to have occurred two thousand years ago, apart from the power such stories have of making us aware of Emmanuel – God with us?

I believe that many Christians (most notably clergymen) are intellectually dishonest in their attitude to the alleged historical events of the gospel story. As scholars they concede that the historical evidence for this and the other event is doubtful, perhaps sometimes showing beyond reasonable doubt that it never happened. But in church they go on speaking and behaving as though it certainly did and there was absolutely no doubt about it. An obvious case in point is the story in the last chapter of St Matthew's gospel of Jesus instructing the disciples to baptize in the name of the Father and of the Son and of the

Holy Spirit. I'm aware that by a great deal of clever wriggling it can be claimed that these words don't mean what they obviously do. But I don't think such cleverness worth considering. The historical Jesus is here represented as instructing his disciples to baptize people in the name of the Trinity. That he couldn't have done. The Trinitarian formula belongs to a later stage of the church's doctrinal development. Yet this passage is the only evidence we have that the historical Jesus instituted the sacrament of baptism. The historical origins of baptism in the Christian church are in fact extremely complicated and obscure. Yet we go on being told in church that Jesus himself instituted the sacrament, in spite of our having no historical evidence that he did and a not inconsiderable amount of evidence which suggests that he didn't.

Such double-think may tide people over temporary difficulties. But the price the Christian church will eventually have to pay for double-think will be damaging in the extreme. Truth may be disconcerting, but when falsehood continues to be deliberately sown the harvest in the end will be devastating.

It is of no importance to me what label is tied to my conviction that the gospel story confronts us with inner realities and is in the end independent of what happened as a matter of history. (People sometimes think that to tie a label round something is to dispose of it.) I am not here following in the footsteps of any philosopher or theologian. I'm merely describing in what direction I was led by joining in the Community's life of worship and prayer.

❦❦25❦❦

AT CAMBRIDGE I had been too busy to think deeply about the Christian faith, and when the day's work was done there were always the distractions provided by the colleagues whose company I enjoyed. And although I was a member of various groups which discussed theological matters like that which produced *Soundings* or Dennis

Nineham's seminar, yet these discussions were by their nature on an intellectual level, and what was discussed remained only one compartment in a fairly crowded life. There was no time to continue thinking consistently about Christianity. I had to move on to the next job, which might be finding a vicar from a college living, sorting out some muddle in which an undergraduate had become involved, making enquiries with a view to appointing the next college chaplain, writing a reference for a former pupil applying for this or the other post, or mastering the latest theory about the composition of the Pentateuch.

At Mirfield my circumstances were entirely different. I had gone there to discover the something infinite in myself and to acquire first-hand experience of those ultimate realities which so far had been for me little more than a matter of talk and theory. And Mirfield provided me with ample opportunity to do precisely that. There was the daily routine of prayer and worship. There were the hours set aside for contemplation. There was plenty of time to read and think. And there were few, if any, distractions. I could no longer by means of work or pleasure evade the fundamental questions which were hovering somewhere in the back of my mind. The whole pattern of life at Mirfield pointed to those questions and demanded that I should face them.

So, for instance, every feast in the liturgical year brought home to me afresh that it wasn't in reality historical events which we were celebrating.

The feast of the Epiphany moved us all deeply, but the story of the three wise men being led by a star is admitted by even conservative New Testament critics to be legendary. It never happened. But its power as present spiritual truth wasn't thereby diminished one iota. The same was true (as I've said) of the feast of the Annunciation. But these two celebrations as a matter of history could be regarded as more or less peripheral.

But how about the resurrection of Jesus – the central and most important feast of the Christian year?

What as a matter of historical fact the resurrection of Jesus was supposed to have been we don't know. It is very far from clear what the New Testament presents us with for belief about the resurrection of Jesus as an historical event. Different passages suggest different things. And here we can't have it both ways: we can't on the one hand insist that the resurrection of Jesus was an historical event and, on the other, claim that this greatest and most mighty of mysteries can't by its nature be subject to the ordinary laws of historical evidence. I became, therefore, more and more convinced that what we celebrated at Easter was God's power to give life to the dead now in the present – a power of which all of us in various ways had had experience. It was of this that I wrote in *True Resurrection*.

It was thus that I became gradually convinced that the gospel events we celebrated had in fact no need of any historical foundation and that their very great importance lay in their providing us with the stories in terms of which God's relationship to us could be set forth in visual imaginative terms, thereby enabling us to assimilate the truth of that relationship and so to deepen and enrich our life in God. Their reference, I was driven to believe, was always to the present. But because of the story form they appeared also to refer to the past. But in the last resort that reference to the past was unnecessary.

❧‖26‖❧

THE ENORMOUS INFLUENCE of these gospel stories upon the Western world is an established fact. What, however, is now becoming more and more clear to us is that the stories don't speak to the peoples of the Far East. Those peoples have their own stories to express the truth of God's relationship with them. Naturally their stories don't seem to us as good as ours, just as our stories don't seem to them as good as theirs. But we can at least understand that their stories are as meaningful to them as ours are to us.

27

I WAS VERY FRIGHTENED of what I was being led to along this road. For it implied that what is called the Christian revelation wasn't the final and ultimate truth about God's relationship with man – a truth which must in the fullness of time replace or supplement other more partial truths. Christianity, it now appeared to me, was only one way of speaking about God among other possible ways. Religion, it has been said, is like language. You can't speak language in general. You have to speak a particular language. So religions can't be amalgamated into one universal religion. Religions have to be particular and will be conditioned by (as well as themselves conditioning) the cultural mould in which they were formed, having their own particular stories and ways of thought. The various religions don't in the end by means of their different stories all say the same thing. The experts in comparative religion are quite certain about that. But when attempts are made to describe the infinite, who would expect the same thing to be said by all peoples and cultures? It is arguable that you can't say exactly the same thing in English and German, since each language has behind it its own history and package of associations. And if that is true of languages in the literal sense, how much more must it be true of the various languages of religion? Each great religion, I believe, has caught some facet of the infinite, but these different facets can't be fitted together into a neat coherent scheme. It is by his own religion that a devotee must be fed. But if he is to keep a sense of proportion he will always bear in mind that other religions have said other things, and that no one religion can claim here to be the judge or referee of the others. Such agreements to differ are, I believe, a sign of spiritual maturity because they show that the infinite has been apprehended as truly infinite and is therefore bound in earthly terms to be many-coloured, some of the colours clashing quite violently with some of the others.

To admit that other religions speak validly of God's

relationship with man doesn't in any way destroy the validity of one's own religion. I can still be a Christian and continue to find the life-giving power of the Christian scheme while at the same time I admit that the Buddha spoke of truths not found in the Christian tradition and maybe inconsistent with them. Ultimately truth is too large, too infinitely wide, to be expressed with mathematical consistency. I can still decide what quality it is which I hold to be supreme. Let us say that that quality is generous, costly, self-giving love. For humankind that love isn't in fact the clear and simple thing it may first appear to be. For generous love, if it is to come to its full fruition, must take into itself and include those apparently contrary qualities which we call the dark side of ourselves, the shadow. So stories in other religions which give expression to the shadow self may not so completely oppose the quality of generous love as at first sight they may seem to do. We have here to use our powers of insight and discrimination – a heavy burden which, like freedom, humankind is called to carry and which we often want to abandon in favour of something easier like submitting to authority, but which we can't abandon without a fundamental loss of integrity.

28

BUT WHAT, THEN, OF JESUS? Here I come to speak of the greatest sacrifice which life at Mirfield called on me to make and which had never previously even entered my imagination. I approached the prospect of it with horror and dread. I felt at first that it would rob life of all meaning and warmth. And it was a sacrifice I had to make alone, since nobody else at Mirfield could begin to understand where God was leading me.

The conclusion to which I was led was a matter to me of such fundamental and supreme importance, and I arrived at it by means of so much distress and travail, that I must repeat it again here in this autobiography as I repeated it a thousand times in my own heart and mind. The repetition may be taken to indicate some of the cost at which it was bought.

Jesus, for the people of Christendom, was the story by means of which they were able to perceive what life was ultimately about, which meant to perceive and appropriate God's relationship with them. It was they who at Christmas were the manger in which God was born. It was they who by means of God's indwelling were able to bring healing and peace to others. It was they (as St Paul said of himself) who in the various adverse circumstances of life were crucified. And it was they who were given new life from the dead.

But Jesus didn't remain only the story by means of which people apprehended what they potentially were and could actually become. The story was externalized and objectified so that it became a single once-for-all event. Jesus was thus no longer the story of what by our relationship with God we could all become. Instead he became a figure of absolute uniqueness who belonged to a different species from ourselves, since, although it was claimed that he was fully man, it was also claimed that at the centre of his person he was God as we ourselves were not and never could be. He was a divine intruder into our world. He came down to earth from heaven. And the result was inevitable: he became a cult-hero who was worshipped and prayed to as he himself had prayed to the God he taught us to call our Father. As a cult-hero he was also the mediator. It was through him, and only through him, that God's children could approach their heavenly Father. It was only through his merits and mediation that they could draw near to the throne of grace. It was only for Jesus Christ's sake that their prayers would be heard.

The cult-hero became the focus for projections. Our extremely partial and relative ideas of what is good and just and pure and lovely were projected upon the cult-hero and thus given an absolute and (so it seems at the time) permanent validity. Christians today often speak of "Christ's standards" with regard to matters about which he said nothing at all. An amusing example of this can be found in the comments of A. C. Benson about a visiting preacher in Magdalene College chapel. "A very foolish sermon," Benson wrote in his diary, "he seemed to imply that Christ approved of horse-racing but disapproved of betting."

That, of course, is trivial. But when a figure revered by millions of people throughout the world as Christ's Vicar and Representative on earth says in effect that it is contrary to Christ's standards for married couples to use contraceptives, the result is more serious. For if anything is going to lead certainly in the end to a nuclear holocaust, it is a world which is overpopulated. That is the cost we may finally have to pay for our cult-hero and the ideas and standards which are inevitably projected upon him.

29

WHAT JESUS in fact was as a matter of history it is extremely difficult to discover since the only evidence we have about him was already doctrinally slanted before it reached anywhere near the pages of our gospels. But to adopt an all-or-nothing attitude here is to be defeatist. Perhaps the best short summary of what Jesus of Nazareth was historically was provided in the early 1950s by W. R. Inge in a letter he wrote towards the end of his life to a clergyman who had become an object of obloquy for his unorthodoxy. Inge wrote:

> "My own view is that the historical Jesus was a supremely great prophet 'full of the Holy Spirit' – and what does Incarnation mean except just that? He made such an overwhelming impression upon His disciples that within a few years of His ignominious death they loaded Him with the highest honours they could think of, the Jews as the Messiah-designate, and the 'Greeks' as a Saviour God of their mysteries, and then as the Logos."

In the end what seemed to me to be the utter loss which

robbed life of its meaning turned out to be gain. Resurrection, as always, followed death. For the words of Jesus the Prophet had about them a freshness and pungency which they had formerly lacked. He showed that the ways of God are both similar to the ways of men and also most disconcertingly different from them. And most notably he constantly called in question accepted religious and ethical ideas. The challenges he threw in front of the institutional church of his day led churchmen in the end to engineer his death. One wonders what the General Synod of the Church of England would have made of him. But that is a question which he himself could be said to have answered:

> "You build the tombs of the prophets and adorn the monuments of the righteous, saying, 'If we had lived in the days of our fathers we would not have taken part with them in shedding the blood of the prophets.' Thus you witness against yourselves that you are the sons of those who murdered the prophets."

It isn't difficult to imagine the reaction to statements of this kind. It would almost certainly be compassionate: "Poor man. He's got an enormous chip on his shoulder."

To have Jesus alive and vigorously kicking was, I finally realized, beyond all comparison better than the mummified cult-hero of the ecclesiastical tradition. And that giving of life to Jesus is perhaps the greatest thing being at Mirfield has done for me.

30

AS ONE FED by the Christian religion I find it necessary to distinguish between the historical Jesus and what could be described as the Christ Reality. I believe that the historical Jesus embodied the Christ Reality to a unique degree. But I don't believe that the Christ Reality was confined to him or that he monopolized it. And I see that if I had been fed by another religion I should call the Christ Reality something else – the Buddha nature, for instance, especially with regard to the compassion shown by the Buddha when he refused Nirvana for himself in order to bring enlightenment to men. Many of the hymns addressed in the Japanese Buddhist tradition to Amida Buddha are in content identical to hymns addressed by Christians to Jesus.

But I can speak here only as a Christian. And for a Christian, what he calls the Christ Reality is recognized as the presence within people and around them of God's costly self-giving love, the love by which people can become fully themselves and the world the place where God reigns.

For a Christian the Christ Reality is found wherever people are no longer the slaves of the changes and chances of this mortal life because they can "in heart and mind thither ascend and with him continually dwell" to use the words of the Prayer Book collect. And this ascent by the Christian into heaven will have practical earthly consequences. It will lead to the active demand that justice overcome injustice, and to compassion overcoming indifference and confidence overcoming suspicion and fear. The Christ Reality, the heaven where in heart and mind we continually dwell, will lead to meanness giving way to generosity, ugliness to beauty, prejudice to an open mind, the demand for simplistic answers to the recognition and acceptance of the inevitable complications and subtleties of human life, fantasy to realism, and, most important of all, the dethronement of the impersonal which destroys human feeling as what is warmly and humanly personal is seen to be infinitely more real.

The historical Jesus embodied and bore witness to the Christ Reality, but it was found in many places centuries before he was born and continued to be found among people who had never heard of him: in the experience of the Hebrew prophet Hosea and the vision of that unknown prophet of the Exile whose words are found in our book of the prophet Isaiah. And in various degrees the Christ Reality was embodied and shown forth by the Buddha, Lao-Tse, Mohammed, Hafiz, Kabir, and countless others who have left no memorial. Nor is the Christ Reality absent from the discoveries and insights of a Charles Darwin, or a Karl Marx, or a Sigmund Freud. Still less from the music of a Mozart or a Beethoven or the plays of a Shakespeare or even a Bernard Shaw. That does not mean that we must accept everything they said as true. Far from it. They often made mistakes and were plain wrong, just as Jesus was wrong about his return to earth in glory in the near future. The demand for all or nothing is mere childishness. The Christ Reality has always to be found among much that contradicts it, of which for us the Christian church itself is the most obvious example with its recurring habit of becoming the anti-Christ. God, it seems, has chosen to be present by means of human fallibility and weakness. That is what is affirmed by those Christians who reject the fundamentalist view of the Bible. It is illogical to reject fundamentalism as far as the Bible is concerned and to demand it in other areas. In doing this we make of the Jesus who has had such an enormous influence upon the ideals and culture of Christendom something of a magical figure who is not human.

That is why it is so immensely important for us to realize that we are not dependent solely upon a figure of the past, because the Christ Reality is all about us in our world today. And He (for the Christ Reality is God) is found not only in people and events reckoned notable but also in unnoticed acts of goodness performed by people who do their duty conscientiously and are generous and merciful souls, giving a helping hand where they can, fully recognizing how very far from perfect (let alone infallible) they are. In them the Christ Reality is present now in our midst as they contribute to the final result which Christians have sometimes called the Christ who is to be. That final consummation is not a future historical event. It belongs to the heavenly order which means that it is beyond the boundaries of space and time. St Paul described it as the state in which God is all in all, and that description is not very far from much that is found in the *Upanishads*.

EPILOGUE

AN AUTOBIOGRAPHY can't be brought to a neat conclusion. For its subject continues to live, and it is only in fiction that people live happily ever after.

But an ideal ending can be set beside a report of what is actually the case. A man's aspirations can be compared with what is in fact his condition. And that seems as good a way as any of bringing this book to a close.

It is in the *Asian Journal* of Thomas Merton, the Trappist monk, that I've found described the person I would like to be.

A day or two before he died he was in Sri Lanka visiting Polonnaruwa, where there are several vast statues of the Buddha. Merton writes:

"I am able to approach the Buddhas barefoot and undisturbed, my feet in wet grass, wet sand. Then the silence of the extraordinary faces. The great smiles. Huge and yet subtle. Filled with every possibility, questioning nothing, knowing everything, rejecting nothing, the peace not of emotional resignation, but [that which] has seen through every question without trying to discredit anyone or anything – *without refutation* – without establishing some other argument."

So much for the ideal. The reality is very different. It is a person who, because of what he has seen, feels increasingly that he is out in the cold, like the old men in T. S. Eliot's poem:

> We returned to our places, these kingdoms,
> But no longer at ease here, in the old dispensation,
> With an alien people clutching their gods.
> I should be glad of another death.

Yet perhaps, after all, were I able to choose, I should choose what I actually am rather than the ideal. Unamuno once wrote to a friend: "God forbid you peace and give you glory." My life so far seems to have been an answer to that prayer. Not that I have attained the glory. But I have caught glimpses of it now and then.

Nothing is for nothing. You always have to pay for what you get. Without pain there can be no birth; without death no resurrection. In that necessity the ideal and the actual are reconciled and seem to belong inescapably to each other.

Books by H. A. Williams

Jesus and the Resurrection, Longman's, London, 1951
God's Wisdom in Christ's Cross, Mowbray's, London, 1960
The Four Last Things, Mowbray's, London, 1960
The True Wilderness, Constable, London, 1965 and Fount Paperbacks, 1979
True Resurrection, Mitchell Beazley, London, 1972 and Fount Paperbacks, 1983
Poverty, Chastity and Obedience, Mitchell Beazley, London, 1975
Tensions, Mitchell Beazley, London, 1976
Becoming What I Am, Darton, Longman & Todd, London, 1977
The Joy of God, Mitchell Beazley, London, 1979

Contributions: *Soundings*, Cambridge University Press, 1962
Objections to Christian Belief, Constable, 1963
The God I Want, Constable, 1967

Also available in Fount Paperbacks

Naught for your Comfort
TREVOR HUDDLESTON

'To recommend a book by such a fascinating and controversial man would be superfluous; to ban it, as the South African censors will certainly do, ineffective. It will be widely read here and – more important – there.'

Colin Welch, Daily Telegraph

Let My People Go
ALBERT LUTHULI

'Luthuli's love for his country transcends his loyalty to any one racial group within it. This book will surely convince the world that the Nobel Prize was most justly awarded to its author.'

Trevor Huddleston, Sunday Times

Instrument of thy Peace
ALAN PATON

'Worthy of a permanent place on the short shelf of enduring classics of the life of the Spirit.'

Henry P. Van Dusen,
Union Theological Seminary

Miracle on the River Kwai
ERNEST GORDON

'This description of the reality of Christian love, discovered in the hell of unspeakable prisoner-of-war conditions, says more to the average man than the most brilliant treatise of apologetics.'

David H. D. Read

Also available in Fount Paperbacks

Journey for a Soul
GEORGE APPLETON

'Wherever you turn in this inexpensive but extraordinarily valuable paperback you will benefit from sharing this man's pilgrimage of the soul.'

Methodist Recorder

The Imitation of Christ
THOMAS A KEMPIS

After the Bible, this is perhaps the most widely read book in the world. It describes the way of the follower of Christ – an intensely practical book, which faces the temptations and difficulties of daily life, but also describes the joys and helps which are found on the way.

Autobiography of a Saint: Thérèse of Lisieux
RONALD KNOX

'Ronald Knox has bequeathed us a wholly lucid, natural and enchanting version . . . the actual process of translating seems to have vanished, and a miracle wrought, as though St Teresa were speaking to us in English . . . his triumphant gift to posterity.'

G. B. Stern, The Sunday Times

The Way of a Disciple
GEORGE APPLETON

'. . . a lovely book and an immensely rewarding one . . . his prayers have proved of help to many.'

Donald Coggan

Also available in Fount Paperbacks

A Gift for God
MOTHER TERESA OF CALCUTTA

'The force of her words is very great . . . the message is always the same, yet always fresh and striking.'

Malcolm Muggeridge

Strength to Love
MARTIN LUTHER KING

'The sermons . . . read easily and reveal a man of great purpose, humility and wisdom . . . in the turbulent context of the American race conflict, Dr King's statements have the ring of social as well as spiritual truth . . .'

Steven Kroll
The Listener

A Book of Comfort
ELIZABETH GOUDGE

'The contents are worth ten of the title: this is a careful, sensitive anthology of the illuminations in prose and verse that have prevented the world from going wholly dark over the centuries.'

Sunday Times

The Desert in the City
CARLO CARRETTO

'. . . we have been in the hands of one of the finest of modern spiritual writers, who helps us on the road of love in Christ.'

Philip Cauvin, the Universe

Also available in Fount Paperbacks

Erasmus of Christendom
R. H. BAINTON

'In this book, which carries lightly and easily the massive Erasmian scholarship of the last half-century, Erasmus comes to life. He speaks for himself, and, speaking, reveals himself.'

Hugh Trevor-Roper, Sunday Times

Calvin
FRANÇOIS WENDEL

'This is the best introduction to Calvin and his theology that has been written, and it is a work of scholarship which one salutes and admires.'

Professor Gordon Rupp

Bonhoeffer: An Illustrated Introduction
EBERHARD BETHGE

'. . . we have facts reviewed which were not generally known before. The number of portraits are really first class.'

Christian Herald

Gateway to God
SIMONE WEIL

'Simone . . . makes everything seem, at once, reassuringly recognizable and so luminous as to be heavenly . . . the great mysteries . . . are seen through a window of time in the perspective of eternity.'

Malcolm Muggeridge

Fount Paperbacks

Fount is one of the leading paperback publishers of religious books and below are some of its recent titles.

- ☐ DISCRETION AND VALOUR (New edition)
  Trevor Beeson £2.95 (LF)
- ☐ ALL THEIR SPLENDOUR David Brown £1.95
- ☐ AN APPROACH TO CHRISTIANITY
  Bishop Butler £2.95 (LF)
- ☐ THE HIDDEN WORLD Leonard Cheshire £1.75
- ☐ MOLCHANIE Catherine Doherty £1.00
- ☐ CHRISTIAN ENGLAND (Vol. 1)
  David Edwards £2.95 (LF)
- ☐ MERTON: A BIOGRAPHY Monica Furlong £2.50 (LF)
- ☐ THE DAY COMES Clifford Hill £2.50
- ☐ THE LITTLE BOOK OF SYLVANUS
  David Kossoff £1.50
- ☐ GERALD PRIESTLAND AT LARGE
  Gerald Priestland £1.75
- ☐ BE STILL AND KNOW Michael Ramsey £1.25
- ☐ JESUS Edward Schillebeeckx £4.95 (LF)
- ☐ THE LOVE OF CHRIST Mother Teresa £1.25
- ☐ PART OF A JOURNEY Philip Toynbee £2.95 (LF)

All Fount paperbacks are available at your bookshop or newsagent, or they can also be ordered by post from Fount Paperbacks, Cash Sales Department, G.P.O. Box 29, Douglas, Isle of Man, British Isles. Please send purchase price, plus 10p per book. Customers outside the U.K. send purchase price, plus 12p per book. Cheque, postal or money order. No currency.

NAME (Block letters) _____

ADDRESS _____

_____

_____